CQ GUIDE TO

CURRENT AMERICAN GOVERNMENT

Spring 1996

CQ GUIDE TO
CURRENT AMERICAN GOVERNMENT

Spring 1996

Congressional Quarterly Inc.
Washington, D.C.

Congressional Quarterly Inc.

Congressional Quarterly Inc., an editorial research service and publishing company, serves clients in the fields of news, education, business, and government. It combines the specific coverage of Congress, government, and politics contained in the *Congressional Quarterly Weekly Report* with the more general subject range of an affiliated service, the *CQ Researcher*.

Congressional Quarterly also publishes a variety of books, including college political science textbooks and public affairs paperbacks on developing issues and events under the CQ Press imprint. CQ Books researches, writes, and publishes information directories and reference books on the federal government, national elections, and politics, including the *Guide to the Presidency,* the *Guide to Congress,* the *Guide to the U.S. Supreme Court,* the *Guide to U.S. Elections,* and *Politics in America. CQ's Encyclopedia of American Government* is a four-volume reference work providing essential information about the U.S. government. The *CQ Almanac,* a compendium of legislation for one session of Congress, is published each year. *Congress and the Nation,* a record of government for a presidential term, is published every four years.

CQ publishes the *Congressional Monitor,* a daily report on current and future activities of congressional committees, and several newsletters. The CQ FaxReport is a daily update available every afternoon when Congress is in session. An electronic online information system, Washington Alert, provides immediate access to CQ's databases of legislative action, votes, schedules, profiles, and analyses.

Printed in the United States of America

Library of Congress Catalog No. 61-16893
International Standard Book No. 0-87187-850-X
International Standard Book No. 1-56802-245-X (supplement to *Governing by Consent,* 2d ed.)
International Standard Serial No. 0196-612X

Editor: Jerry Orvedahl
Associate Editor: Megan Q. Davis
Production: Michael Emanuel, Jhonnie G. Bailey

CONTENTS

Introduction

Congressional Quarterly's *Guide to Current American Government* is divided into four sections—foundations of American government, political participation, government institutions, and politics and public policy—that correspond with the framework of standard introductory American government textbooks. Articles have been selected from the *Congressional Quarterly Weekly Report* to complement existing texts with up-to-date examinations of current issues and controversies.

Foundations of American Government. This section focuses on the Supreme Court's role in interpreting the Constitution. The first two articles—on congressional districting and affirmative action—relate to the 14th Amendment guarantee of equal protection under the laws. In a third case, relating to the Takings Clause of the 5th Amendment, the Court rules that the government may, within limits, make laws and regulations that have the effect of reducing property values or limiting land use without compensating the landowner.

Political Participation. This section addresses parties; elections, campaigns, and voters; and interest groups. Specifically, the 1994 congressional midterm elections and the Supreme Court's decision on majority-minority congressional districts are reviewed for their impact on party politics and the political landscape. Then, the 1996 congressional and presidential elections are previewed from several different angles. This section of the *Guide* concludes with analyses of two interest group coalitions, the cotton industry and the Medicare lobby.

Government Institutions. Aspects of the presidency, Congress, and judiciary are discussed in turn. During the 102nd Congress Democrats controlled Congress and a Republican occupied the White House; in the 104th Congress the situation is reversed. The implications of partisan realignment for the institutions themselves as well as for issue formulation are addressed. The section concludes with overviews of presidential powers and the Supreme Court's role in confusing the issue of majority-minority districts.

Politics and Public Policy. CQ editors present an overview of the major issues of the day: Medicare and Medicaid reform, welfare reform, overhaul of sixty-year-old agriculture programs, and other topics. At press time, none of the major reform bills had passed, many had been rolled into a massive budget reconciliation bill, and President Clinton was threatening to veto that. With events developing rapidly and the outcome uncertain, editors of the *Guide* intend these overviews to assist the reader in understanding the eventual outcome, whatever it may be.

By reprinting articles largely as they appeared originally in the *Weekly Report,* the *Guide*'s editors provide a handy source of information about contemporary political issues. The date of original publication is noted with each article to give the reader a time frame for the events that are described. Although new developments may have occurred subsequently, updates of the articles are provided only when they are essential to an understanding of the basic operations of American government. Page number references to related and background articles in the *Weekly Report* and the *CQ Almanac* are provided to facilitate additional research on topical events. Both are available at many school and public libraries.

FOUNDATIONS OF
AMERICAN GOVERNMENT

Nothing is more central to constitutional government than fair and equal representation in the national legislature. The boundaries of congressional districts are redrawn every ten years to account for a shifting population so that each member of Congress is representing roughly the same number of citizens. Redrawing the boundaries, however, is a contentious business, particularly in the South where African Americans were systematically discriminated against for many years. The Voting Rights Act of 1964, passed in an effort to end discrimination in congressional districting, required a number of Southern states to clear their maps in advance with the Justice Department or a federal district court. Vigorous enforcement of the act by the Justice Department to enhance the chances of minorities being elected to Congress is now being questioned by an increasingly conservative Supreme Court. Since 1993 the Court has been struggling to determine at what point a race-conscious redistricting process weighted to ameliorate past discrimination violates the 14th Amendment's requirement of equal protection under the law.

The second article in this section concerns a similar 14th Amendment issue: affirmative action. The Court handed down a ruling that questioned the constitutional permissibility of "set asides" for selected groups in federal contracts. This case, like that on redistricting, was decided on a 5-4 vote, indicating wide disagreement among the justices.

Another issue brewing on Capitol Hill as well as in the courts concerns the Takings Clause of the 5th Amendment. The federal government often passes legislation, such as the Endangered Species Act of 1973, that directly or indirectly limits a property-owner's use of his or her property. The courts and Congress are increasingly sensitive to such uncompensated takings.

These issues, likely to be debated in this decade and beyond, introduce *Guide* readers to the complexities of the Constitution and of constitutional interpretation.

Court Takes a Harder Line On Minority Voting Blocs

Tougher standard for districts drawn around race may undermine new diversity in Congress

In its latest attempt to balance the Voting Rights Act of 1965 with constitutional principles of equal treatment, the Supreme Court has sharpened its objections to race-based political boundaries — even when drawn to increase, rather than suppress, the power of racial minorities.

By so doing, the court may have limited minorities' chance to maintain or expand their numbers in Congress. And it may have created more electoral anxiety for some Republican members.

The court June 29 struck down Georgia's congressional district map as racial gerrymandering that violates the Constitution's guarantees of equal protection under the law. The 5-4 decision in the case, *Miller v. Johnson,* firmed up the court's 1993 ruling in *Shaw v. Reno,* which had questioned race-based redistricting but seemed primarily disturbed by the "bizarrely shaped" districts drawn to aggregate minority voters. *(Weekly Report, p. 1133; 1993 Almanac, p. 325; 1993 Weekly Report, 1761; 1990 Weekly Report, p. 2786)*

Now, the court clearly has moved beyond district shape to cast heavy doubt on any district lines for which race was the "predominant factor."

The decision is expected to prompt legal challenges to other controversial districts in several states. The Supreme Court already has agreed to hear pending challenges to minority-dominant districts in North Carolina and Texas.

While predictions vary widely, some

CQ Weekly Report July 1, 1995

analysts believe a dozen minority-dominant districts could be invalidated, forcing the affected states to redraw their maps with less emphasis on race.

That could jeopardize the historic gains blacks and Hispanics made after the census of 1990 and the election of 1992: In the 103rd Congress (1993-94), the number of black, Hispanic and Asian members increased by more than 50 percent compared with the 102nd Congress.

At the same time, grouping minority voters in districts tended to concentrate the Democratic vote and leave neighboring districts correspondingly more Republican.

This effect contributed to the loss of some traditionally Democratic seats in the South in the elections of 1992 and 1994 and reduced the vote share of some Democrats who were re-elected.

That suggests that any major dis-

mantling of the post-1990 districts, in Georgia and elsewhere, might help Democrats recover some of the electoral ground they recently lost.

Sharpening Shaw

In the *Shaw v. Reno* ruling in 1993, written by Justice Sandra Day O'Connor, a 5-4 majority of the court indicated its discomfort with the aggressive drawing of elongated districts for the clear purpose of aggregating minority voters.

In *Miller v. Johnson,* the same five justices backed an opinion written by Justice Anthony M. Kennedy questioning any districting plan in which race was the "predominant factor."

The ruling does not forbid states from taking race into account when drawing political districts and explicitly concedes it may at times be appropriate. But districting that relies heavily on racial demographics will be subject to the court's most stringent level of review — strict scrutiny. And the decision takes aim at the philosophical premise that minorities benefit when they are placed in minority-dominant voting districts.

In his opinion, Kennedy said the goal of opening the political system to minorities "is neither assured nor well served, however, by carving electorates into racial blocs."

Joining in Kennedy's opinion were Chief Justice William H. Rehnquist and Justices O'Connor, Antonin Scalia and Clarence Thomas. The same five justices constituted the majority in a recent ruling that cast doubt on federal affirmative action programs. *(Weekly Report, p. 1743)*

Open Invitation

The ruling is a clear slap at the Justice Department, which pushed minority-dominant districts aggressively under President George Bush and has continued to do so under President Clinton. The Voting Rights Act requires that states with a history of racially discriminatory voting, including Georgia, must "preclear" new districting plans with the Justice Department or a federal district court. Critics, and in this case the Supreme Court, claim that Justice officials have abused this authority and improperly forced states to maximize the number of minority-dominant districts.

Still, the court left much unanswered about when race can factor into states' districting considerations. When is race not simply present, but "predominant" in the districting process? Even when race is a predominant factor, maps may be defensible because of a compelling need to eradicate discrimination, but the ruling does not spell out how states can pass that test.

Justice Ruth Bader Ginsburg dissented, joined by Justices Stephen G. Breyer, David H. Souter and John Paul Stevens.

Ginsburg wrote that the *Miller* ruling would create chaos in the redistricting process and implicate federal judges in complex map-drawing that properly should be left to politicians. "The court's disposition renders redistricting perilous work for state legislatures," she wrote.

She read portions of her dissent from the bench and cautioned that "the court has not yet spoken a final word" on the difficult issues raised in the *Miller* case.

Ginsburg said the court majority seems to be placing a greater burden on districts drawn to promote racial, rather than ethnic, identity.

"Until now, no constitutional infirmity has been seen in districting Irish or Italian voters together, for example, so long as the delineation does not abandon familiar apportionment practices," she wrote in her dissent.

Ginsburg also cited the long history of white efforts to stifle black voting power and said that history requires different judicial protections for minority voters than for white voters.

Just hours after handing down the Georgia ruling, the court agreed to hear two additional cases — from Texas and North Carolina — involving the proper scope of race-conscious

State Maps Become Legal Battlegrounds

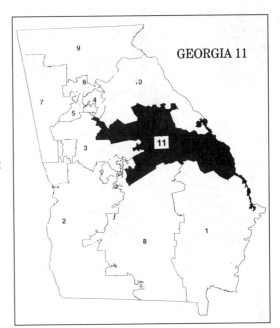

The 11th was one of two new black-majority districts created in Georgia. The district is not one of the most irregularly shaped of the new minority districts. However, at its extremes, it reaches thin fingers to take in widely separated black populations near Atlanta and in Augusta and Savannah. Democrat Cynthia A. McKinney represents the 11th.

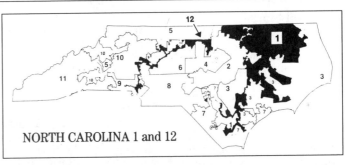

Two black-majority districts were created in North Carolina, which previously had none. The 12th, represented by Democrat Melvin Watt, narrowly follows the route of Interstate 85, incorporating black communities in most of the state's major cities. The 1st, held by Democrat Eva Clayton, has numerous nooks and crannies along its edges.

districting. The court summarily dismissed a challenge to California's congressional district map, indicating it found no evidence of harm to the principles discussed in *Miller*.

Civil rights advocates were dismayed by the *Miller* ruling.

"This is the worst possible decision short of saying these districts are absolutely unconstitutional," said Laughlin McDonald, director of the American Civil Liberties Union's voting rights project. McDonald predicted that many new districts that have elected minority representatives could be in jeopardy.

But some analysts, such as University of Virginia law Professor Pamela Karlan, think those predictions are premature. Karlan pointed to the

court's decision to hear the Texas and North Carolina cases as evidence that there is more, and unpredictable, law to come: "The court is so divided on the issue that some of the justices want to hear every case."

Abigail Thernstrom, a senior fellow at the Manhattan Institute and the author of a book critical of race-conscious redistricting, welcomed the ruling as an overdue check on the Justice Department role in state map-drawing. "The Justice Department has totally distorted the Voting Rights Act," she said.

The Justice Department has denied it was or is pursuing a "maximization" policy, saying it was simply carrying out the mandates of the Voting Rights Act. Karlan agreed, but

In his majority opinion, Justice Anthony M. Kennedy wrote, "The end is neither assured nor well served ... by carving electorates into racial blocs."

Justice Ruth Bader Ginsburg, after reading her dissenting opinion in *Miller v. Johnson*, said, "The court has not yet spoken a final word."

predicted the department would have no choice now but to ease up on its enforcement recommendations or leave states in an untenable position.

Earlier voting rights cases had focused on the portion of the Voting Rights Act that allows voters or the Justice Department to challenge state actions that dilute minority voting power.

The Supreme Court laid out many of the rules for race-conscious districting under the Voting Rights Act in the 1986 case *Thornburg v. Gingles*.

Legislatures generally are required to draw a minority-dominant district when there is evidence that the minority voters are sufficiently compact, numerous and politically cohesive and where there is evidence that white voters tend to vote along racial lines.

The Justice Department interpreted those mandates fairly aggressively in the redistricting that followed the 1990 census, often prodding states to draw additional districts in which minorities would make up a majority of the voting age population.

This was the trend arrested by *Shaw v. Reno*, which challenged North Carolina's map. That districting plan led to two blacks being elected to Congress from the state in 1992 (the first African-Americans to represent North Carolina since 1901). In O'Connor's

opinion, race-conscious maps of this sort have the potential of violating constitutional guarantees of equal protection under the 14th Amendment.

The ruling was vague but provocative, and a string of challenges followed. Two of those cases reached the U.S. Supreme Court this term — a Louisiana case called *United States v. Hays* and the *Miller* case from Georgia. In both, lower federal courts had rejected congressional districting maps designed to provide new, black-majority districts. The high court heard oral arguments on both appeals April 19 and handed down rulings in both on June 29.

In Louisiana, white voters challenged a newly drawn congressional district that in 1992 elected Democrat Cleo Fields, an African-American. Federal judges have rejected two different versions of that black-majority district, prompting the state to appeal to the Supreme Court.

The Supreme Court sidestepped the core of the *Hays* case, instead ruling that the white plaintiffs had no grounds to sue because they lived outside the controversial 4th District. That saves Fields' district for now, but voters within his district could revive the complaint.

Role of Justice

Georgia initially had drawn a district map with two black-majority congressional districts. Under pressure from the Bush administration's Justice Department, however, it redrew the map to provide three such districts. Rep. Cynthia A. McKinney, a black Democrat, was elected from that additional black-majority district, the 11th District.

Because McKinney's district had a more regular shape than the district at issue in *Shaw*, and because it was drawn to meet the Justice Department's view of the Voting Rights Act requirements, state officials and its defenders had thought the 11th District could survive in court.

But Kennedy quashed both lines of argument.

An odd shape is just a clue that race may have been behind district lines, he wrote, not a necessary requirement to mount a legal challenge under the equal protection clause. Kennedy set forth a new standard for such challenges, namely showing that race was the "predominant factor" in shaping the district.

To meet this standard, Kennedy

said, "a plaintiff must prove that the legislature subordinated traditional race-neutral districting principles ... to racial considerations." Some of the traditional principles recognized by the court majority include compactness, contiguity, adherence to political subdivisions and "actual shared interests."

And the opinion states that while shared racial identity may in some cases reflect shared interests, it cannot be assumed to do so.

Even where race was the predominant factor, Kennedy said, states can still defend their district lines if they can prove they were crafted to serve a "compelling interest." Kennedy did not specify what would meet this standard, but he did make it clear that adhering to Justice Department directives did not suffice.

In the Georgia case, Kennedy concluded that the Justice Department had overstepped the requirements of the Voting Rights Act when it pressed the state to create a third black-majority district.

However, several legal analysts said they believe a state could withstand an equal protection challenge if it could show that it had to draw a race-conscious district or risk a plausible vote-dilution lawsuit by minority voters under the Voting Rights Act. ∎

Ruling Rocks Foundation Of Affirmative Action

Federal programs now must pass 'strict scrutiny' test even as challenges to policy build in Congress

Republican lawmakers are pushing ahead with efforts to unravel affirmative action, encouraged and empowered by a dramatic Supreme Court ruling that cast doubt on federal programs seeking to advance women and minorities.

The high court June 12 handed down a 5-4 opinion in a closely watched case, *Adarand Constructors v. Pena,* that challenged a federal affirmative action program.

The majority opinion, written by Justice Sandra Day O'Connor, did not actually strike down any affirmative action programs — not even the special considerations for minority subcontractors that were at issue in the case. But it criticized the moral justification for affirmative action, saying that race-conscious programs can amount to unconstitutional reverse discrimination and even harm those they seek to advance. The ruling puts these programs on far more tenuous legal footing. From now on, federal affirmative action programs will be subject to the most rigorous level of court review — a test that has proved difficult to pass.

At a minimum, the ruling seems certain to invite legal challenges to other federal affirmative action programs.

But Congress, or even President Clinton, might get there first.

Republicans had been preparing a legislative assault on federal affirmative action, either by eliminating programs or with a sweeping measure to outlaw virtually all federal preferences on the basis of race or gender. Their targets include scores of congressional and executive branch initiatives that offer special consideration or set-asides for

CQ Weekly Report June 17, 1995

O'Connor, left, said the Constitution guarantees equal protection to individuals, not groups. Stevens led the dissent.

women, minorities and others in federal contracting and hiring. *(Guide to Current American Government, p. 112)*

The *Adarand* decision should embolden this camp, adding political and intellectual heft to its position.

"The Supreme Court's decision today is one more reason for the federal government to get out of the race-preference business," Senate Majority Leader Bob Dole, R-Kan., said in a prepared statement. "It's now our responsibility in Congress to follow the court's lead and put the federal government's own house in order."

Dole traditionally supported affirmative action, but in recent months has criticized the policy and pledged to curtail or eliminate federal preferences.

Some advocates of affirmative action conceded that their task would be more difficult in the months ahead.

Yet many hastened to underscore that the debate is far from over.

All but two justices indicated that affirmative action is sometimes appropriate to address ongoing problems of discrimination.

By fencing out race-conscious programs that cannot meet the new rules, many supporters said, the court simultaneously has drawn a protective line

around a permissible zone for affirmative action. Rep. Melvin Watt, D-N.C., said he hopes the ruling will undercut Republicans who want to abolish affirmative action. "The Supreme Court has boxed some of my colleagues in," he said.

Clinton, whose administration is reviewing affirmative action efforts, June 13 released a statement stressing this view. "The court has approved affirmative action that is narrowly tailored to achieve a compelling interest," Clinton said. "The constitutional test is now tougher than it was, but I am confident that the test can be met in many cases."

Rather than ending the debate on affirmative action, the court ruling may have sharpened it.

"I think there are people on the Hill who will wrap themselves in the court decision," said William L. Taylor, vice chairman of the Leadership Conference on Civil Rights. But because the court indicated there is room for some affirmative action, Taylor said, lawmakers cannot pretend that the *Adarand* decision settles the issue.

"Their choices are their choices and not the court's," he said. If they abandon affirmative action, Taylor said, "they will be responsible for the consequences of what they do."

Shifting Standard

The *Adarand* case concerned a Department of Transportation policy that gave contractors a bonus if they hired minority subcontractors.

Under the program, the bonus applied to any "disadvantaged business enterprise." Racial minorities were presumed to meet the "disadvantaged" criterion, subject to a challenge proving otherwise. Non-minorities could become eligible for the program if they

Excerpts From Court Decision

*F*ollowing *are excerpts from the Supreme Court decision June 12 in* Adarand Constructors v. Pena. *In the 5-4 decision, the court said federal affirmative action programs must meet a standard known as strict scrutiny, which requires them to be "narrowly tailored" to meet "a compelling government interest."* (Story, p. 12)

The majority opinion was written by Justice Sandra Day O'Connor and joined by Chief Justice William H. Rehnquist and Justices Anthony M. Kennedy, Antonin Scalia and Clarence Thomas. O'Connor wrote:

... All governmental action based on race — a group classification long recognized as in most circumstances irrelevant and therefore prohibited — should be subjected to detailed judicial inquiry to insure that the personal right to equal protection of the laws has not been infringed. These ideas have long been central to this Court's understanding of equal protection, and holding "benign" state and Federal racial classifications to different standards does not square with them. "[A] free people whose institutions are founded upon the doctrine of equality" should tolerate no retreat from the principle that government may treat people differently because of their race only for the most compelling reasons. Accordingly, we hold today that all racial classifications, imposed by whatever Federal, state, or local governmental actor, must be analyzed by a reviewing court under strict scrutiny. In other words, such classifications are constitutional only if they are narrowly tailored measures that further compelling governmental interests....

By requiring strict scrutiny of racial classifications, we require courts to make sure that a governmental classification based on race, which "so seldom provide(s) a relevant basis for disparate treatment" is legitimate, before permitting unequal treatment based on race to proceed....

We think that requiring strict scrutiny is the best way to ensure that courts will consistently give racial classifications that kind of detailed examination, both as to ends and as to means....

Finally, we wish to dispel the notion that strict scrutiny is "strict in theory, but fatal in fact." The unhappy persistence of both the practical and the lingering effects of racial discrimination against minority groups in this country is an unfortunate reality, and government is not disqualified from acting in response to it....

When race-based action is necessary to further a compelling interest, such action is within constitutional constraints if it satisfies the "narrow tailoring" test this Court has set out in previous cases.

Concurring, Thomas wrote:

I believe that there is a "moral (and) constitutional equivalence" between laws designed to subjugate a race and those that distribute benefits on the basis of race in order to foster some current notion of equality. Government cannot make us equal; it can only recognize, respect and protect us as equal before the law.

That these programs may have been motivated, in part, by good intentions cannot provide refuge from the principle that under our Constitution, the Government may not make distinctions on the basis of race. As far as the Constitution is concerned, it is irrelevant whether a government's racial classifications are drawn by those who wish to oppress a race or by those who have a sincere desire to help those thought to be disadvantaged. There can be no doubt that the paternalism that appears to lie at the heart of this program is at war with the principle of inherent equality that underlies and infuses our Constitution....

Dissenting Views

Dissenting from the ruling were Justices John Paul Stevens, David H. Souter, Ruth Bader Ginsburg and Stephen G. Breyer. Stevens wrote:

The consistency that the Court espouses would disregard the difference between a "No Trespassing" sign and a welcome mat.... It would equate a law that made black citizens ineligible for military service with a program aimed at recruiting black soldiers. An attempt by the majority to exclude members of a minority race from a regulated market is fundamentally different from a subsidy that enables a relatively small group of newcomers to enter that market. An interest in "consistency" does not justify treating differences as though they were similarities.

The Court's explanation for treating dissimilar race-based decisions as though they were equally objectionable is a supposed inability to differentiate between "invidious" and "benign" discrimination. But the term "affirmative action" is common and well understood. Its presence in everyday parlance shows that people understand the difference between good intentions and bad....

It is one thing to question the wisdom of affirmative action programs; there are many responsible arguments against them, including the one based upon stigma, that Congress might find persuasive when it decides whether to enact or retain race-based preferences. It is another thing altogether to equate the many well-meaning and intelligent lawmakers and their constituents, whether members of majority or minority races, who have supported affirmative action over the years to segregationists and bigots....

In a separate dissent, Ginsburg wrote:

The divisions in this difficult case should not obscure the Court's recognition of the persistence of racial inequality and a majority's acknowledgment of Congress's authority to act affirmatively, not only to end discrimination, but also to counteract discrimination's lingering effects. Those effects, reflective of a system of racial caste only recently ended, are evident in our work places, markets and neighborhoods. Job applicants with identical resumes, qualifications and interview styles still experience different receptions, depending on their race. White and African-American consumers still encounter different deals....

could show how they were socially and economically disadvantaged.

A white contractor challenged the policy in court after losing a contract to build guardrails, despite offering the lowest bid.

A federal appeals court upheld the program as within the proper bounds of affirmative action. The Supreme Court decision did not uphold or reject that ruling, but instead sent the case back for further review under new, tougher rules.

At the core of the court's decision are the words "strict scrutiny" — a legal term that means the policy in question is on dubious constitutional ground and must be extremely well justified to survive a court challenge.

Since 1989, the Supreme Court has required that state and local affirmative action programs pass the strict scrutiny test.

To survive strict scrutiny, a policy must serve a "compelling" governmental interest and employ the most narrowly tailored means to that end.

The federal government, however, has operated under a somewhat looser standard that gives it more leeway in implementing affirmative action. This intermediate standard requires that a policy serve important goals and be "substantially related" to those ends.

As recently as 1990, the high court upheld a program to grant minority broadcasters a preference in obtaining federal licenses. There, the majority said that when the federal government makes racial distinctions for a benign or remedial purpose, such programs need only survive intermediate-level scrutiny by the federal courts. *(1990 Almanac, p. 379)*

Now the court is taking a new tack.

O'Connor said the federal government must meet the same standards as state and local governments when it takes race into account, even if its programs are meant to advance rather than harm the affected group.

She wrote that the Fifth and 14th amendments to the Constitution guarantee equal protection to individuals rather than to groups. "It follows from that principle that all governmental action based on race — a group classification long recognized as 'in most circumstances irrelevant and therefore prohibited' . . . should be subjected to detailed judicial inquiry to ensure that the personal right to equal protection of the laws has not been infringed."

(Excerpts from the opinion, p. 6)

O'Connor did not specify whether the Transportation Department program would meet the new test. Nor did her opinion rule out the potential for some constitutionally valid affirmative action programs. "The unhappy persistence of both the practice and the lingering effects of racial discrimination . . . is an unfortunate reality," she wrote, "and government is not disqualified from acting in response to it."

SCOTT J. FERRELL

Canady plans to introduce a bill outlawing most federal affirmative action programs.

Two justices, Clarence Thomas and Antonin Scalia, would have gone further and outlawed any use of racial preferences. "Government can never have a compelling interest in discriminating on the basis of race in order to 'make up' for past racial discrimination in the opposite direction," Scalia wrote.

The four dissenting justices said the main opinion went too far.

Justice John Paul Stevens wrote a lengthy dissent, taking issue with almost every step in the majority's reasoning. "There is no moral or constitutional equivalence between a policy that is designed to perpetuate a caste system and one that seeks to eradicate racial subordination."

Stevens said Congress should have more leeway than state or local governments. He noted that the 14th Amendment, while prohibiting the states from discriminating against racial minorities, explicitly empowers Congress to take action necessary to make equal protection a reality.

Justices Stephen G. Breyer, Ruth Bader Ginsburg and David H. Souter also dissented.

Stevens pointed out that the ruling may wind up sustaining affirmative action for women while outlawing it, in most cases, for racial minorities.

Gender distinctions traditionally have been scrutinized in the court under intermediate rather than strict scrutiny.

The Next Chapter

The court decision likely will delay a long-awaited administration review of federal affirmative action programs.

Clinton ordered the review in February, saying he wanted to see if some programs needed to be strengthened or discarded.

Administration officials are expected to re-evaluate the programs in light of the new legal rules.

There is considerable debate about how many of the programs can withstand that test. Some analysts, such as conservative activist Clint Bolick, predicted that few programs would pass muster. However, Judith Lichtman, president of the Women's Legal Defense Fund, said dozens of state and local affirmative action programs have been upheld under the "strict scrutiny" standard.

Generally, that standard has meant the government must show that an affirmative action policy responds to specific past discrimination, rather than general societal prejudices, and that the problem cannot be overcome through race-neutral measures.

Watt said he hopes lawmakers will let the administration conduct the review and adjust the programs — many of which are executive branch directives — itself.

GOP leaders do not have the issue on a fast-track summer agenda, and House Speaker Newt Gingrich, R-Ga., said he might prefer to proceed slowly.

Still, some Republicans appear prepared to take an active role, and soon.

Besides Dole's renewed pledge to go after affirmative action programs, another GOP presidential candidate, Sen. Phil Gramm of Texas, has said he would try to block affirmative action via the must-pass appropriations bills.

In the House, Rep. Charles T. Canady, R-Fla., is moving ahead with plans to introduce and mark up a major bill outlawing virtually all federal affirmative action programs. Canady chairs the House Judiciary Subcommittee on the Constitution.

Meanwhile, Small Business Committee Chairman Jan Meyers, R-Kan., said she has been preparing to excise the Small Business Administration's well-established set-aside program for minority subcontractors from an upcoming reauthorization bill. ■

JUDICIAL REVIEW

Court Upholds Law Protecting Species on Private Property

Decision bolsters environmentalists' cause but may rally landowners' supporters

Environmentalists, who see their cause as under siege in the 104th Congress, got a boost from the judicial branch June 29, when the Supreme Court upheld a key regulatory tenet of the Endangered Species Act.

The ruling enables the Interior Department to continue barring damage to vital species' habitats on private property, as well as preventing intentional physical injury to endangered plants and animals.

But the court's 6-3 ruling in the case of *Babbitt v. Sweet Home Chapter of Communities for a Greater Oregon* will not forestall nascent efforts by many congressional Republicans and conservative Democrats to overhaul the 1973 Endangered Species Act (PL 93-205), making changes that would effectively overturn the court's decision.

Efforts to rewrite the act are based on the contention that the law has allowed the federal government to deprive individuals of their property rights in the name of protecting animals and plants.

"Today's decision will serve as a rallying cry for ... reform from communities across the country that have been hurt by the current law," said Sen. Slade Gorton, R-Wash., the author of a bill (S 768) that would revise the law and limit the government's ability to place private lands off limits to development. *(Weekly Report, p. 1324)*

The *Sweet Home* case centered on the federal government's enforcement on privately owned lands of the law's prohibition against any act that would "harm" an animal or plant species that faces an imminent or likely threat of extinction.

A regulation enforced by the Interior Department's Fish and Wildlife Service since 1975 defines harm to include "significant habitat modification and degradation where it actually kills or injures wildlife."

Critics, including the Oregon for-

esters who filed the *Sweet Home* case, argued that the regulation is wrong on its face and should have defined harm to mean only direct injury to a species.

They also contended that federal actions under the habitat protection regulation had cost many jobs and damaged property values by preventing landowners from cutting trees, even when there was no evidence of direct threat to a species.

The U.S. Court of Appeals for the District of Columbia Circuit agreed with the foresters in March 1994, issuing a 2-1 ruling that overturned the regulation. The Supreme Court decision June 29 reversed the lower court ruling.

Representing the majority, Justice John Paul Stevens wrote, "Given Congress' clear expression of the [law's] broad purpose to protect endangered and threatened wildlife, the [Interior] Secretary's definition of 'harm' is reasonable." Joining Stevens in the majority were Justices Sandra Day O'Connor, Anthony M. Kennedy, David H. Souter, Ruth Bader Ginsburg and Stephen G. Breyer.

In his dissent, Justice Antonin Scalia took a strong position in support of property rights advocates.

"The Court's holding that the hunting and killing prohibition incidentally preserves habitat on private lands imposes unfairness to the point of financial ruin — not just upon the rich, but upon the simplest farmer who finds his land conscripted to national zoological use," Scalia wrote. Joining Scalia in the minority were Chief Justice William H. Rehnquist and Justice Clarence Thomas.

Congressional Backlash

Environmental activists hailed the court's ruling. "This historic decision confirms what Congress has said for 20 years, that habitat protection is essential to species conservation," said Rodger Schlickeisen, president of the Defenders of Wildlife, an environmentalist group based in Washington, D.C.

Such opinions were echoed by congressional advocates of the law. "If we can't protect the dinner tables that feed species or the nurseries where they shelter their young, we can't protect endangered species," said Rep. Gerry E. Studds, D-Mass.

But critics of the "harm" regulation said the decision would fuel their efforts to overhaul the law.

Rep. Richard W. Pombo, R-Calif., who is drafting an endangered species revision bill as head of a House Resources Committee task force, said he was disappointed by the ruling. "Congress needs to establish policy and clarify the intent of the law, or the court system and the bureaucracy will do it for us," he said.

Gorton took a slightly different tack while reaching the same conclusion. He said the court had correctly interpreted the validity of the regulation under the current law. But he said it only proved that the law is wrong and needs to be revised.

The 104th Congress has already shown a strong inclination to make at least some modification to the Endangered Species Act.

An amendment by Sen. Kay Bailey Hutchison, R-Texas, to place a moratorium through the end of fiscal 1995 on new listings of plant and animal species as endangered was enacted as part of a supplemental spending bill for defense programs (HR 889 — PL 104-6). *(Weekly Report, p. 827)*

The fiscal 1996 Interior spending bill approved June 27 by the House Appropriations Committee would extend the listings freeze for one year.

The law also has been singled out by private property rights advocates in the House. An omnibus regulatory overhaul bill (HR 9) passed by the House on March 3 names the Endangered Species Act as one of a handful of environment-related laws under which the federal government would have to compensate landowners for regulatory actions that result in decreased property values. *(Weekly Report, p. 679)* ■

POLITICAL PARTICIPATION

The historic turnaround in the fortunes of the Republican Party in the 1994 midterm elections changed the face of politics. It affected not only the tenor and agenda of the 104th Congress but also the outlook for the 1996 congressional and presidential elections. CQ editors begin this section of the *Guide* with an overview of the 1994 elections and their impact on the parties and the political landscape.

Adding to the Democratic Party's electoral woes is a Supreme Court on the verge of overturning majority-minority congressional districts. The reelection prospects of roughly a dozen minority members of Congress—all Democrats—were thrown into doubt when the Supreme Court ruled 5-4 to disallow the map used in Georgia's 11th congressional district in the 1992 and 1994 elections. The ruling does not automatically invalidate similarly drawn districts in other states, but it clearly shows the direction in which the Court is leaning. If suits are brought challenging other districts drawn largely along racial lines, the Democratic Party might be hard pressed to retain those seats.

The *Guide*'s coverage of the 1996 presidential election begins with a topic that gives Republicans as well as Democrats cause for concern: widespread disaffection among the American people with both major parties. In 1992 Ross Perot and other independent candidates claimed 20 percent of the popular vote in the greatest defection from the major parties since 1912. But unlike the situation in 1912, the voters show no signs of returning to the fold. Ross Perot, Colin Powell, and a half dozen other independent or third-party candidates could figure prominently come November.

As in 1992, the primary calendar will influence the selection of the major party candidates. The primaries and caucuses are early and tightly clustered—circumstances that favor the frontrunners, who have the name recognition, financial resources, and organization to battle in many states simultaneously. After reviewing the calendar, CQ editors profile the frontrunners: President Bill Clinton and Senate Majority Leader Robert Dole.

Before turning to interest groups, which along with parties and voters is a key element in political participation, CQ editors provide a cautionary tale about the use of statistics in politics and review the steps the GOP freshmen are taking to prepare for their first reelection bids.

An interest group is an organized body of individuals who share some goals and try to influence public policy to meet those goals. The cotton industry is one such group. The growers, ginners, cooperatives, warehouse workers, merchants, crushers, and manufacturers coordinate their efforts to gain favorable treatment on Capitol Hill. Another diverse group—the elderly, doctors, hospitals, and health insurers—watches carefully how Congress handles Medicare reform.

ELECTION '94 ASSESSMENT

Rare Combination of Forces May Make History of '94

Democratic apathy and Republican strength suggest landslide may have ushered in a lasting change

Great partisan shifts in Congress can have different origins. Sometimes they are caused by great surges in voter support for one party or by widespread apathy that debilitates the other.

The powerful Republican tide of 1994 combined elements of both. Voters flocked to GOP congressional candidates in record numbers in the election that marked the middle of the term that President Clinton had won in 1992. At the same time, the president's own party had difficulty motivating its core constituents.

That extraordinary combination could give the 1994 election, which turned over the House and Senate to GOP control, a long-term significance well beyond that of other recent landslides in Congress.

It may augur a return of the White House to Republican control in 1996. Beyond that, it could signal a new era of sustained Republican domination on Capitol Hill, a state of affairs not seen since the 1920s.

At a minimum, the 1994 election provided an abrupt change from the electoral arithmetic to which both parties had long since become accustomed. And the results of that shift were evident in the agenda pursued by House Republicans, and bequeathed to their Senate brethren, in the first 100 days of the 104th Congress.

Up and Down

Republicans, whose nationwide vote for House seats had never totaled more than 28 million in a midterm election, won 36.6 million votes in 1994. That was nearly 9 million more than the GOP won in 1990 and represented the largest midterm-to-midterm increase in one party's vote total in the nation's history.

Democratic House candidates, on the other hand, drew almost 1 million

CQ Weekly Report April 15, 1995

Voter Turnout: Upswing in the '90s
(Turnout Rate as Percentage of Voting-Age Population)

SOURCE: Census Bureau, 1960-92; Congressional Quarterly, 1994, using voting-age population projections from the Census Bureau. Midterm House turnout rate since 1972 includes vote cast for delegate in the District of Columbia.

MARILYN GATES-DAVIS

fewer votes than in 1990, continuing a general downward slide in their congressional voting strength that had begun in the mid-1980s. In 1982, when recession politics were putting a brake on the popularity of Republican President Ronald Reagan, Democratic candidates for House seats collected more than 35 million votes. In 1994, they drew less than 32 million.

"I think it was a realigning election," says Republican demographer John Morgan. "The Democrats have not stopped hemorrhaging."

It will take another election or two to see the full ramifications of the 1994 vote. But it was clear on Election Day that something big had happened.

The combination of shrinking vote totals for the Democrats with an exploding GOP vote (nearly one-third larger than 1990) was unparalleled since the Democrats' own growth spurt during the Depression and early days of the New Deal.

Then the number of votes won by Democratic House candidates grew by one-third from 1926 to 1930 and increased again by more than 50 percent

from 1930 to 1934. In the process, the Democrats went from being a hopeless minority to unassailable status as the nation's majority party for the next generation. Indeed, after 1934, the Democrats dominated in the House for all but four of the next 60 years.

Republicans may be poised for a run of their own. At the moment, however, the standing of the GOP more closely resembles the Democrats on the eve of their hegemony (1930) rather than at its height.

By 1930, the Democrats had the momentum but the GOP still held the White House. It took the election of Franklin D. Roosevelt in 1932 and a pro-Democratic vote in the midterm election of 1934 to cement the Democratic majority.

Positive Landslides

Elections like those of 1930, 1934 and 1994 can be considered "positive" landslides because of the large surge in votes for one party. They do not happen very often.

The decisive Democratic midterm victories of 1958 and 1974 were basically "negative" landslides, driven by apathy and a corresponding lack of votes on the Republican side. *(Weekly Report, p. 1061)*

The big Republican midterm victories of 1946 and 1966 featured vote increases for both parties. It just so happened that the GOP vote total showed a greater increase each time.

A cautionary note for Republicans is that midterm elections, even one-sided ones, are not always a reliable harbinger of the next presidential election. The legendary example is the midterm of 1946. Large GOP congressional gains that year were overturned by a Democratic comeback two years later, which allowed the party to regain control of Congress and returned embattled President Harry S Truman

The GOP's Historic Surge

Republican House candidates in 1994 drew nearly 9 million more votes than in 1990. That gain easily eclipsed the largest previous increase ever recorded by one party from one midterm House election to another.

Prior to 1994, the largest increase was 6.3 million votes, registered by the Democrats from 1930 to 1934.

Much of the GOP vote increase in November 1994 was in the South, although the party scored dramatic gains in every region. *(Vote totals shown below are in thousands)*

| | 1994 House Vote | | Votes Gained or Lost, 1990-94 | |
	Republicans	Democrats	Republicans	Democrats
South	10,322	7,861	+ 3,798	- 798
Midwest	10,147	8,414	+ 2,176	- 956
West	8,237	7,424	+ 1,692	+ 403
East	7,885	7,999	+ 1,319	+ 583
NATIONAL TOTAL	36,590	31,698	+ 8,985	- 769

SOURCE: Congressional Quarterly calculations based on official state-by-state election results. Some totals do not add due to rounding.

to office. *(Weekly Report, p. 503)*

Yet the contests of 1946 and 1948 were fought in an era when the Democrats were still the majority party. That is not the case now.

Republicans not only won majorities in both chambers of Congress in 1994 but also achieved a dominant 30-seat share of the governorships and climbed to their highest share of state legislative seats in more than a generation.

Elephant Romp

Ever since Clinton's election, the GOP has been on a sustained elephant romp. Before 1992 had ended, Republicans had picked up a Senate seat (Paul Coverdell) in a runoff election in Georgia. In 1993, they added another (Kay Bailey Hutchison) in a special election in Texas. The same year, they swept to victory in the gubernatorial contests in New Jersey and Virginia.

In 1994, Republicans took away Democratic House seats in districts in Oklahoma and Kentucky, the latter of which had never sent a Republican to the House before. And in the fall, Republicans outpolled Democrats by more than 7 million votes in gubernatorial races, by nearly 5 million votes in House elections and by almost 4 million votes in Senate races.

The 1994 election was historic, says former Republican National Committee Chairman Frank J. Fahrenkopf Jr., for the "depth and reach" of the Republican success. *(1994 Vote count, p. 13)*

Conversely, the Democratic debacle was truly national in scope. In 1992, the Democrats had won more House votes than the Republicans in every region of the country. But in 1994, the Democrats were outpolled in every region except the East and in every state with at least 10 congressional districts except Massachusetts.

In a number of megastates, the GOP edge was substantial. Republicans took 59 percent of the congressional ballots cast in Florida, 58 percent in Ohio, 57 percent in North Carolina, 56 percent in Texas, 54 percent in New Jersey and Pennsylvania, and a plurality 49 percent share in California and New York (even though Democrats wound up with more seats in California, New York, Texas and Pennsylvania).

The Democrats won more House votes than the Republicans in only a dozen small to medium-sized states. In terms of electoral votes — soon to be the coin of the realm in the 1996 presidential contest — the states where the Democrats won more votes totaled just 73 electoral votes. The states where Republicans had the edge totaled 450 electoral votes. (The District of Columbia and Louisiana, which elected members in October, were not included in the tally.) *(1994 House vote map, p. 12)*

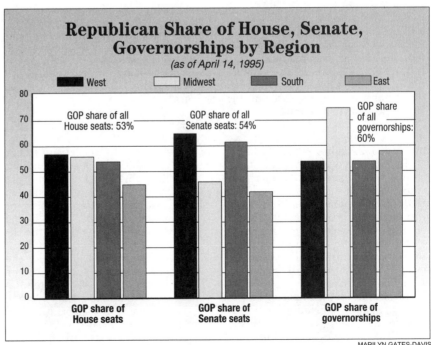

Republican Share of House, Senate, Governorships by Region
(as of April 14, 1995)

■ West □ Midwest ▨ South ▨ East

GOP share of all House seats: 53%

GOP share of all Senate seats: 54%

GOP share of all governorships: 60%

GOP share of House seats

GOP share of Senate seats

GOP share of governorships

MARILYN GATES-DAVIS

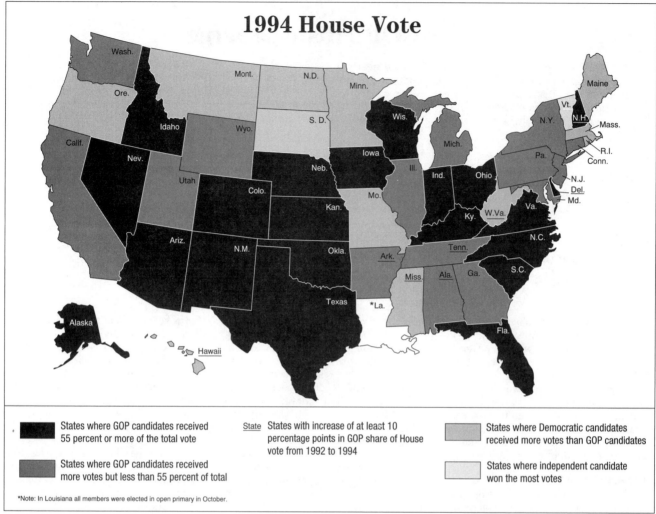

1994 House Vote

States where GOP candidates received 55 percent or more of the total vote

State — States with increase of at least 10 percentage points in GOP share of House vote from 1992 to 1994

States where Democratic candidates received more votes than GOP candidates

States where GOP candidates received more votes but less than 55 percent of total

States where independent candidate won the most votes

*Note: In Louisiana all members were elected in open primary in October.

MARILYN GATES-DAVIS

Nothing Cheap

And GOP success last fall was not accomplished in the milieu of a low turnout election. For a midterm contest, the turnout was relatively high. In spite of media talk of an electorate turned off by negative campaigning, the number of ballots cast for the House jumped from 61 million in 1990 (which represented 33 percent of the nation's voting-age population) to nearly 70 million in 1994 (36 percent).

Republicans were the almost exclusive beneficiaries of the increased vote. The total number of votes that GOP congressional candidates won was up dramatically from 1990 in every region of the country — by nearly 4 million votes in the South, by more than 2 million in the Midwest, by almost 1.7 million in the West and by 1.3 million in the East.

Meanwhile, the number of ballots cast for Democratic House candidates was up marginally from 1990 on the East Coast and West Coast but down elsewhere. Democrats won nearly 600,000 more House votes in the East, and 400,000 more in the West. But the Democratic House vote collapsed in the nation's heartland. It was down by nearly 1 million from four years earlier in the Midwest and by 800,000 in the South.

The number of votes won by Republican House candidates was higher than in 1990 in all but four isolated states — Connecticut, Rhode Island, North Carolina and Montana. Meanwhile, the Democratic vote total was down from 1990 in most states. Where the Democrats did show an increase in their vote total, it was usually dwarfed by the rise in the Republican vote.

In California, for instance, the Democrats won nearly 400,000 more House votes than in 1990, but the Republicans were up more than 700,000. In New York, the Democratic total was also nearly 400,000 votes higher than it was four years earlier, but the GOP total jumped almost 600,000.

And in Washington, where the Democrats suffered more carnage per district than any other state — losing former House Speaker Thomas S. Foley, four other incumbents and a formerly Democratic open seat — the Democrats actually drew 130,000 more House votes than in 1990. But it was just half the size of the increase in the Republican vote.

Heartland Collapse

More typical of 1994, though, was the vote in the bellwether state of Ohio, which has supported the winning candidate in the past eight presidential elections. There, the number of House votes for Republicans was up more than 300,000 from the previous midterm, while the Democratic vote was off by nearly 500,000.

Republicans not only picked up four House seats in Ohio, they easily won the Senate seat vacated by Democrat Howard M. Metzenbaum. And they re-elected Gov. George V. Voino-

Counting the Vote: 1994 Totals

Republicans dominated the 1994 elections, winning 53 percent of the House seats (230 out of 435), 60 percent of the Senate seats (21 of 35) and 67 percent of the governorships (24 of 36) that were at stake.

There were 382 head-to-head House races in November — 195 won by the Republicans, 187 by the Demo-

crats. Of the other 53 races, Republicans won 35 and the Democrats 17, with one seat won by an independent.

Vote totals in the chart below are based on official returns as provided by state election boards.

Percentages in this table do not always add to 100 due to rounding.

	Total Vote	Republicans Vote	%	Democrats Vote	%	Others Vote	%	Plurality
House								
All races	69,774,163	36,590,396	*52.4*	31,698,017	*45.4*	1,485,750	*2.1*	R 4,892,379
Head to head	64,566,048	32,781,359	*50.8*	30,643,383	*47.5*	1,141,306	*1.8*	R 2,137,976
Senate	59,204,131	30,312,301	*51.2*	26,589,323	*44.9*	2,302,507	*3.9*	R 3,722,978
Governor	60,141,074	32,264,674	*53.6*	24,972,007	*41.5*	2,904,393	*4.8*	R 7,292,667

The House vote from all races includes results from the 422 districts in which votes were tallied in the November election. Not included are seven districts in Louisiana, where the House members were elected in the state's open primary in October, and six districts in Florida, where candidates ran unopposed in November and no vote was recorded.

The head-to-head House races are those in which both major parties fielded candidates in November.

SOURCE: Congressional Quarterly calculations based on official state-by-state election results.

---

vich with 72 percent of the vote, the highest share for any Ohio gubernatorial candidate since 1826.

"The Republican victories in Ohio were extraordinary and far greater than many of us anticipated," says John C. Green, the director of the Ray C. Bliss Institute of Applied Politics at the University of Akron.

By way of explanation, Green points to a united Republican Party with good candidates, a divided Democratic Party with weak candidates and the backdrop of an unpopular Democratic president and unpopular Democratic Congress.

Green says he believes it could be awhile before the Democrats are a competitive force again in Ohio. While GOP fissures have been masked by Voinovich's popular management-oriented style, Democratic divisions have been laid bare by a void in party leadership.

Differences have been exposed between socially conservative blue-collar Democrats who still embrace New Deal economic programs and socially liberal suburban professionals who favor more efficient government.

"The Democrats have real serious organizational problems in this state," says Green, "and it will be tough for them to come back in 1996."

Ohio, though, was not a unique problem area for the Democrats in the Midwest last fall. Republicans picked

up 15 House seats in the region, won all four open Senate races and swept eight of the nine governorships, six of them with more than 60 percent of the vote. In the process, the GOP re-established its hegemony in the region where it was born.

Dixie Debacle

For unrelieved misery for Democrats, though, no region could touch the South. The party historically rooted in

Dixie won only one Senate race and three gubernatorial contests there (with two of the winners, Florida's Lawton Chiles and Georgia's Zell Miller, taking only 51 percent of the vote).

Democrats were outpolled by Republican House candidates in every Southern state except Mississippi, where most of the Democratic members are so conservative they could just as readily be Republicans.

Profile of the Defeated

Of the 34 House incumbents who were defeated for re-election this past November:

Foley

- All were Democrats.
- 29 had voted for the 1994 Clinton crime bill.
- 28 had voted for the 1993 Clinton budget-reconciliation bill.
- 21 had won in 1992 with less than 55 percent of the vote.
- 16 were freshmen.
- 16 had voted for NAFTA.
- 15 represented districts that voted for President George Bush in 1992.
- 13 had at least one overdraft at the House bank.
- 9 were outspent by their Republican challengers.
- 5 were from the state of Washington, including House Speaker Thomas S. Foley, the first Speaker to be defeated for re-election since 1862.

In a number of districts, the Democrats went down without a fight. They conceded 21 seats across the region, including nine in Florida, five in Texas and three in Virginia.

By contrast, Democrats were offered free rides by the GOP in only four Southern districts — two minority-oriented constituencies in south Florida, represented by Carrie P. Meek and Alcee L. Hastings, plus the districts of veterans Tom Bevill in north Alabama and W. J. "Billy" Tauzin in the Cajun country of Louisiana.

Altogether, the Democrats lost 19 House seats across the South last fall, more than in any other region. Many of the seats may be gone for good, as Republicans won most of them by comfortable margins in politically congenial terrain. "I think the changes in the South are permanent," says University of California at San Diego political scientist Gary C. Jacobson.

Republicans picked up another seat April 10, when Democratic Rep. Nathan Deal of Georgia announced that he was switching to the GOP. That transforms a delegation that was 9-1 Democratic just three years ago into 8-3 Republican. The three Georgia Democrats that remain represent minority districts.

It would not be surprising if the Democrats lost a number of other seats in the next few years. Sixteen Southern Democrats in the 104th Congress represent districts that were won by President George Bush in 1992.

The party's future in the South may have been writ large in last fall's Senate races, where six GOP candidates easily won seats that not long ago had been held by Democrats. The region's lone Democratic winner was Sen. Charles S. Robb of Virginia, who needed a split in GOP ranks to eke out a plurality victory over Republican Oliver L. North with 46 percent of the vote.

Coastal Comfort

Compared to the decisive Republican trends in the South and Midwest, the voting on the two coasts was not quite so severe for the Democrats.

They lost 15 House seats in the West, including six in Washington alone. But Democrats also scored some high-profile victories across the region, from Sen. Dianne Feinstein's triumph over the $30 million candidacy of then-GOP Rep. Michael Huffington in California, to Democratic gubernatorial wins in Alaska, Colorado, Hawaii, Nevada and Oregon.

There was a potentially ominous

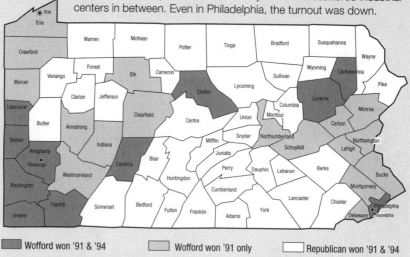

Changing Democratic Fortunes
Wofford Senate Races, 1991-94

The defeat of Sen. Harris Wofford, D-Pa., in 1994 was a microcosm of the Democrats' national decline. Wofford had scored an upset victory in 1991 by reaching beyond the Democratic base into the Republican suburbs of Philadelphia and the politically marginal counties beyond. In 1994, however, he won only the Democratic strongholds: Philadelphia, western Pennsylvania and scattered industrial centers in between. Even in Philadelphia, the turnout was down.

Wofford won '91 & '94   Wofford won '91 only   Republican won '91 & '94

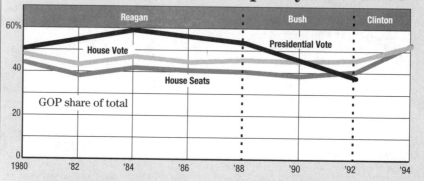

GOP House Vote-Seat Disparity Since 1980

For decades, Republicans had complained that their share of seats in the House did not fully reflect their share of the total vote in House elections. The disparity was redressed in some measure by redistricting after the 1990 census. But the real difference came with the surge in the GOP vote in 1994.

Republican share of:

Years	Presidential Vote	House Vote	House Seats
1980	50.7%	48.0%	44.1%
1982		43.3	38.2
1984	58.8	47.0	41.8
1986		44.6	40.7
1988	53.4	45.5	40.2
1990		45.0	38.4
1992	37.4	45.6	40.5
1994		52.4	52.9

MARILYN GATES-DAVIS

Speaker-to-be Newt Gingrich comments on election results.

1994 Election Highlights

- Nearly 70 million ballots were cast in the 1994 House elections, the highest number in any midterm election.

- Republican House candidates won 36.6 million votes, the most for one party in any midterm.

- Republican House candidates drew nearly 9 million more votes than in 1990, the largest increase ever in one party's vote total from one midterm to another.

- The vote for Democratic House candidates fell nearly 1 million from 1990 to a level more than 3 million votes below the party's total in 1982.

- The GOP's 52.4 percent share of the House vote was the party's largest since 1946. It was also the first time since 1946 that GOP House candidates received a majority of the total House vote.

- In another historic reversal, Republican House candidates received more free rides than the Democrats. In the South alone, 21 GOP winners had no Democratic opposition.

- Voter turnout was up for the second straight election: Fifty-five percent of the voting-age population cast ballots for president in 1992, the highest turnout rate in 20 years; 36 percent cast ballots in 1994 House elections, the highest turnout rate for a midterm since 1982.

- In spite of the GOP success, Democrat Daniel K. Akaka of Hawaii paced the senators, winning re-election with 72 percent of the vote. Democrat Ben Nelson of Nebraska led the governors, winning re-election with 73 percent of the vote.

sign for the GOP in Oregon, where former Republican Rep. Denny Smith could not come close to beating former Democratic state Sen. John Kitzhaber in the governor's race, in spite of the favorable Republican mood.

Smith was backed by the conservative wing that increasingly dominates Oregon GOP primaries, but he was unable to substantially expand his base in the fall. Oregon Republicans are "marching off to the right very resolutely and reducing their chance

to win the general election," says Oregon State University political scientist Bill Lunch.

Meanwhile, the Democrats' base in the Northeast was penetrated but not demolished by the 1994 vote. Democrats lost only three House seats in the East, retaining a regional majority.

Most of the incumbents in both parties won re-election to the Senate. And though the GOP picked up governorships in New York, Pennsylvania, Connecticut and Rhode Island, none

of those seats were won with a majority of the vote.

The independent movement, which elected Lowell P. Weicker Jr. to the governorship of Connecticut in 1990, remained strong across the Northeast. Independent Angus King won the governorship in Maine, a pair of independent candidates garnered 30 percent of the gubernatorial vote in Connecticut and an independent right-to-life candidate drew 13 percent of the vote for governor of Pennsylvania.

Poster Child Loses

The only incumbent senator in the East to lose his re-election bid was Democrat Harris Wofford of Pennsylvania, whose brief Senate career closely reflected the ups and downs of the Democratic Party in the 1990s. Wofford's upset victory in a 1991 special election proved a harbinger of the party's success nationally the following year; his loss in 1994 typified the Democrats' collapse.

Wofford won in 1991 by running as a champion of the "forgotten middle class" against former GOP Gov. and U.S. Attorney General Dick Thornburgh, who allowed himself to be painted as a Washington insider.

Wofford rolled up a big lead in the Democratic strongholds of Philadelphia and western Pennsylvania, cut down the normal Democratic deficit in the rural central portion of the state and ran even with Thornburgh in the Republican suburbs of Philadelphia. (Map, p. 14)

Democratic strategists were impressed by Wofford's campaign, which included an emphasis on the health care issue, and he emerged as a finalist for the Democratic vice presidential nomination in 1992.

But in 1994, Wofford was thrown on the defensive by his aggressive young GOP foe, then-Rep. Rick Santorum, who pounded away at Wofford as a friend of Clinton and big government.

Santorum easily won the Republican countryside, reclaimed the Philadelphia suburbs and made deep inroads among socially conservative Democrats in his home base of western Pennsylvania.

"There was palpable fear in 1991," says Wofford, and people were apt to vote their economic interests. In 1994, he adds, "there was a lot of itchiness but not fear" and issues such as guns and abortion swung votes to the Republicans' advantage. ∎

REPRESENTATION

Court Ruling Expected To Spark More Suits

The Supreme Court's deepening disapproval of race-based redistricting is expected to spark more lawsuits against existing majority-minority districts in the South and elsewhere, thinning the ranks of black and Hispanic members and making life more difficult for Republicans in adjacent districts.

The court's 5-4 ruling June 29 only disallowed the congressional map used in Georgia in 1992 and 1994, where the court found fault with the 11th District, won by Democratic Rep. Cynthia A. McKinney.

But if the ruling itself addressed only one state map, the principle established appeared to endanger about a dozen other districts with black or Hispanic majorities. Any or all of these might eventually have to be redrawn in Texas, North Carolina, Florida, Louisiana, Illinois and New York, with a resulting effect on nearby districts. Other states might be affected in the future.

Attorneys for the states involved, and for the Justice Department, would have to meet a "strict scrutiny" test in court in order to preserve the current districts if challenged in court under the criteria set June 29.

If they were unable to do so, the courts or state legislatures would redraw the maps. And in at least some of those districts, incumbents would have difficulty holding the seats if the current racial composition were to change.

"We will certainly lose some minorities" in Congress, said Lisa Handley, a senior research analyst at Election Data Services, a private firm involved in redistricting. That prospect, as well as the doubt cast on the creation of additional majority-minority districts, prompted angry protests

CQ Weekly Report July 1, 1995

SCOTT J. FERRELL

Among the Democrats protesting the Georgia ruling June 29 were, left to right, Charles B. Rangel of New York, Cynthia A. McKinney of Georgia, and Bobby L. Rush and Luis V. Gutierrez of Illinois.

from civil rights activists.

McKinney, the one member most immediately affected, called the ruling "a setback for democracy."

"It is a shame that we are even here arguing whether or not we have gone overboard on perfecting democracy," McKinney said.

But other observers of the political mapping process were less sure about the extent of the damage, and the full political implications of the court's ruling may be more difficult to predict.

Handley said the effect would depend on how many challenges are filed and, eventually, how drastically minority districts are redrawn by judges or by state legislatures.

Some analysts said that even if the minority populations are decreased in some districts, some of the current black or Hispanic officeholders could survive, in part with the built-in advantages of incumbency.

"I think you'll see more lawsuits on broader grounds, but I don't think we'll see the demise of black districts in the U.S.," said Allan J. Lichtman, a history professor at American University who had been following the case closely.

Also easy to find were those who applauded the decision.

"It's exactly what we were hoping for," said A. Lee Parks, the attorney who argued the case before the Supreme Court in behalf of the Georgia plaintiffs. "[I]f you're gonna use race, you have to establish the need for it."

"I cannot argue with the court's ruling... primarily because I believe the Voting Rights Act was designed to create possibilities not guarantees," said Rep. W. J. "Billy" Tauzin, a conservative white Democrat from Louisiana.

And Rep. Gary A. Franks of Connecticut, a black Republican who represents a majority-white district, has long been a critic of majority-minority districts, saying they are essentially "set-asides" for minorities.

"You should not be looking at race as the prominent factor.... It's very sensible that we cannot allow districts to be race-driven," Franks said.

Effect on GOP Gains

Prior to the 1992 election, 17 new majority black or hispanic districts were drawn with the intention of electing a minority to Congress. The initial result in 1992 was that minorities made huge net gains: The ranks of African-Americans in the House swelled from 26 to 39, of Hispanics from 12 to 19. The gains were particularly significant in the South, where the delegations of Alabama, Florida, North Carolina, South Carolina and Virginia included black members for the first time since the turn of the century.

In creating these districts, minority voters were siphoned off from surrounding districts, removing a portion of the base that helped keep many Southern Democrats in office.

The controversy intensified in 1994, when the GOP won its first majority of House seats in the South since Reconstruction.

But some observers dispute the degree to which majority-minority districts hurt white Democratic incumbents. A study by the NAACP Legal Defense Fund attributed the loss of only one seat to the creation of majority-minority districts.

Other analysts dispute this, setting the number as high as 10 seats.

In Georgia's 8th District, for example, the black population was reduced from 35 percent to 21 percent after redistricting. In 1992, the incumbent, Democrat J. Roy Rowland, was reelected with only 56 percent of the vote after winning with 69 percent or higher in previous years. Rowland retired after the 103rd Congress and his open seat was picked up in 1994 by Republican Saxby Chambliss, who was elected with 63 percent of the vote.

Democrats could become more competitive in some districts if some minority-majority districts are diluted, but as David Bositis of the Joint Center for Political Studies said, "Democrats aren't going to take back the House based on this."

Georgia: Starting Over?

The Georgia case has been handed back to a three-judge federal panel, which will have to decide whether to redraw congressional lines itself or have the legislature do it.

Charles Bullock, a political science professor at the University of Georgia in Athens, said courts usually will give state legislatures a chance at redrawing the maps first.

If the legislature is charged with redrawing the map, it could pit Republicans and black Democrats against white Democrats, who have gone from completely dominating the House delegation to being shut out.

As recently as 1992, Newt Gingrich, who was elevated to House Speaker at the start of the 104th Congress, was the state's only GOP House member and John Lewis, was the only black Democratic House member.

Georgia now sends eight white Republicans and three black Democrats to represent the state in the House.

"When they go back to the drawing board, Republicans and black members have a lot in common in preserving these districts," Bositis said.

Republicans and blacks could be looking to make only minor changes to the state's map. Democrat Tom Murphy, the speaker of the Georgia House of Representatives has indicated he would like to redraw the whole map, according to Bullock.

Either way, more black voters are likely to be added to the 1st District of GOP Rep. Jack Kingston; and more may also be added to the 10th District of freshman GOP Rep. Charlie Norwood. That would make both districts more competitive, although both Republicans won with at least 65 percent of the vote in 1994.

Other States

The court dismissed a challenge to the race-based map in Louisiana because the plaintiffs did not reside in the district in question (the 4th Dis-

Urban Districts in Line of Fire

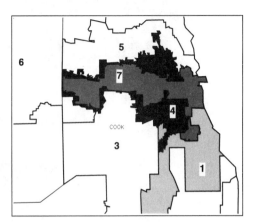

Illinois' 4th District was created to accommodate Chicago's growing Hispanic population. But the city's Hispanics mainly live in two blocs separated by a portion of a black-majority district. To avoid bisecting that district, the mapmakers drew a thin band around it connecting the Hispanic sections of the 4th, which in 1992 and 1994 elected Democrat Luis V. Gutierrez.

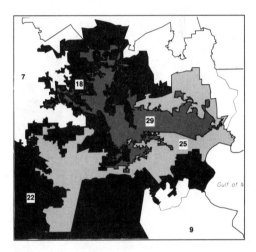

Texas's 29th District meanders through Houston and into its suburbs, picking up pockets of Hispanic voters. One of the most serrated districts in the country, the 29th is said to resemble a giant bird with outstretched wings. Hispanics make up 61 percent of the district's population. But "Anglo" Democrat Gene Green has carried the district in two elections.

trict, represented by two-term Democratic Rep. Cleo Fields).

But Edward W. Warren, the attorney who represented the Louisiana plaintiffs, said he expects to file another suit in the near future, using the criteria from the Georgia ruling.

Louisiana Attorney General Richard P. Ieyoub said he is confident that the state plan will be upheld. "It doesn't change our position" that the Louisiana Legislature considered neutral principles in drawing the 4th, he said.

The court has already agreed to review challenges to majority-minority districts in Texas and North Carolina and will hear arguments later in 1995. A decision is not expected in either case until 1996.

"We hope that the North Carolina case will provide the vehicle for the Supreme Court to give clear and concise directions for state legislatures to follow in drawing these plans," said North Carolina Attorney General Michael F. Easley.

Both the affected incumbents in North Carolina, Melvin Watt and Eva Clayton, believe their districts can pass the strict standard set by the Supreme Court in the Georgia case.

"The 1st Congressional District, I believe, is a community. The population is homogeneous, with cultural, social and economic similarities throughout," Clayton said.

The Texas case involves three districts that were struck down by a lower court as racially gerrymandered. The state has argued that the districts were drawn primarily on incumbency protection.

In addition, challenges to congressional districts in Florida, Illinois and New York are pending at the lower federal court level and may well be affected by the court's ruling in the Georgia case. ∎

PRESIDENTIAL CAMPAIGN

Two-Party System Under Assault in '96 Campaign

*Staying power of voters' discontent generates
calls for independents to step into ring*

While they fight each other for the presidency in 1996, the two major parties will also be fighting another battle, in which their interests coincide—a battle to maintain their joint control of the American political process.

How they manage this second challenge may be just as important in the long run as who wins the presidency in 1996.

American politics has been a story of two-party domination. In the beginning, there were the Federalists and the Jeffersonian Democrats. They were followed by Whigs and Jacksonian Democrats. Since the 1850s, the two teams have been known as Republicans and Democrats.

But after two centuries, that two-party domination has shown signs of weakening. Twenty percent of the ballots in the 1992 presidential election were withheld from the major parties (19 percent went for independent Ross Perot, nearly 1 percent for a collection of third parties, led by the Libertarians).

Perot's vote was remarkably consistent across all regions of the country. But because it was not concentrated in certain strongholds, he won no states and therefore no Electoral College votes. He did not even win a single congressional district.

Still, the Texas billionaire led a defection from the two major parties that was the second-largest since the Civil War, surpassed only by the 35 percent that went for an array of third parties in 1912. That year, the assault on the two-party system was led by former President Theodore Roosevelt's Progressive Party.

Perot's movement is also unusual in that it survived the presidential cycle. In the past, major disaffection with the two parties has

Ross Perot on Election Night 1992.

Historic Highs

Only eight independent or third-party candidates have ever received more than 10 percent of the popular vote in a U.S. presidential election.

Theodore Roosevelt (Progressive, 1912)	27.4%
Millard Fillmore (Whig-American, 1856)	21.5
Ross Perot (Independent, 1992)	18.9
John C. Breckinridge (Southern Democrat, 1860)	18.1
Robert M. LaFolette (Progressive, 1924)	16.6
George C. Wallace (American Independent, 1968)	13.5
John Bell (Constitutional Union, 1860)	12.6
Martin Van Buren (Free Soil, 1848)	10.1

SOURCE: CQ Guide to U.S. Elections

been short-lived. Significant third parties have been like shooting stars, brilliant but brief. Their supporters are usually reabsorbed into the two-party system by the next election.

Before Perot, all the major independent or third-party candidates this century—Roosevelt in 1912, Robert M. La Follette in 1924, George C. Wallace in 1968 and John B. Anderson in 1980—had either died, retired from the political scene or gone back to their original party by the time of the next presidential election.

But there are signs that 1996 may break dramatically from this pattern. Perot continues to demand attention, both as a prospective candidate and as the source of support for a third party. Moreover, one of the candidates some Republicans wanted to lure into their primary contests, retired Army Gen. Colin L. Powell, could affect the outcome unpredictably by running as an independent.

Moreover, politicians from Jesse Jackson to former Connecticut Gov. Lowell P. Weicker Jr. have mentioned the possibility of mounting independent candidacies themselves in 1996. So has retiring Democratic Sen. Bill Bradley of New Jersey, who, like Jackson, has expressed interest in an independent bid rather than a challenge to President Clinton in the Democratic primaries.

Some see commentator Patrick J. Buchanan leading an independent movement on the right in 1996 if he loses in the primaries and the Republican nomination goes to someone he considers too liberal on abortion.

And elements of the populist left have talked of drafting former California Gov. Edmund G. "Jerry" Brown Jr. in 1996, despite his apparent lack of interest so far in this cycle. Brown has run three times in the Democratic primaries.

Historical Circumstances

The attractiveness of the independent route for the 1996 cycle reflects the power of incumbency in the presidential nominating process. No matter how much any Democrat may want the nomination, the fact remains that President Bill Clinton will almost certainly have it. No president in this century who wanted another term has been denied renomination by his party. And Clinton, despite being mired in an approval rating of less than 50 percent in most opinion polls, approached the last year of his term with a commanding lead in funds and commitments.

Still, the interest shown by Jackson and Bradley reflects a political climate that is increasingly restive and dissatisfied with the candidates and policy choices put forward by the major parties. Weicker has already tapped that mood on the state level, winning an election as governor of Connecticut as an independent in 1990 (he did not run for a second term in 1994).

According to Everett Carll Ladd, president of the Roper Center for Public Opinion Research at the University of Connecticut, public sentiment for alternatives to the two major parties has been fueled by a powerful confluence of events.

Americans always have had a relatively weak party system, says Ladd, and it has grown even weaker in the television age. The electorate is less and less likely to express a distinct partisan identification. The media are increasingly critical of centralized authority.

Ladd says these trends have been demonstrated recently not only in the support for Perot's candidacy in 1992 but also in the nationwide movement in support of term limits. (Term limits for members of Congress have been adopted in each of the 23 states where they have been put to a vote, although the Supreme Court on May 22 declared such limits unconstitutional.)

And many voters are unlikely to be mollified by the alternatives that the major parties are expected to offer in 1996, Ladd says. "The weakness of Clinton. The weakness of [Kansas Republican Sen. Bob] Dole. The weakness of everyone else adds to the other factors."

1992 Also-Rans

President George Bush, Bill Clinton and Ross Perot divided 99.4 percent of the 1992 presidential vote, with the rest scattered among other independents, minor parties and write-ins. The eight candidates who received more than 20,000 votes were:

Libertarian (Andre V. Marrou)	291,627
America First (James Gritz)	107,014
New Alliance (Lenora B. Fulani)	73,714
Taxpayers (Howard Phillips)	43,434
Natural Law (John Hagelin)	39,179
Peace and Freedom (Ron Daniels)	27,961
Economic Recovery (Lyndon H. LaRouche)	26,333
Socialist Workers (James Warren)	23,096

Overcoming Obstacles

Still, those who dream of breaking generations of political precedent must produce answers to several daunting questions. A third-option candidate must replace the organization and money that usually accrue to major-party nominees by virtue of their nominations.

Perot was able to level the playing field in 1992 by spending about $63 million out of his own pocket. But for candidates who lack such a fortune, the fund-raising process can be slow and difficult. Contributions from individuals cannot exceed $1,000; contributions from political action committees cannot exceed $5,000. And if, unlike Perot in 1992, a candidate chooses to accept public financing, he cannot contribute more than $50,000 of his own money to his presidential campaign.

Even then, a candidate can receive public money only after the election and then only by winning at least 5 percent of the nationwide popular vote. The amount of public money he would collect would be tied to his share of the vote.

Even well-financed independent candidates such as Perot must divert much of their time and money to gaining a spot on the ballot. It is an intricate process with deadlines and petition requirements that vary from state to state.

Richard Winger, the publisher of Ballot Access News, says a candidate seeking to run nationwide in 1996 would need to collect at a minimum an aggregate of nearly 700,000 signatures

---

to get on the ballot nationwide as an independent. A candidate interested in forming a new third party would need to gather even more signatures to meet the requirements of some states.

History of the Challenge

In the past, the preferred method of challenging the major parties was to create a full-blown third party. Roosevelt did so in 1912 with the Progressive Party (popularly known as the Bull Moose Party), which elected roughly a dozen members to Congress that year.

But in recent times, major challenges to the two major parties have been by independents. The American Independent Party was almost exclusively a vehicle for Wallace's presidential candidacy in 1968, and Anderson and Perot made no effort to form third parties during their candidacies.

An independent presidential candidacy is easier to launch than a third party and possibly better reflects an electorate dissatisfied with most large political institutions.

But there are several small third parties that are positioning themselves to tap the mood for change in 1996. According to Winger, the Libertarian Party will be holding its nominating convention in July, culminating a nominating process that will feature presidential primaries in nearly a dozen states. And the U.S. Taxpayers Party, which ran Howard Phillips (the longtime head of the Conservative Caucus) for president in 1992, has scheduled its convention for San Diego in August, immediately after the Republican National Convention there closes.

Disaffected Center

But much of the disaffection with the two parties in the mid-1990s arises not from the extremes of the left-right continuum but from the center. It has not always been this way. Most significant third parties of the past championed a particular cause and had a base of support largely limited to a specific region.

America's first significant third party in the early 19th century, the Anti-Masons, emerged in the Northeast. The agrarian Populist Party of the late 19th century was a powerful force that grew up almost exclusively west of the Mississippi River. And the states' rights campaigns of Strom

Thurmond in 1948 and Wallace in 1968 showed little pull beyond their home base in the South.

But the recent independent candidacies of Anderson and Perot were more national in their appeal. Both men spoke to voters in the center of the political spectrum by stressing the need for more honest and efficient government.

The disaffected middle has grown larger as the years have passed. Anderson peaked at about 25 percent in a Gallup Poll in June 1980 before slumping to 6.6 percent on Election Day as his campaign ran low on money. Perot reached 35 percent in presidential trial heats in the spring of 1992 and finished with 19 percent after exiting and re-entering the presidential race. But what was most remarkable about Perot was not the degree to which he faded in the late fall but the degree to which he sustained his hold.

Previous third-party candidacies had tended to lose altitude as Election Day neared, deflated by massive defections by voters who did not want to waste their vote on a candidate who had no chance of winning. But while it was clear during the final days of the 1992 campaign that Perot could not win, his support actually increased. The final pre-election surveys by most of the major polling organizations undervalued Perot's actual Election Day showing by 2 percentage points to 5 percentage points.

Part of his late surge was due, no doubt, to the millions of dollars that Perot threw into a fall media blitz—money that previous third-party candidates did not have. But it also reflected the willingness of many voters to suspend the normal political practice of limiting their choice to the Democratic or Republican nominees.

Even more voters appear ready to consider options beyond the two major parties in 1996, making it quite possible that there could be a three, four or even five-way race for the White House.

And if that happens, it would signal something significant unfolding within the American political system beyond the Democrats' and Republicans' control. The only previous time that the two parties lost even 10 percent of the presidential vote in back-to-back elections was in 1856 and 1860, on the eve of the Civil War. That was a period of great political turbulence that featured the demise of one major party (the Whigs) and the birth of another (the Republicans).

Such a striking result is hard to imagine in the late 1990s. Still, the decade has already seen political upheavals that few would have predicted. And after the election of a Democratic president in 1992 and a Republican Congress in 1994, voters may not be finished rearranging the political landscape.

PRESIDENTIAL CAMPAIGN

Earlier Voting in 1996 Forecasts Fast and Furious Campaigns

With many states moving up their primaries and caucuses, party choices are likely to be quick and decisive

PATT CHISHOLM

Each presidential nominating season is different from the last, but rarely have the changes been as dramatic from one cycle to the next as they will be in 1996.

Some aspects of next year's process remain to be settled, but the thrust is clear. More states will be voting earlier than ever before, with an overwhelming likelihood that the nominations will be decided quickly.

Not long ago, states scattered their primaries or caucuses across the calendar from February to June, giving candidates that survived the opening contests time to raise money and hone their strategies.

But in 1996, roughly two-thirds of the states will vote before the end of March, including seven of the 10 largest. Candidates will have to be prepared for a quick-starting, fast-paced campaign. Early financing is more prerequisite than ever: By the start of the primary season a candidate will almost certainly need to have raised millions of dollars — some say as much as $20 million — to compete effectively.

On its face, the new schedule would seem to benefit the obvious front-runners of the two major parties: Democratic President Clinton and Republican Senate Majority Leader Bob Dole of Kansas. Clinton has yet to attract a meaningful challenger, and Dole has a commanding lead in opinion polls and other campaign assets.

But the quick-fire process could mean pitfalls for Dole if he disappoints in early tests or suffers other adverse events. There will be little time for a stumbling front-runner to recover.

Yet the new calendar is not all that will be different about 1996. Some of the states are being boldly innovative; Oregon and possibly Nevada will hold March primaries by mail.

In addition, many of the states will be grouped in regional clusters; so instead of just one "Super Tuesday" there will be an entire March of Super Tuesdays.

Pennsylvania is the last large state to decide its primary date. But even if the state chooses to keep the date in late

April rather than join the move to March, roughly two-thirds of the voting delegates to both national nominating conventions will have been decided by April 1.

Winter Battles

After a series of winter events highlighted by the contests in Iowa and New Hampshire, the first small regional grouping occurs when North and South Dakota vote on Feb. 27.

The votes will be quickly decided by much bigger events. March 5 will be "Junior Tuesday," dominated by primaries in all the New England states except New Hampshire, with neighboring New York providing an additional voice from the Northeast two days later.

March 12 will be Super Tuesday, with the spotlight on a half-dozen Southern states from Florida to Texas.

March 19 will be "Big 10" Tuesday, with primaries in the heart of the Midwest — Illinois, Michigan, Ohio and Wisconsin.

And March 26 will be California, a regional primary all by itself, joined by Washington on the Republican side.

It will be a grueling gantlet that no field of candidates has ever had to run. As recently as 1992, the California and Ohio primaries were in June, while New York and Wisconsin cast ballots in April.

Even the familiar starting points of the nominating process, Iowa and New Hampshire, are having to fend off challenges to their leadoff positions.

Republican parties in Alaska, Hawaii and Louisiana have set dates ahead of the Iowa caucuses, scheduled for Feb. 12. And New Hampshire (Feb. 20) is at odds with Delaware for scheduling a primary within the Granite State's self-defined seven-day territorial limit. Both early kingpins have threatened to move their events forward to secure their primacy.

Candidates and the media, though, have made Iowa and New Hampshire the accepted starting points, even if other states vote before them. And while it is hard to say whether they will set the course of the campaign as they have in the

CQ Weekly Report August 19, 1995

1996 Presidential Nominating Calendar

Step One: Winter Events

Step Two: "Junior Tuesday" Week

Step Three: "Super Tuesday" Week

Step Four: "Big 10 Tuesday" Week

Step Five: California and Beyond

past, none of the candidates is taking the chance that they will not.

More than ever, Iowa and New Hampshire are the states where candidates have some control over their destinies. They can woo voters one-on-one, whether in bowling alleys, coffee shops or the frequent gatherings in neighborhood living rooms. For if there is one thing certain about 1996, it is that once the New Hampshire primary is over, there will be a frenetic burst of tarmac-to-tarmac campaigning heavily dependent on media advertising.

It may be that Iowa and New Hampshire will be even more important in 1996 because the slingshot effect from a strong showing in them will cover a broader number of states.

But it might also work the opposite way. With the terrain changing quickly week by week, there could be quick swings in momentum, and trailing candidates may be reluctant to quit the race as quickly as they have in the past. Certainly with California and its winner-take-all primary beckoning at the end of March like the Million Dollar Lotto, many of the Republican candidates may stay in the race just to try their luck at winning such a big prize.

If the nomination is not settled by the time Californians take part, then the states voting afterwards would suddenly become important, with Pennsylvania (April 23), North Carolina (May 7) and New Jersey (June 4) shaping up as critical events in the end game.

But it would be unusual if the race lasted that long. Recent presidential nominating contests have followed a pattern. The early votes in Iowa and New Hampshire have winnowed the field to a handful of candidates. Then, after a short period of unpredictability, one candidate has scored

a knockout, with his victory ratified by a string of primary votes at the end of the nominating process.

The 1992 Experience

That is what happened in 1992. The first five Democratic primaries that year produced four different winners. But Bill Clinton broke from the pack with a sweep of the Super Tuesday South and ended up winning 23 of the 24 primaries that followed.

Neither party has had an elongated tug-of-war since 1984, when Walter F. Mondale and Gary Hart battled for the Democratic nomination into the final week of the primary season. And neither party has had a nominating contest that was even vaguely competitive by the time of its national convention since the 1976 Republican race between President Gerald R. Ford and Ronald Reagan.

Occasionally, candidates have tried to skip Iowa and New Hampshire and launch their campaigns on terrain more to their choosing. Democrat George C. Wallace did that in 1976. So, to a degree, did Democrat Al Gore in 1988. But that streak of independence did not yield visible benefits for either of them, and none of the current Republican candidates has shown any indication of taking that less-traveled path next year.

Indeed, some of the long-shot GOP contenders are having to focus their campaigns almost exclusively on the early states, because it could be Iowa, New Hampshire and out.

But well-heeled candidates with national followings can think both bigger and bolder. Dole is pursuing a big-name endorsement strategy similar to the one George Bush followed in beating Dole for the nomination in 1988.

Bush had the active support of well-placed GOP governors — John H. Sununu in New Hampshire, Carroll A. Campbell in

Nominating Season at a Glance

	Date of Main GOP Event	Delegate Count D	R	Form of Delegate Selection	GOP Delegate Allocation
Alabama	June 4	66	40	Open Primary	TBD
Alaska	Jan. 26-29	19	19	Closed Caucus (D) / Open Caucus(R)*	NFS
Arizona	Feb. 27	52	39	Open Caucus(D)* / Closed Primary(R)	WTA
Arkansas	May 21	48	20	Open Primary	PR
California	March 26	423	163	Closed Primary	WTA
Colorado	March 5	58	27	Open Primary*	PR
Connecticut	March 5	65	27	Closed Primary	TBD
Delaware	Feb. 24	21	12	Closed Primary	WTA
District of Columbia	May 7	38	14	Closed Primary	WTA
Florida	March 12	177	98	Closed Primary	WTA
Georgia	March 5	91	42	Open Primary	WTA
Hawaii	Jan. 25-31	30	14	Closed Caucus	NFS
Idaho	May 28	24	23	Open Caucus(D) / Open Primary(R)	PR
Illinois	March 19	194	69	Open Primary	DE
Indiana	May 7	89	52	Open Primary	WTA
Iowa	Feb. 12	56	25	Open Caucus*	NFS
Kansas	April 2	41	31	Open Primary*	TBD
Kentucky	May 28	61	26	Closed Primary	PR
Louisiana	Feb. 6	75	28	Closed Caucus(R) / Closed Primary	NFS / WTA
Maine	March 5	32	15	Open Primary*	TBD
Maryland	March 5	85	32	Closed Primary	WTA
Massachusetts	March 5	114	37	Open Primary*	WTA
Michigan	March 19	158	57	Open Caucus (D) / Open Primary (R)	PR
Minnesota	March 5	92	33	Open Caucus	NFS
Mississippi	March 12	49	32	Open Primary	WTA
Missouri	March 9	93	36	Open Caucus	NFS
Montana	June 4	25	14	Open Primary (D) / Open Caucus (R)	NFS
Nebraska	May 14	33	24	Open Primary*	DE
Nevada	March	27	14	Closed Caucus	NFS
New Hampshire	Feb. 20	26	16	Open Primary*	PR
New Jersey	June 4	120	48	Open Primary*	DE
New Mexico	June 4	34	18	Closed Primary	PR
New York	March 7	288	102	Closed Primary	DE
North Carolina	May 7	98	58	Closed Primary(D) / Open Primary(R)*	TBD
North Dakota	Feb. 27	22	18	Open Caucus (D) / Open Primary (R)	PR
Ohio	March 19	171	67	Open Primary	WTA
Oklahoma	March 12	53	38	Closed Primary	WTA
Oregon	March 12	56	23	Closed Primary	PR
Pennsylvania	April 23	195	73	Closed Primary	DE
Rhode Island	March 5	31	16	Open Primary*	PR
South Carolina	March 2	52	37	Open Caucus (D) / Open Primary (R)	WTA
South Dakota	Feb. 27	23	18	Closed Primary	PR
Tennessee	March 12	83	37	Open Primary	WTA / PR
Texas	March 12	230	123	Open Caucus (D) / Open Primary	WTA / PR
Utah	March 25	30	28	Open Caucus	NFS
Vermont	March 5	22	12	Open Primary	WTA
Virginia	April 13	96	53	Open Caucus	NFS
Washington	March 26	91	36	Open Caucus (D) / Open Primary (R)	PR
West Virginia	May 14	42	18	Closed Primary(D) / Open Primary(R)*	DE
Wisconsin	March 19	93	36	Open Primary	WTA
Wyoming	March 23	19	20	Closed Caucus	NFS
Puerto Rico	March 3	58	14	Open Primary	WTA
U.S. Territories		16	12		
Democrats Abroad		9			
Unassigned		1			
TOTAL		**4,295**	**1,984**		

Independents or voters willing to switch parties may participate; voters registered by party may participate only in their party's primary or caucus.

NOTE: Democrats require proportional representation in allocating delegates. Republicans allow a variety of methods:

WTA — winner-take-all; all delegates go to the statewide winner or are split between the statewide winner and each district winner.

DE — direct election of delegates (preference vote for candidates is non-binding).

PR — proportional representation; delegates divided to reflect candidates' share of the vote (thresholds vary from state to state).

NFS — no formal system; determined by participants in caucus process.

TBD — to be determined.

The Bradley Factor

Not all Democrats are satisfied with President Clinton as their presumptive 1996 nominee, and some thought they had glimpsed an alternative when New Jersey Democrat Bill Bradley announced he would not seek a fourth Senate term in 1996.

But Bradley quickly ruled out a primary challenge to Clinton, indicating he was more interested in exploring an independent candidacy. Among those he said he called after deciding to retire was Colin L. Powell Jr., former chairman of the Joint Chiefs of Staff. Powell is often mentioned as a potential independent candidate for president or vice president.

Bradley

On Aug. 16, Bradley said he had tried to lead from the Senate and "make a difference in people's lives" but added that he believes he could do both elsewhere.

"I am leaving the U.S. Senate but I am not leaving public life," he added. "I will expand my dialogue with the American people."

Bradley, 52, has been mentioned as a prospective White House contender since his early years in the Senate. He was a household name even before entering politics, based on his basketball career. An All-American at Princeton University, he won a gold medal at the 1964 Olympics, studied at Oxford as a Rhodes scholar and was a Hall of Fame forward for the professional New York Knicks.

He moved into politics statewide in 1978, winning a Senate seat largely with his own money (some called him "Dollar Bill"). Re-elected despite the GOP year of 1984, Bradley had a political near-death experience in 1990,

when he beat an upstart Republican by 3 percentage points after outspending her 2-to-1. That upstart, Christine Todd Whitman, was elected governor three years later.

Bradley's Senate career had its highpoint in the 99th Congress (1985-86), when his hard work and careful politicking helped enact a tax overhaul on the lower rates, fewer loopholes model he had long espoused.

But otherwise, Bradley was rarely at the center of action. In 1988 he opted out of the presidential chase and showed no interest when his party's top leadership post came vacant. In the next presidential cycle, he again demurred.

Nonetheless, Bradley stirred a brief flurry of interest in February when he criticized Clinton's State of the Union address. Bradley suggested at the time that Clinton might well face opposition for renomination, although he was at pains to say he was not threatening to run.

In the spring, former Pennsylvania Gov. Robert P. Casey entered the presidential field as an exploratory candidate. Casey was expected to contrast his conservatism on social issues such as abortion with his party's prevailing politics. But after a few weeks, he withdrew.

Former presidential candidate Jesse Jackson has also spoken of running in 1996, either in the primaries or as an independent. The latter route is now considered by far the likelier. Also thought to be interested in independent candidacies are Ross Perot, who took 19 percent of the presidential vote in 1992, and former senator and governor Lowell P. Weicker Jr. of Connecticut.

South Carolina and James R. Thompson in Illinois. All helped Bush in critical primary states that he won.

Dole is hoping to construct a similar front with his own phalanx of governors, which includes Terry E. Branstad in Iowa, George E. Pataki in New York, Jim Edgar in Illinois and George V. Voinovich in Ohio.

In many states, Dole's prime competition is coming from Phil Gramm, whose strategy is more dependent on wooing conservative party activists. Unlike Dole, Gramm has been a frequent participant on this year's straw vote circuit, winning a number of these events in the South and West that have demonstrated varying degrees of organizational muscle.

With a large field of Republicans already in campaign mode, the race for the Democratic nomination is an afterthought. Clinton is unchallenged.

If the incumbent remains alone in the field, the only outlet for disgruntled Democrats may be to mark the "uncommitted" line in the states that provide one on the ballot. In 1992, nearly two dozen states offered such an option, and 750,000 Democratic primary voters chose it.

But should a more active challenge to Clinton develop, one fact would become apparent: the Democrats and Republicans operate under different sets of nominating rules.

In some cases, the two parties do not even vote on the same day. In Arizona, Republicans will take part in the new state-run primary Feb. 27, while Democrats will have their

own party-run affair March 9. In Washington, Democrats will elect their delegates through a caucus process that begins March 5, while Republicans will hold a primary March 26. In Michigan, Democrats have scheduled a party-run vote for March 16, while Republicans will take part in "Big 10 Tuesday" on March 19.

But there are other points of divergence as well:

● Republicans do not reserve delegate seats for party and elected officials. Democrats will set aside nearly 20 percent of the slots at their 1996 convention for the Democratic governors and members of Congress, as well as for every member of the Democratic National Committee. Such automatic "superdelegate" slots are even reserved for President Clinton and Vice President Al Gore, who theoretically could take to the convention floor next summer in Chicago to vote for their own renomination.

● Democrats also do not allow primaries or first-round caucuses (with the exception of those in Iowa and New Hampshire) before the first Tuesday in March. Republicans have no such restriction and allow their state parties to schedule primaries or caucuses in January or February without the national party's consent.

● Democrats are much stricter about who may participate in their primaries and caucuses. They limit participation to voters who either are registered Democrats or are willing to be publicly identified as casting a Democratic ballot.

State-by-State Methodology

In recent years, the national parties have tried to exercise varying degrees of supervision over their presidential nominating processes, but winning either the Republican or the Democratic nod remains in essence a state-by-state battle. So the guide on the pages that follow presents the overall mosaic piece by piece, emphasizing the individual states, their people, their parties and their rules.

The states appear in the chronological order in which their primary or first-round caucus is currently scheduled. Where the parties' dates differ, the Republican date has been used because that is where the action is expected to be.

Each state has a "statistical profile box." The latest state population totals reflect Census Bureau population estimates from 1994.

Minority population percentages are based on population projections for 1995.

Voter registration figures were gathered this summer and were the latest available at the time.

Each state has a "rules box" with filing dates, meeting times or polling hours (in local time) and the latest information available on party rules for delegate selection.

Democrats in most states limit primary and caucus participation to party members or to those who are willing to be recorded as taking part in the Democratic event. Republicans generally accede to state law or state party rules.

Republicans elect delegates from congressional districts and statewide (at large).

To these two categories Democrats add pledged party and elected officials (PEOs) and unpledged party and elected officials ("superdelegates").

The PEOs, like Democratic district and at-large delegates, must reflect the state's primary or caucus vote. Superdelegates are free agents.

Each party's delegate count is subject to revision. The Republicans, in particular, could change slightly with the results from gubernatorial and state legislative elections this fall.

Accompanying nearly all states are charts and maps presenting the 1992 results in sample counties (or in the case of New England, cities and towns).

These data are chosen to illustrate voting patterns with actual votes rather than surveys, exit polls or other projections.

The charts begin with results from leading population centers (highlighted on the maps) — usually counties with 5 percent or more of the state's 1994 estimated population.

Other groupings are included to emphasize elements of a state's demographics, such as high-growth suburbs and smaller industrial centers.

The charts include Ross Perot's best county in each state: They are listed as "Perot Country" where he received 30 percent or more and as "Perot Toehold" counties where he received less than 30 percent.

The primary results almost always have been based on a preference vote in which the names of presidential hopefuls themselves (and not just delegates) are on the ballot.

Caucus results reflect the outcome of first-round mass meetings, the only stage open to grass-roots participation.

In almost every state, primary returns are tabulated and certified by a state election board, but results from a caucus are often less precise. The vast majority of states, though, now use primaries.

Generally, the sample county charts include: candidates who drew at least 10 percent of the Democratic primary or caucus vote in 1992; the vote share for George Bush, Bob Dole and Pat Robertson in each state where there was a competitive Republican primary or caucus vote in 1988; the name and vote percentage of the winning candidate in the 1992 Republican primary or caucus; and the November 1992 vote percentages for Bill Clinton, George Bush and Ross Perot.

Percentages in all cases are based on total votes cast.

● Democrats require that delegates from every state be divided proportionally to reflect the candidates' share of the primary or caucus vote. The exception is that candidates must win at least 15 percent of the vote in a state or district to qualify for delegates.

Republicans allow their state parties to award delegates on a winner-take-all basis, and many of the GOP primary states expect to employ some variation of this system in 1996.

California Republicans have traditionally had a statewide winner-take-all system, with the high vote-getter winning all the delegates. They will be joined by a number of other states that will either have statewide winner-take-all or variation that easily could result in one candidate winning the delegates.

The greater incidence of winner-take-all should fuel the momentum of any Republican candidate who breaks out early in the process. A clear front-runner may well extend his lead in the delegate count far beyond what would be possible with proportional representation.

Still in Flux

By now, most states have their nominating rules in place for 1996. But a few do not, and a state or two could still make a date change. Pennsylvania, for instance, has not totally closed the door on moving its primary from April 23 to "Big 10 Tuesday" on March 19. Both parties in Nevada have to decide whether to take part in the state's new ballot-by-mail primary March 26.

And Republican parties in several states have yet to determine how they will award their delegates — through proportional representation or some variation of winner-take-all.

Even the delegate counts of both parties are subject to small changes. The defection in early August of Rep. W. J. "Billy" Tauzin to the Republicans, for instance, cost Democrats a delegate in his home state of Louisiana and added one for Louisiana Republicans.

Also, the GOP delegate totals for states with guberna-

Presidential Campaign Funding

While Congress continues to reject calls to change the way its own campaigns are financed, the public funding of presidential campaigns will celebrate its 20th anniversary in 1996.

In 1976, in the first presidential election following the Watergate scandal and the subsequent resignation of President Richard M. Nixon, President Gerald R. Ford and Democratic challenger Jimmy Carter each received $21.8 million in taxpayer money to spend on their fall campaigns. This election cycle, the major party nominees will each receive $60.1 million, plus a cost-of-living adjustment.

The two major parties in 1976 also got $2.2 million each to put on their national conventions; this time around, the parties already have received $12 million apiece.

Inflation has increased the amount of taxpayer money going to the candidates and parties in each election cycle, but the statutory method for funding this commitment has not always kept pace.

From the fund's beginning in 1973 until 1994, taxpayers voluntarily could earmark $1 of their federal income taxes to pay for the presidential campaigns. In 1992, federal election officials worried that there would not be enough money to give all of the presidential candidates their matching funds during the crucial primary months. But those concerns proved unfounded because of the campaign's late start.

In 1994, the checkoff was increased to $3, alleviating the pressure on the fund. This year, the Senate voted to keep public financing of presidential campaigns, which would have been eliminated under the version of the budget resolution (S Con Res 13) adopted by the Senate Budget Committee. *(Weekly Report, p. 1527)*

But if the fund is secure for 1996, its long range future may be threatened by a decline in taxpayer participation. In 1993, only 14.5 percent of tax returns were checked off for the presidential campaign fund, down from 18.9 percent in 1992.

"You've got a whole new class of taxpayers who don't have the same concerns or memories of Watergate," said Sharon Snyder, spokeswoman for the Federal Election Commission.

"It's the only time you as a taxpayer can tell the government how you want your money spent," Snyder said. Many taxpayers simply did not want their money spent on presidential elections, she said.

The presidential fund also provides millions of dollars to candidates trying to capture the nomination. In 1976, 15 Democratic and Republican candidates received $24.8 million in federal funds to help pay for their primary campaigns. In 1992, 12 candidates shared $43.4 million.

To qualify for the federal matching funds, candidates must raise at least $5,000 in 20 different states in amounts of no more than $250 from any one individual. That is a minimum of $100,000.

In exchange for the federal matching funds, candidates agree to abide by limits on how much they can spend nationally and in each state, excluding legal and accounting costs.

So far this year, four candidates, all Republicans, have qualified for the money: Senate Majority Leader Bob Dole of Kansas, Sen. Phil Gramm of Texas, former Tennessee Gov. Lamar Alexander and former presidential aide Patrick J. Buchanan.

Three other GOP candidates are awaiting certification from the Federal Election Commission to become eligible for the funds: Sens. Richard G. Lugar of Indiana and Arlen Specter of Pennsylvania and California Gov. Pete Wilson. The money will begin to flow Jan. 2, 1996.

Gramm so far has been the most successful fundraiser among the Republicans, pulling in $16.2 million between Jan. 1 and June 30. Dole was second at $13.3 million. Alexander reported raising $7.5 million; Wilson, $3.4 million; Lugar, $2.9 million; and Buchanan, $2.2 million.

The other GOP candidates, Sen. Arlen Specter of Pennsylvania, former Maryland senatorial candidate Alan Keyes, and Rep. Robert K. Dornan of California, all reported raising less than $1 million.

torial and legislative elections this November could go up if Republicans win.

But that should not be enough to prevent the 1996 GOP convention in San Diego from being the smallest Republican nominating event since 1972. At present, GOP delegates are expected to total fewer than 2,000.

Even though Republicans in 1994 took control of both houses of Congress, a majority of governorships and dozens of state legislative chambers around the country, GOP delegate totals accent the outcome of the previous presidential election. So the 22 states that voted for Bush in 1988 but not in 1992 almost invariably will have fewer delegates in 1996 than they did in 1992.

That is bad news for some of the candidates for the nomination. California Gov. Pete Wilson's home state will have 38 fewer delegates in 1992. Sen. Arlen Specter's home state of Pennsylvania will have 18 fewer. And former Gov. Lamar Alexander's home state of Tennessee will have eight fewer delegates.

Even the home state of the GOP's most mediagenic Republican, House Speaker Newt Gingrich (who was not a candidate for the nomination as of the summer of 1995) will send a smaller delegation than it did in 1992, even though the state now has a GOP congressional majority. Georgia had 52 delegates at the 1992 convention. But because Clinton carried the state that fall, its 1996 total is now set at 42.

The problem of the shrinking convention could be a boon if the physical limitations of the convention hall prove severe. It is, nonetheless, a trend the party plans to correct before 2000. ∎

CANDIDATE PROFILE

GOP Congress Could Boost Chances for Clinton

*President takes on a more centrist look
in contrast with conservative agenda*

Bill Clinton is gearing up to seek a prize that only one of the last four occupants of the White House has achieved: re-election.

No Democrat has been elected president and then re-elected to a second full term since Franklin D. Roosevelt more than half a century ago.

By conventional standards, Clinton's prospects of overcoming these historical odds would seem poor. His party lost control of both chambers of Congress in the 1994 midterm elections, a debacle for which many Democrats hold him responsible.

Clinton's presidency has never gained much altitude, nor has his base significantly expanded beyond the 43 percent of the vote he won in 1992.

While the economy has flourished by most measures, Clinton has received little credit. His management of foreign relations has flirted with disaster in Somalia, the Caribbean, the Balkans and the Far East. He has been hounded by allegations both legal and personal that stem from his years as governor of Arkansas.

Clinton's presidential approval rating in the Gallup Poll has never reached 60 percent, a standard that most presidents easily surpass during the traditional "honeymoon" of their first months in office.

Clinton has spent much of his term mired below 50 percent. His Gallup approval rating in late August stood at 46 percent, roughly where it has been over the past year and not much different from the 43 percent share of the vote he received in 1992.

Yet even his most partisan adversaries on Capitol Hill are loath to write him off. "He has a very realistic opportunity to get re-elected," said House Speaker Newt Gingrich, R-Ga., in September.

Few politicians of any stripe were saying that at the end of 1994. After Republicans took control of both houses of Congress for the first time in 40 years, the opinion was widespread that Clinton

SCOTT J. FERRELL

himself would be voted out in 1996.

But the president's position has stabilized during 1995, to the point that he probably has a better chance to win re-election next year than his Democratic colleagues in Congress have of recapturing control in either the House or Senate.

Clinton has benefited from a shifting of the spotlight. Attention has turned from his rocky relationship with the Democratic-controlled 103rd Congress to the controversial initiatives of the Republican 104th Congress, with its social conservatism and budget-cutting zeal.

As the new majority tackles its agenda, it takes risks before a skeptical public. Some recent polling shows trust in the new Congress declining as apprehension over its direction grows. A Gallup measure in August for CNN and USA TODAY found only 30 percent of respondents approved of the way Congress was handling its job.

This focus on Congress has enabled Clinton to appear more centrist than he ever did during his first two years in office. And the thematic underpinnings of a re-election campaign have become visible.

Georgetown University political scientist Stephen Wayne says Clinton is less apt to run on his own record than as a safer alternative to the GOP agenda and whomever it nominates against him.

In this role, said Wayne, Clinton would portray himself as "a mainstreamer ... a non-ideologue ... a moderate."

Up From the Depths

Clinton's political fortunes struck a low point with his party's devastating losses in the 1994 elections.

Republicans made the midterm a referendum on Clinton, airing television ads in which a given Democratic candidate's face was slowly transformed into Clinton's.

"After some months of shock and floundering, I think the president has found his sea legs in this new environment," said Thomas E. Mann, director of governmental studies at the Brookings Institution.

EXECUTIVE PROFILE	
Candidate vita	28
Gallup approval rating	28
Where Clinton won in 1992	29
Pending investigations	30
Campaign team for 1996	31
Clinton in the 103rd Congress	32
Presidential success scores	34

Rep. Sherwood Boehlert, a moderate Republican from New York, however, said he believes "the jury is still out" on how Clinton has related to the new order in Congress and on Clinton's own prospects for re-election.

In many ways, Clinton's chances for re-election may have improved under a GOP-led Congress, some Democrats and observers say.

If Democrats had remained in control with a reduced majority, Clinton might still have been expected to produce on his agenda. But with Republicans running Congress, Mann argued, Clinton may now be judged on his ability "to control the Republican extremism and channel it in a constructive way."

In addition, Clinton now has something to run against from the outset of the 1996 cycle. After searching for a strategy, he has moved into painting the GOP as having gone too far in their efforts to reduce government spending and slim down the federal bureaucracy.

"The president's fortunes are improving daily; I think that in large part because ... the Republican House and Senate is making it easier for the president to define and differentiate his policies from those of the Republican led-Congress," said Rep. Cal Dooley, a three-term conservative Democrat from California.

Dooley and other Clinton supporters say the president is re-establishing himself as the centrist they knew in 1992.

Clinton can, for example, present a more gradual approach to Medicare cost-cutting than the GOP proposal to cut $270 billion over seven years.

bate will have a big effect on (Clinton's) re-election," said Sen. Tom Harkin, D-Iowa. "I think lot of elderly people who vote are going to be upset when they see exactly what the GOP plans to do."

Clinton appears to be betting that the public will reward him for restraining an overzealous GOP.

"He's going to be able to say that he stopped the extremism of the right-wing Republicans ... that he kept the country from moving too far to the right and off the cliff," said Rep. Robert T. Matsui, D-Calif.

Even Republicans acknowledge that Clinton is a

Bill Clinton

Democrat of Little Rock, Ark.

Born: Aug. 19, 1946; Hope, Ark.

Education: Georgetown University, B.S.F.S., 1968; Rhodes scholar, Oxford University, 1968-70; Yale Law School, J.D. 1973.

Family: Wife, Hillary Rodham Clinton; one child, Chelsea.

Religion: Baptist.

Political career: Nominee for U.S. House, 1974; state attorney general, 1977-79; governor, 1979-81; nominee for governor, 1980; governor, 1983-93; president, 1993 —

Professional career: Law professor, University of Arkansas, 1973-76.

likable, engaging campaigner. And, for the moment at least, he can point to a comparatively peaceful stasis in world affairs and a stream of good news on the economic front. Not only have the financial markets enjoyed a banner year, but the economy as a whole has shown sustainable growth with low inflation and low unemployment.

Ron Walters, a Howard University political scientist, foresees the president saying that "the first two years he got things done [and] the second two years he prevented things from being done that would hurt you."

Walters notes that, "where possible, [Clinton would say he] compromised with Republicans to get bipartisan legislation." But he expects it to be even more important for Clinton to have resisted the new congressional majority.

In the end, Walters says, Clinton's own record will be less important than what voters feel about the actions of the GOP Congress. "The only thing keeping him afloat," said Walters, is the prospect that "Americans will perceive the Republicans have gone too far."

Taking Both Sides

But finding this footing has been a slow and painful struggle. The Republican victory caught the White House off guard, and it showed in Clinton's reaction to the "Contract With America" and its balanced-budget amendment, tax cuts and term limits.

"Republicans were very certain about what the election meant and the president was uncertain about what the election meant," said Richard F. Fenno, a political scientist at the University of Rochester. "That uncertainty has been underlying in his behavior since."

The best Clinton could do in the first blush of Republican success was to adopt a "me too" attitude, said Martha Phillips, executive director of the Concord Coalition, an anti-deficit lobbying group.

"He was bidding for a position in the game the Republicans had organized," Phillips said.

Five weeks after the 1994 elections, Clinton jumped on the tax cut bandwagon with his own proposal for $60 billion worth of tax cuts over five years targeted primarily at middle-income earners.

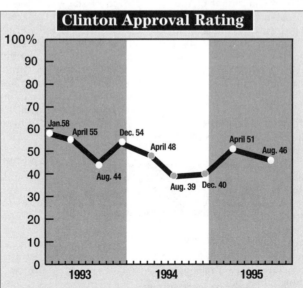

Clinton Approval Rating

Jan.58
April 55
Dec. 54
April 48
Aug. 44
Aug. 39
Dec. 40
April 51
Aug. 46

1993   1994   1995

President Clinton's most recent peak in his Gallup approval rating followed his victory on the North American Free Trade Agreement late in 1993. His lowpoint came in the summer of 1994, when his legislative progam in Congress was foundering.

SOURCE: The Gallup Organization

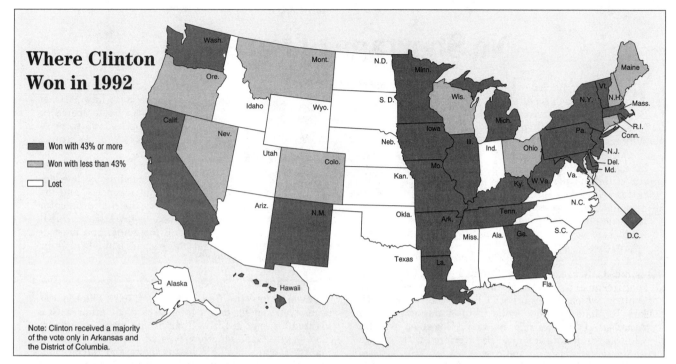

Where Clinton Won in 1992

- ■ Won with 43% or more
- ▨ Won with less than 43%
- □ Lost

Note: Clinton received a majority of the vote only in Arkansas and the District of Columbia.

When Gingrich began promising a vote on a school prayer amendment in the GOP-led 104th Congress, Clinton offered some positive comments on the issue. But he later said he opposed a constitutional amendment and favored clarifying what was already permissible under the Constitution.

In June, he offered his own 10-year balanced budget, which included cuts in Medicare and taxes, as a substitute to the budget he had proposed in February (and which had been almost totally ignored). Mann and some Democrats say the 10-year budget was a good move because it has provided Clinton with an alternative to contrast with Republican cuts he says go too deep.

Since then, however, Clinton has joined congressional Democrats in attacking several of the majority's spending bills.

Clinton has vetoed one of the 13 appropriations bills and said he might veto several more, as well as the reconciliation legislation that enforces long-term decisions made earlier in the budget resolution (H Rept 104-159).

Clinton has criticized Republicans for making deep cuts in some of the bills in such areas as education and health and adding provisions, as the House did, that would limit the Environmental Protection Agency from enforcing a variety of anti-pollution laws. GOP appropriators also took aim at two of Clinton's most cherished programs by approving spending bills in the House that kill funding for the National Service initiative and Goals 2000 education reform program (the Senate has agreed to stop funding National Service).

Veto Total: Three

Clinton cast his third veto Oct. 3, making good a threat made months earlier against the legislative appropriations bill that funds Congress and its support agencies. Clinton did not quarrel with the bill itself but said Congress should not be taking care of its own funding ahead of the other appropriations categories.

In his first 33 months in office, Clinton had vetoed just two bills, both in the summer of 1995. The first veto forced Republicans to scale back somewhat on the amount of 1995

spending they wanted to rescind in midyear. The second preserved U.S. cooperation with the international arms embargo on the Muslim-led government of Bosnia.

In vetoing the rescissions bill, Clinton cited specific cuts and also the language that would accelerate certain timber sales in national forests. But in the end he angered some of his strongest supporters in the environmental movement by signing a modified bill that restored some funding and essentially left the controversial timber language intact.

Clinton also has threatened a veto over the size of the Medicare cuts proposed by the GOP.

Republicans claim that the double-digit growth of Medicare and Medicaid, which the GOP also has proposed has agreed that cutting by $182 billion over seven years, will bankrupt the government. The GOP has proposed putting its Medicare and Medicaid plans in the budget-reconciliation bill.

Clinton, who himself proposed cutting Medicare by $128 billion and Medicaid by $54 billion in his 10-year budget plan, has argued that the GOP's proposal is too extreme and is being manufactured to pay for tax cuts for the wealthy. Medicare provides health care coverage for senior citizens and Medicaid offers basic health care for the poor and disabled.

"This is not what it takes to save Medicare," Clinton said Sept. 15. "If these health care cuts come to my desk, of this size, I would have no choice but to veto it."

But David M. Mason, a political analyst from the conservative think tank the Heritage Foundation, said Clinton has already given up ground by offering Medicare cuts of his own. "This is not the issue that will get him re-elected," Mason said.

Mason added, however, that the overall budget battle provides Clinton with an opportunity to improve his standing. "It will come to how deft of a politician he can be [in withstanding] what will be a substantive defeat."

Too Many Maneuvers?

Clinton critics are often wary of counting him out because he has shown a knack for finding his way back in. But with this facility the incumbent president risks appearing unprincipled.

No Shortage of Scrutiny

Few presidents have survived as much scandal as Bill Clinton had survived before he even reached the White House.

And while 1995 has brought no new stories to sully Clinton's personal reputation, investigations that began earlier have continued to burden his administration.

Leach   D'Amato   Starr

And there is no end in sight as the campaign year approaches.

On Oct. 2, Sen. Alfonse M. D'Amato, R-N.Y., announced that the Senate Banking Committee would soon resume its probe of the Whitewater real estate venture, which involved both Clinton and his wife, Hillary Rodham Clinton, while Clinton was governor of Arkansas. D'Amato said he would focus on whether Clinton administration officials interfered with savings-and-loan regulators in the case.

Whitewater is also the subject of an investigation by special federal prosecutor Kenneth W. Starr. D'Amato rejected Starr's request that no further hearings be held until the special prosecutor's investigation has been completed. Starr has already obtained grand jury indictments of several Arkansas figures with Clinton ties and has indicated he has not finished.

Also looking into Whitewater, and the role played by a now-bankrupt savings and loan, is the House Banking Committee, led by Chairman Jim Leach, R-Iowa. Leach's panel held a week of hearings in August. *(Weekly Report, p. 2420)*

Earlier in the summer, D'Amato held two weeks of hearings inquiring into the Whitewater implications of another event, the suicide of Vincent W. Foster. A for-

mer law partner of Mrs. Clinton at the Rose Law Firm in Little Rock, Foster came to Washington in 1993 to serve as deputy White House counsel.

Foster's death has been ruled a suicide by law enforcement agencies and by the first special prosecutor tapped to investigate. But it remains a source of fascination for many, and it occupied D'Amato's panel for more than a week in July. *(Weekly Report, p. 2243)*

Affairs Alleged

Even before the first primary of 1992, Clinton was accused of having had a long-term illicit affair with a nightclub singer in Little Rock during his governorship. The singer, Gennifer Flowers, sold her story to supermarket tabloids and TV gossip shows and forced Clinton and his wife, Hillary, to submit to long broadcast interviews on the subject.

Although Flowers faded after the campaign, another woman, Paula Jones, filed a lawsuit in 1994 charging that she had been sexually harassed by Clinton several years earlier when he was governor of Arkansas.

In December 1994, a federal court granted a stay in the Jones matter, accepting the White House contention that the president should not be subject to civil suits while in office. That ruling has been appealed.

The Clinton administration has also been bruised by investigations into the behavior of the FBI and the Bureau of Alcohol, Tobacco and Firearms at the Branch Davidian compound near Waco, Texas, in 1993. *(Weekly Report, p. 2377)*

When Clinton completed a policy review regarding affirmative action in July 1995 by announcing support for such programs, he received as much applause for having taken a foursquare position as for the position he took. *(Weekly Report, p. 2194)*

"There is a lack of consistency in terms of themes and action," said Boehlert, echoing a criticism heard from members of both parties on issues from the budget to foreign policy.

After Clinton offered his 10-year plan to balance the budget, Wisconsin Rep. David R. Obey, the ranking Democrat on the House Appropriations Committee, said: "Most of us learned some time ago that if you don't like the president's position on a particular issue, you simply need to wait a few weeks."

On foreign policy, Clinton's actions to achieve peace in Bosnia-Herzegovina have been criticized as indecisive and ineffective. Congress approved legislation in August to require the president to unilaterally lift the international arms embargo against the Bosnian government, leading to Clinton's second veto.

But in the last few weeks, Clinton appeared to turn a

corner on this issue after the United States and its NATO allies launched a bombing campaign that seemed to force the defiant Bosnian Serbs to withdraw some of their heavy weapons from the siege of Sarajevo. *(Weekly Report, p. 2928)*

In addition, Clinton has had some measure of success in advancing peace negotiations in Northern Ireland and, most notably, in the Middle East. An agreement providing for greater Palestinian control of the West Bank was signed Sept. 28 under his aegis in Washington.

Given these successes, voter irritation with Clinton's perceived lack of focus seems to be muted. He "goes about four ways at once," said Lawrence Longley, a Lawrence University, Wisconsin, political scientist and a member of the Democratic National Committee. But that, Longley adds, may be an effective contrast to a conservative-led, litmus-test-oriented GOP. "He is diffuse and that may be his strength in 1996."

Mann said Clinton has been using powers at his disposal, such as issuing executive orders and taking a more aggressive stance as a foreign policy leader. "He's acting more and more like a president," he said.

Campaign: Who's In, Out

President Clinton has been casting a wide net as he assembles a political team for his 1996 re-election bid.

Among those already on board, the most controversial is Connecticut-based political consultant Richard Morris. Although he advised Clinton on his gubernatorial comeback in 1982, Morris is better known for such high-profile Republican clients as Senate Majority Whip Trent Lott of Mississippi.

Morris is an "indication that the president is trying to position himself into the bell-shaped curve of American voters," said James A. Thurber, director of American University's Center for Congressional and Presidential Studies.

Morris has been advising the president on policy issues and has helped craft a more centrist message for Clinton.

"I think it's valuable to have someone who comes from outside of the Beltway and is kind of a renegade," said Saul Shorr, a Democratic consultant from Philadelphia, of Morris.

Still, Morris's presence at the White House has created a stir. One Democratic political consultant, who spoke on condition of anonymity, described Morris as the "flavor of the month" who could fall out of favor with Clinton again as he has before.

Changes in the Cast

Several of the better known players from Clinton's 1992 campaign are unlikely to reprise their roles. One key consultant, Paul Begala, is already out of the mix. Begala has returned to his native Texas to write, teach and consult for corporations. In an interview, Begala said he would continue to be a strong supporter of the president but have no formal part in the campaign.

It remains unclear what role James Carville, Begala's former partner and Clinton's top political strategist in 1992, will have in Clinton's campaign team. Carville reportedly has had differences with Morris.

Clinton's chief pollster in 1992, Stanley Greenberg, is also unlikely to be as prominent as in 1992. Doug Schoen of the Democratic polling firm Penn & Schoen is said to be favored by Morris and is expected to be the campaign's top pollster.

Another 1992 veteran now in the background is media consultant Mandy Grunwald. Democratic consultant Bob Squier is expected to be among Clinton's leading media advisers.

Within the White House proper, Deputy Chief of

Clinton

Gore

Stephanopoulos

Ickes

Staff Harold Ickes is the lead political tactician. The in-house political staff includes operatives such as political affairs director Doug Sosnik, a former political director at the Democratic Congressional Campaign Committee, and Craig Smith, who opened Clinton's first presidential campaign headquarters in Little Rock, Ark., in 1991.

Some of the political operatives, such as senior adviser George Stephanopoulos, who moved into governmental roles with Clinton after the 1992 election, may move back into campaign mode.

Stephanopoulos has, by some reports, reached a kind of operating partnership with Morris that would serve to enhance the standing of both.

But Begala cautions that at this point "everything is etched in sand, not stone."

At the Top

Clinton will continue to be advised by his wife, Hillary Rodham Clinton, and by Vice President Al Gore. Both were unusually important to Clinton's strategy in both the campaign of 1992 and the 103rd Congress.

Gore has already weighed in on the 1996 campaign, hitting the road in recent months to urge the president's re-election in highly partisan tones. In September, he went to Iowa, site of the nation's first major delegate-selecting event of the nominating season, telling Democratic activists that the GOP's extreme and narrow message will work to the president's advantage.

And at a recent appearance before a labor union convention in Chicago, Gore pitched the same message, describing the Republican congressional leadership as "right-wing extremists."

The first lady, however, has been far less vocal and far less visible in 1995 than she had been previously. She became a lightning rod for criticism during the 103rd Congress, when some critics held her responsible for her husband's perceived shift to the left. She also directed the writing of the health care overhaul plan, which later collapsed in Congress.

Since the Democratic debacle in the midterm elections of 1994, Mrs. Clinton has performed as a more traditional president's wife. Aside from writing a weekly column for newspapers, her most public effort has been her trip to the international women's conference in China, where she criticized China's human rights record.

All the same, the first lady will remain influential. She "is always going to get the last word," Thurber said.

Wins Did More To Fuel Critics' Fires . . .

When President Clinton presents his record to voters in 1996, much of the legislative agenda he fought for in the 103rd Congress (1993-94) will have been superseded by the battles of the 104th (1995-96).

Clinton will still trumpet a few hard-fought triumphs from the 103rd, and be forced to revisit its bitter defeats. But if the 1994 midterm elections are any indication, the president may suffer more political damage for his victories than for his setbacks.

His record from the 103rd ranges from the narrow passage of the massive budget-reconciliation bill in 1993 to the collapse of his efforts to pass a comprehensive health care reform package in 1994.

He pressed for a tax increase on higher incomes and gasoline, as well as for tighter restrictions on handguns and assault weapons. Both issues galvanized opposition far more than a declining budget deficit and healthy economy growth stimulated support.

Clinton began the first session of the 103rd Congress stumbling with embarrassing controversies over his first choice for attorney general, Zoë Baird, who admitted hiring undocumented aliens to care for her child, and his plan to lift the ban on homosexuals in the military. On both issues, Clinton was forced to back down.

The first substantive bill Clinton signed, in February 1993, was the Family and Medical Leave Act, which required employers to give unpaid leave to workers with newborn children or other pressing circumstances. But the bill had been passed in nearly identical form in the previous Congress, and required no effort from Clinton

REUTERS

Clinton signs the Brady bill as former White House press secretary James Brady, the bill's namesake, looks on.

other than his signature.

Two months later, the first piece of his economic plan, a $16.3 billion economic stimulus package, was killed in the Senate by Republican opposition and lukewarm Democratic support.

But the biggest battle and greatest success of his administration came in August of his first year in office with the passage of the deficit-reducing budget reconciliation bill of 1993.

As passed, the bill was expected to cut the deficit by $496 billion over five years through a mix of tax increases and budget cuts. While Clinton got much of what he asked for, House and Senate negotiators forced him to retreat in several areas. His proposal for a $71.5 billion tax on almost all forms of energy was whittled down to a small boost in the gasoline tax.

The conference report on the bill was adopted by the House without a vote to spare; the Senate cleared the bill with Vice President Al Gore breaking a tie.

While the bill's tax increases fell primarily on the wealthiest taxpayers, Republicans in the 1994 campaign characterized the bill as a burden on all income brackets and attacked it as "the biggest tax increase in history." Several Democrats who voted for the bill were defeated for re-election in 1994.

The budget victory was followed a few months later by Clinton's first major success on trade with the passage in November of the North American Free Trade Agreement (NAFTA). Clinton once again launched a major public relations campaign and pleaded with Democrats by saying his presidency was on the line. This time,

Underlying Weakness

But if the political breezes of the autumn seem friendlier to the president, it is by no means clear that his storms are behind him.

He has been bedeviled by questions about his personal character since the early stages of his 1992 presidential campaign. The Whitewater real estate affair has produced criminal indictments against some of his former associates in Arkansas, and investigations continue. A potentially embarrassing court proceeding on charges of sexual harassment also hovers on the horizon.

And if Clinton has benefited in some respects from the Republican management of Congress in 1995, he is still suffering politically for what happened during the last two years of Democratic control.

Any list of the memorable events from that period would include Clinton's effort to permit gays to serve openly in the military, his push for tax increases and his failure to move his overhaul of the health-care system even close to enactment.

To the extent that he has come back, said Emory Uni-

versity political scientist Merle Black, he has "played off his opponents, not [shown] inherent strength of his own."

The Electoral Problem

It must also be remembered that presidential elections are not conducted by poll, and the winner is not elected by the popular vote. What is essential is a majority in the Electoral College, and this challenge at times looks all the more daunting for Clinton.

When looking at the current electoral vote map, it is far easier to see how Republicans reach the 270 votes needed for victory than Clinton. Republicans enjoy a long head start in most of the South, the Plains states and the Rocky Mountain West. George Bush won much of this territory in 1992 and GOP presidential candidates have dominated it over the last quarter-century.

If that remains the case again next year, then Clinton would need to draw to an inside straight in the rest of the country — the Northeast, the industrial Midwest and the Pacific West. "Democrats are back to an 18-to-20 state Electoral College strategy," said Wayne.

...Than To Help President's Ratings

however, the tactic did not work. Clinton had to turn to the House Republicans, led by GOP Whip Newt Gingrich of Georgia, to find the votes for passage.

A few days after NAFTA was adopted, the administration chalked up another win when the Senate cleared the Brady bill, a measure requiring a five-day waiting period for the purchase of a handgun.

Other successes in the 1993 session included passage of the "motor voter" law, which eased voter registration by linking it to the driver's license process. Clinton also got his much-touted Americorps program national service system by which college grants could be earned through community service.

After his shaky start, Clinton was perceived as having found his footing as the 1993 legislative session ended. Some thought he had positioned himself for greater success in 1994. But the second session would prove acutely disappointing.

In March, Congress approved the administration's Goals 2000 program, a measure that for the first time established national education goals for the country's schools. But from then on, Clinton's fortunes on the Hill steadily declined.

His top legislative priority — a sweeping plan to restructure the nation's health care system — limped through the summer and died in September. The plan divided Democrats, who could not agree on the contents of the bill, and generally united Republicans. A bipartisan proposal to make incremental changes in the system came too late in the

R. MICHAEL JENKINS

Clinton holds up a model for a "national health card" during his address to Congress on health care reform in the fall of 1993.

year to marshal majority support.

Clinton did eke out a victory on the $30.2 billion crime bill, another of his top priorities. It included the ban on assault weapons, as well as funding for prevention programs, prison construction and additional police officers. But even this victory was arguably a Pyrrhic one.

En route to final passage in August, the House-Senate compromise on the bill hit a snag when Democrat leaders could not muster the votes to bring it to the floor for a vote. Once again, Clinton had to deal with Gingrich and his troops, reshaping the bill to gain their votes.

The gun provisions contributed mightily to the defeat of several incumbents, including Speaker Thomas S. Foley of Washington and Judiciary Committee Chairman Jack Brooks of Texas.

Emboldened by the crime bill drama and unified behind the "Contract With America" campaign theme they sounded in September, Hill Republicans closed ranks in the fall weeks to frustrate Democratic efforts on campaign finance, lobbying disclosure, telecommunications and toxic waste.

The only other major piece of legislation enacted with administration backing in the 103rd was a bill implementing a renewal of the General Agreement on Tariffs and Trade. This victory, however, came during a lame duck session following Democrats' devastating losses in November.

Clinton benefited from the independent candidacy of Ross Perot in 1992, whose supporters were disproportionately Republican-leaning. With Perot taking nearly one-fifth of the popular vote, Clinton was able to win the White House with just 43 percent, the fourth-lowest winning percentage in American history.

Perot now wants to start a third party, which presumably would be interested in nominating Perot. This is widely viewed as foreshadowing a replay of 1992. A Los Angeles Times poll taken in mid-September showed Clinton with 43 percent to 35 percent for Senate Majority Leader Bob Dole, R-Kan., and 20 percent for Perot. In 1992, Clinton got 43 percent of the vote to 37 percent for President George Bush and 19 percent for Perot.

But Clinton cannot count on prospective independent candidates in 1996 to be as helpful. Running as independents, either Jesse Jackson or retired Gen. Colin L. Powell would surely cut into the Democrats' traditional base among racial minorities. Democratic Sen. Bill Bradley of New Jersey would presumably carve into other parts of the Democratic coalition.

Weakened Institution

Not long ago, the powers of the presidency and the respect attending them were so great that voters almost automatically gave Oval Office occupants a second term. From Franklin D. Roosevelt in 1936 to Richard M. Nixon in 1972, presidents were not only re-elected but rewarded with decisive margins.

Presidential victories ranged from a comfortable 4.5 percentage points for Harry S Truman in his come-from-behind win in 1948, to landslide triumphs of at least 15 percentage points for FDR in 1936, Dwight D. Eisenhower in 1956, Lyndon B. Johnson in 1964 and Nixon in 1972.

But Clinton must seek re-election in a more demanding era. In the last 20 years, Ronald Reagan has been the only president to win re-election. The others — Gerald R. Ford, Carter and Bush — all lost re-election bids. They made history in the process. Never before have so many presidents suffered rejection at the ballot box in so short a period of time.

For a time in early 1995, Clinton looked as though he would draw a primary challenge from former Pennsylvania

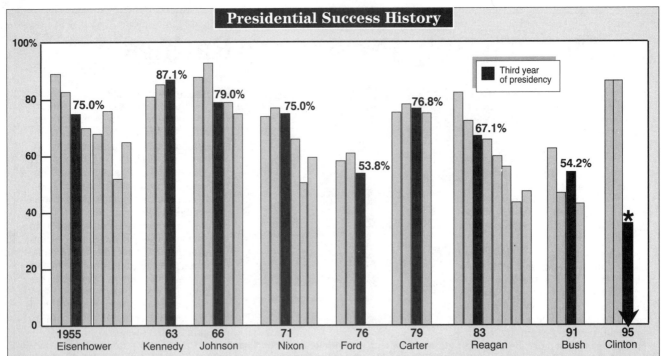

Presidential Success History

Third year of presidency

75.0% — 87.1% — 79.0% — 75.0% — 53.8% — 76.8% — 67.1% — 54.2%

| 1955 Eisenhower | 63 Kennedy | 66 Johnson | 71 Nixon | 76 Ford | 79 Carter | 83 Reagan | 91 Bush | 95 Clinton |

✱ Congressional Quarterly's presidential success rate is a measure of how often the president prevails after taking a clear position on a vote in the House or Senate. President Clinton's score was 86.4% in 1993 and again in 1994— among the highest ever recorded. The success rate is an annual score and so cannot be calculated until the session ends, and the flurry of remaining votes could change it dramatically. But preliminary indications suggest Clinton's success rate will be reduced by roughly half in the Republican 104th Congress.

Gov. Robert P. Casey, an outspoken foe of abortion. But Casey ended his nascent campaign in April, citing health reasons.

That has left Clinton, at least for the time being, without opposition for renomination, just as Reagan was when he ran for re-election in 1984. And Clinton has been quickly raising millions of campaign dollars to increase his likelihood of remaining unopposed. The president's campaign committee is expected to raise as much as $20 million in 1995.

The absence of an intraparty challenge also has freed Clinton to focus on convincing voters that no matter what their doubts about him, he is growing into the role of president. The Clinton campaign has already done some spot advertising in potential battleground states such as Colorado promoting the administration's anti-crime legislation.

At the same time, the crowded Republican race has grown increasingly contentious. And an array of national polls have shown Clinton moving well ahead of Republican front-runner Dole.

Firming Up the Base

The assertive nature of the Republican Congress seems to have helped Clinton solidify support within the Democratic coalition. A clear majority of liberals, minorities and low-income voters approved of Clinton's job performance in the late August Gallup approval ratings.

Clinton also drew majority support from young voters (18 to 29 years old), self-described moderates, and Easterners (the regional building block for Democrats in fashioning Electoral College majorities).

On the discouraging side, Clinton's performance won the approval of only one-third of Perot voters, roughly the

same percentage that backed Democratic congressional candidates during the party's disastrous showing at the ballot box in 1994.

From his vantage point in Ohio, University of Akron political scientist John C. Green sees many voters taking a "wait and see attitude" toward both Clinton and the Republican Congress. "They kicked out George Bush and they kicked out the Democratic Congress," says Green. The feeling for now is "let's give [both of] them a little room."

But that mood could change quickly in the weeks ahead. The fall before a presidential election year is often when trend lines are established for the year to come.

"It was in the fourth quarter of 1991," writes Lydia Saad, managing editor of The Gallup Poll, "that George Bush's ratings tumbled 16 points, ending his Gulf War bonanza, after which he descended sharply, and permanently, below 50 percent."

"Conversely," she continues, "it was in this quarter of 1983 that Ronald Reagan broke out of a seven-quarter slump and reached approval levels above 50 percent, which he then maintained throughout the election campaign."

Reagan was boosted by an economy rapidly recovering from recession; Bush was burdened by the perception of an economy sinking into recession.

But though the state of the economy is a staple of politics, far more than pocketbook concerns will be affecting voter opinions of Clinton in the months ahead, as the Democrats at one end of Pennsylvania Avenue and the Republicans at the other struggle to define the role of government.

"At this point," said Stephen Hess of the Brookings Institution, "I wouldn't bet on him but I would not necessarily bet against him. It's a crazy year." ∎

Dole Turns GOP Majority Status Into Front-Runner Position

Republican leader's new legislative power, seniority and survival skills make him party's man to beat

Whether or not Senate Majority Leader Bob Dole is elected president in 1996, he already has achieved in the first six months of 1995 a pinnacle few could have imagined for him even a few short years ago.

Late in 1992, with the White House about to fall to the Democrats and the Senate elections just as gloomy for the GOP, the Kansas Republican spoke bitterly of ending his long career. Dole saw nothing but frustration ahead if the number of minority Senate Republicans was going to be "down in the 30s somewhere."

But Dole persevered. In the 103rd Congress he led a highly successful rear guard action against President Clinton and the majority Democrats. His immediate reward was a historic midterm election in 1994 that produced the most Republican Congress in nearly half a century.

After eight years as Senate minority leader, Dole has returned to the majority with his parliamentary skills undiminished.

He proved that in June, when he scuttled Clinton's most prominent nomination of the year (Dr. Henry W. Foster Jr. for surgeon general), eclipsed the efforts of a presidential rival (Sen. Phil Gramm, R-Texas) to do the same, struck a bargain with House Speaker Newt Gingrich, R-Ga., guaranteeing a budget resolution with a tax cut and a balanced budget (by 2002) and saw through the Senate a monumental revision of telecommunications law — all in the span of seven days. *(Weekly Report, pp. 1845, 1814, 1727)*

Now, Dole approaches his 72nd birthday (July 22) as the clear front-runner for the Republican presidential nomination in 1996 — a year when that nomination may well be the inside track to the White House.

In three national polls done for

SCOTT J. FERRELL

Dole greets Capitol visitors outside his office suite on June 22.

EXECUTIVE PROFILE

news organizations in June, Dole led Gramm, his closest rival, by at least 30 percentage points. In Iowa, site of the first delegate-selecting caucuses, Dole's lead was 40 points.

Some say these numbers will waste away before Christmas or be shattered by Dole's first failure to meet expectations. Already, some erosion in the polls is visible in Dole's favorability rating, which typically falls below 50 percent. The nominating dynamic of any cycle can be unpredictable.

"Dole is where the smart money might be now," says Fred Greenstein, a political science professor at Princeton University and a leading scholar of presidential politics. "It's hard to see anything or anyone that stands dramatically in his way. But the current primary process continues to be full of surprises."

Greenstein says conversations with his colleagues leave him particularly cautious about the "sharply compressed" calendar for choosing delegates to the nominating convention in 1996. Because several of the largest states have moved their voting dates into March — including California, New York, and probably Pennsylvania — more than two-thirds of the delegates will be chosen by the end of that month.

"You have to take a lead like this at least somewhat at face value," argues Burdett Loomis, professor of political science at the University of Kansas and a longtime Dole watcher.

"The surprise is that no one of the fiftyish generation has really emerged yet," adds Loomis. "But if there's a vacuum, Dole can fill it with a lot more than just seniority. He has substance, and he has a lot of IOUs, and he has to be taken seriously."

Early leads have been known to evaporate for Democratic presidential hopefuls, but Republicans have tended to honor order and seniority to the degree that winning the nomination has been a matter of knowing one's time and waiting one's turn. In every cycle since 1940 the Republicans have nominated the presidential contender who entered the election year as the best known and most widely supported in opinion polls. Barring a health problem or an unforeseen reversal of equal gravity, Dole is likely to enter 1996 as both.

"More and more, the nomination is being determined by what happens in the year before the primaries," says political scientist Paul Green of Governors

State University in Illinois. "What's more, I don't see anyone else besides Dole with the bench strength to survive if he takes a hit early."

Dole knows survival. He came back from mortal wounds in World War II and a three-year ordeal in Veterans Administration hospitals. He entered politics in 1950 while still an undergraduate on the GI bill and has held elected public office continuously since.

This will be his fourth time around in presidential politics, having been the vice presidential nominee in 1976 and an entrant in the primaries in 1980 and 1988. The difference is that this time he is the front-runner. That fact has enabled him to raise more money at the start of his campaign (more than $13 million after the first six months of 1995) than in the 1988 cycle (when he had raised less than $4 million at the comparable juncture).

But rather than protect his lead, Dole has elected to press his advantage. He might have stepped down as majority leader of the Senate and campaigned full time as his party's senior statesman. Instead he has chosen to brave the slings and arrows in an era of great controversy and intraparty struggle.

At the same time, Dole has shown himself willing to do what he must and to sacrifice what he must to assure himself of the nomination. He has returned to his own conservative roots on social issues such as gun control, civil rights and welfare. He has strenuously courted moral activists by taking on sex and violence in Hollywood — and by extension the humanism and permissive attitudes that are anathema to religious conservatives. And he has voluntarily signed a pledge not to raise taxes, shrugging off the curse some believe cost him the nomination in 1988.

Meeting the Minuses

The knock on Dole as a national campaigner has been threefold. Conservative purists call him a pragmatist who lacks an overarching ideology. His campaigns have lacked organization, both nationally and at the local level. And he has had a

Bob Dole

Republican of Russell, Kan.

Born: July 22, 1923; Russell, Kan.

Education: University of Kansas, 1941-1943; Washburn University, A.B. 1952, LL.B. 1952.

Family: Wife, Mary Elizabeth Hanford; one child.

Religion: Methodist

Political Career: Kansas House, 1951-53; Russell County attorney, 1953-61; U.S. House, 1961-69; Republican nominee for vice president, 1976; sought Republican nomination for president, 1980, 1988.

Occupation: Lawyer

Military Service: Army, 1943-48.

burdensome reputation for being acerbic to the point of meanness. This last trait has been exacerbated by his frequent inability or unwillingness to curb his own tongue.

Dole will never be the champion of those conservatives who have been described over the years as the New Right, "movement conservatives" or, most recently, "Contract Republicans," so named for the House GOP's "Contract With America."

Dole in the 104th

After Republicans recaptured the majority in November 1994, Bob Dole, R-Kan., resumed his position as Senate majority leader in January 1995. Stories on Dole in the 1995 *CQ Weekly Report* include:

Dole-tied foundation details contributions, *p. 1806.*
Dole and the Foster nomination, *p. 1845.*
Dole and the budget resolution, *p. 1814.*
Dole and the telecommunications bill, *p. 1727.*
Dole releases financial summary, *p. 1710.*

Dole stakes out stand on Bosnia, *pp. 1766, 1653, 761.*
Dole gets behind push for a new course on regulatory policy, *pp. 1925, 1836, 1693.*
Dole and farm subsidies, *p. 1316.*
Dole and the product liability bill, *pp. 1233, 1221.*
Dole and lobbyists on product liability, *p. 1219.*

Dole tackles budget, Medicare cuts, *p. 1227.*
Presidential announcement, *pp. 1102, 1082.*
Dole and the line-item veto, *pp. 854, 359.*
Dole confronts intraparty rebellion, *p. 729.*
Dole and the balanced-budget amendment, *p. 671.*

Dole will never be entirely forgiven for the tax bills he pushed on President Ronald Reagan as chairman of the Senate Finance Committee in 1982 and 1983, nor the things he said about tax-cutting "supply-side" economics and its enthusiasts along the way. (Example: "A busload of supply-siders went off a cliff; the bad news is there were two empty seats.")

Specific issues aside, it seems implausible that a Republican electorate enamored of term limits and fresh faces in Washington would turn over the White House to a man who has been in government without interruption for 45 years and in Congress for 35 of them — a man who is the second longest-serving Republican on Capitol Hill.

But Dole by most measures has been a consistent conservative. His annual rating from the liberal Americans for Democratic Action has usually been below 10 (and never higher than 22). He rose to national politics as an acolyte of President Richard M. Nixon, and he was chosen as President Gerald R. Ford's running mate in 1976 largely to cover Ford's right and appeal to Sun Belt Republicans.

And while he has adopted a variety of positions on affirmative action, civil rights, guns and some other social issues, he has been a consistent opponent of abortion and a consistent supporter of school prayer. Most important at the present, he has shown great willingness to work with the Christian Coalition and other religious groups eager to effect changes in federal statutes.

Tellingly, conservative Christian activists also have reached out to him. When the Christian Coalition brought forth its 10-point agenda at the Capitol in May, other Republican leaders came to the news conference; Dole waited in his office for Ralph Reed and other Coalition leaders to come to him. He was cordial and welcoming but did not commit himself to all of the coalition's "Contract With the American Family."

The Nixon Connection

President Richard M. Nixon had enormous influence over the politics of the postwar era in American history, and one of the ways he wielded that influence was by elevating the career of Bob Dole.

The two first met in the 1950s. In the mid-1960s, when Nixon was traveling the country repairing the damage from his losing campaigns of 1960 and 1962 (when he ran for president and governor of California, respectively), he came to Kansas twice to help Dole win re-election to the House. The journalist Richard Ben Cramer, in his study of the 1988 presidential candidates, quotes Dole as remembering Nixon as "the only guy in Washington who remembered to shake with his left hand." (Dole lost the use of his right hand to his World War II wounds.)

The alliance persists even now. On May 7, The Los Angeles Times reported that Dole "has leaned heavily on detailed advice from Nixon, one of his oldest and closest political friends" prior to the former president's death in 1994.

Among other things, Nixon urged Dole to run "as far as you can to the right because that's where 40 percent of the people who decide the nomination are." After that, Nixon was said to have advised, "you have to run as fast as you can back to the middle, because only about 4 percent of the nation's voters are on the extreme right wing."

Bonding in 1969

Dole was first elected to the Senate in 1968, the year Nixon first won the White House. As a freshman in the exclusive chamber, Dole found his first role as the new president's most ardent and frequent defender.

Cramer wrote that Dole would receive speeches from the White House with red flags marked URGENT and head for the Senate floor to deliver them.

Dole was among the few who fought hard for Nixon's ill-fated Supreme Court nominees, F. Clement Haynsworth Jr. in 1969 and G. Harrold Carswell in 1970. One Nixon aide described the 47-year-old Dole as "a hungry Doberman pinscher."

Nixon

Elizabeth Dole

Ford

Bob Dole (1973)

That turned out to be just the pedigree the White House wanted for its new Republican National Committee chairman in January 1971, and Dole got the job. He embarked on a nonstop traveling schedule that would bring him his first real national attention and bring his 24-year marriage to an end in 1972. (Dole's first wife, Phyllis, told reporters that after he took the RNC job Dole was home for dinner just twice in an entire year.)

Dole was at odds with Nixon's campaign staff in 1972, constantly urging that in his landslide re-election the president ought to do more to help other Republicans. His reward was to be eased out of the RNC chairmanship early in 1973. That turned out to be fortunate because the Nixon presidency would soon be destroyed by the Watergate scandal.

Dole continued to defend Nixon until the president resigned. But having established his distance from the Nixon White House, he also could joke that "Watergate happened on my night off" and get away with it.

Lasting Benefits

Dole emerged from that era with two benefits of incalculable importance. He established his bona fides as a loyal and indefatigable combatant with President Gerald R. Ford, Nixon's successor, who would choose Dole as his running mate in 1976.

Moreover, in the Nixon administration, Dole met a woman from North Carolina (a former Democrat) who had sub-Cabinet rank and an obvious future of her own in politics. Elizabeth Hanford would become secretary of Transportation for President Ronald Reagan and secretary of Labor for President George Bush, but in 1975 she became the second wife of Bob Dole.

Advising Dole nearly 20 years later, Nixon would say the Kansan had the "brains, heart and guts" to be president.

Loyal to Nixon to the end, Dole gave a tearful eulogy at Nixon's funeral in which he said the second half of the 20th century would be known as "the Age of Nixon."

Still, Dole is clearly loath to offend these forces in the party. He and his wife, Elizabeth, have stopped attending the Foundry United Methodist Church in Washington (where the Clinton family goes many Sundays). The Associated Press reported in May that the Doles were seeking an evangelical church because the minister at Foundry, a supporter of feminism and gay rights, was

too liberal. The Doles refused comment. Elizabeth Dole, president of the American Red Cross, had become a member at Foundry during the tenure of an earlier minister.

All on the Altar

As for his campaign organization, Dole is finally benefiting from the dynamic that makes all front-runners look

well-organized and well-financed. He has also been successful at turning bad stories around with a minimum of damage. When adviser Edward J. Rollins made a joking reference to two Jewish members of Congress as "Hymie boys," he was separated from the campaign.

When questions were raised about contributions to a think tank ancillary to Dole's political organization, Dole

After Years of Building Consensus . . .

Through 35 years in Congress, Bob Dole has been known as a negotiator and a legislative broker, a master of the inside compromise that gets the job done. Small wonder then that his own philosophy has been described as an "ideological blur."

But as the leader of congressional opposition to President Clinton in 1993 and 1994, Dole, R-Kan., toughened his stand on issues almost across the board.

And now, with the 1996 presidential nomination on the line, he has striven to prove his fealty to conservative doctrine — not only on taxes, government spending and foreign policy, but also on social questions such as abortion, gun control and civil rights.

Dole has gone back and forth over his long career on the issue of gun control. As a House member, he voted for the Gun Control Act of 1968 in the aftermath of the assassinations of Robert Kennedy and the Rev. Dr. Martin Luther King Jr. But as a senator in the mid-1980s he supported efforts to weaken that act's restrictions on mail-order or interstate shipment of firearms and ammunition and its licensing procedures for firearms production, sale and possession.

During Republican President George Bush's term, Dole supported a crime bill that would have mandated a three-year prohibition on the production, sale and possession of semiautomatic assault weapons. As recently as 1991, he supported a version of the Brady bill, which imposed a five-day waiting period for the purchase of handguns and a mandatory background check on purchasers.

In 1993, however, after the election of Clinton, Dole no longer felt obliged to seek a middle ground in behalf of a Republican president. He voted against a second consideration of the Brady bill. He also voted against banning 19 semiautomatic weapons.

Hardened Line

Dole has hardened his line against gun control in the 104th Congress, competing directly for the votes of National Rifle Association (NRA) members and other Second Amendment enthusiasts.

In a March 10 letter to the NRA's chief lobbyist, Tanya Metaksa, Dole pledged to lead an effort to repeal the 1994 law banning 19 semiautomatic assault weapons. "Gun control is a completely ineffective approach to the lack of safety and security in our communities," Dole wrote. "Disarming law-abiding citizens only places them at the mercy of those who break the law."

Most recently, Dole has rebuffed Democratic attempts to attach firearm restrictions to the anti-terrorism bill passed June 7. "They do not want to pass anti-terrorism legislation. They have already forgotten what has happened in Oklahoma City," Dole said. The Republicans ultimately prevailed.

A recent Los Angeles Times poll estimated that gun owners would constitute nearly half (48 percent) of the Republican primary vote. And although many of these votes may already belong to Dole's rival for the presidency, Sen. Phil Gramm of Texas, the competition is not over.

"If we could keep the NRA from endorsing Phil Gramm, we'll consider it a victory," Dole campaign manager Scott Reed has said.

Civil Rights

On civil rights, Dole moved to the left in the mid-1960s but soon returned to a conservative line. In the 1980s, he adopted a middle-of-the-road position and facilitated compromises on the civil rights bill of 1991.

Dole voted for both the 1964 Civil Rights Act and the 1965 Voting Rights Act. The next year, however, Dole conspicuously reversed his position and voted against the Civil Rights Act of 1966 and the Equal Employment Opportunity Act of 1966.

The Civil Rights Act of 1966, which passed the House but not the Senate, would have barred discrimination in the selection of juries and in the sale or rental of some housing.

Dole seemed to shift again when he came to the Senate in 1969. Although he consistently voted against forced busing to desegregate schools, he supported the 1975 extension of the Voting Rights Act, and he became

---

quickly closed the fund. The Better America Foundation returned about $2.5 million that was left from more than $4.6 million collected from corporations and wealthy individuals since its founding in 1993.

The mean-streak criticism is muted, at least for the moment, by Dole's own somewhat cooler demeanor. This restraint contrasts with the hot talk coming from other Republicans in the new Congress, including Gingrich and Gramm, as well as from talk-show hosts and commentators in general.

But if Dole seems to have his personal demons under control, he gains only so long as he keeps them under control. The floor leader was clearly straining to keep his cool early in July when confronted with a filibuster mounted awkwardly by Sens. Paul Wellstone, D-Minn., and Carol Moseley-Braun, D-Ill.

"This debate doesn't make any sense to me," Dole growled as he glowered at Wellstone.

But the front-runner must know that the day his temper flares in a

debate or at a media event, he will see all his worst moments replayed on television again and again.

He hurt his own cause in 1976 by referring to the four wars Americans had fought in the 20th century as "Democrat wars." He warned his Senate colleagues in 1985 to pass the Gramm-Rudman deficit reduction law fast or else "people may start to read it." And in 1988 he seemed to scotch his own fading chance for the nomination when he snapped at New Hampshire primary winner George Bush:

...Dole Takes Uncompromising Stance

something of a champion for civil rights bills in the 1980s. In 1982, he shepherded the Voting Rights Act extension through a hostile Senate, crafting a compromise that was applauded by President Ronald Reagan, liberal Sen. Joseph R. Biden Jr., D-Del., and civil rights groups.

In 1983, Dole led the floor fight to make Martin Luther King Day a national holiday. In 1984, he forged a compromise on the "Grove City" issue, which arose after the U.S. Supreme Court, in a case named for Grove City College in Pennsylvania, narrowed the scope of legislation regarding sex bias and discrimination based on color, race or national origin. Civil rights groups accepted Dole's compromise, but other Republicans did not.

Dole also voted in favor of the Civil Rights Act of 1991, a bill that sought to reverse a series of Supreme Court decisions that had made it difficult for workers to win job discrimination suits. Included in the legislation was an expansion of Title IX of the Civil Rights Act of 1964, which had been affected by the Grove City College case. Bush threatened to veto the measure but feared that moderate Republicans would join with Democrats to override a veto. Dole acted as an intermediary and brought in a deal.

Affirmative Action

Dole's standing with civil rights proponents has slipped recently because of his changing position on affirmative action. Earlier this year, Dole made headlines by pressing an attack on affirmative action programs authorized under a presidential order issued in 1965.

Dole singled out the executive order on federal contractors and the Small Business Administration's set-aside program for what are called "small and disadvantaged businesses."

But in 1985, Dole had been one of 69 senators who asked Reagan not to rescind that same order. Among others urging retention of the order at that time was Dole's wife, Elizabeth, who was then Reagan's secretary of transportation.

Dole was also a 1991 co-sponsor of the Glass Ceiling

Commission, which rewards companies for bringing minorities and women into high-level positions.

Responding to criticism of his apparent turnaround on the issue, Dole said he still favored affirmative action "if it means remedying proven past discrimination against individuals."

"If affirmative action means recruitment of qualified minorities and women to give them an opportunity to compete without guaranteeing the results, then I'm for that, too," he added.

"But if affirmative action means quotas, set-asides and other preferences that favor individuals simply because they happen to belong to certain groups, then that's where I draw the line."

Abortion Issues

Dole consistently votes against abortion rights supporters. But he has softened his rhetoric since the 1970s, when he won his closest re-election battle largely by attacking his opponent as a supporter of abortion rights.

In 1983, he voted to overturn the Supreme Court decision that legalized abortion, and in 1986 he supported an amendment to tax-overhaul legislation that would have taxed nonprofit clinics and hospitals that perform abortions. The measure did not pass.

Throughout the '90s, Dole voted in favor of anti-abortion provisions. In 1990, he voted against a measure that allowed minors to seek abortions without parental notification; in 1992, he voted to lift the fetal tissue research ban but against abortion counseling at federally funded clinics.

Dole also has taken a strong position against federally funded abortion, and in 1994 he voted against the act that safeguarded access to abortion clinics.

His rhetoric, however, has become significantly less aggressive. In 1989, Dole called for a more moderate party stance on the abortion issue; he said he feared that rejecting members who advocate abortion rights could divide the Republicans. Dole also said he agreed with Bush's position that abortion is permissible in cases of rape, incest or when the woman's life is in danger.

"Stop lying about my record."

But in the 1996 cycle, in a last hurrah he himself might have thought impossible after 1988, the well-seasoned Dole strives to apply all the lessons he has learned. He seems finally willing to put it all on the altar, holding back nothing — not even his right to speak his mind in blunt terms.

Time To Remember

There is another side to the new, more controlled Dole, something beyond mere self-restraint. It is a new-found willingness to talk about his own past, his youth and most especially his wartime wounds. The shift was made plain when Dole made his official declaration in April on the 50th anniversary of the week when his life nearly ended on a battlefield in northern Italy.

In the waning days of World War II, as a second lieutenant in the Army, Dole was part of an assault on well-entrenched German troops that left every man in his platoon wounded. Dole was caught in machine gun fire and an explosion that shattered his

right shoulder and arm and broke five vertebrae. After hours on the ground, he was dragged to safety by another soldier. When Dole reached a hospital back in the United States, he had lost more than 60 pounds, one kidney, all use of his right arm and most of the feeling in his left. He endured more than three years of surgery and rehabilitation in a succession of VA hospitals. Half a century later, he still has no use of his right arm and less than full feeling in his left.

He carries a pen or a paper in his

How Dole Voted . . .

Congressional Quarterly each year selects a series of key votes on major issues and records how every member voted on each.

The following examples were culled from the annual lists during the last two dozen years of Dole's 35-year career on Capitol Hill.

1995

Allow vote on Henry Foster as surgeon general	N
Approve balanced-budget constitutional amendment *(switched vote to N so as to permit motion to reconsider)*	N
Approve budget resolution eliminating deficit by 2002	Y

1994

Safeguard access to abortion clinics	N
Require risk assessment of some new EPA regulations	Y
Invoke cloture on bill to limit product liability	Y
Bar military action in Haiti without vote in Congress	Y
End U.S. arms embargo on Bosnia	Y
Waive Senate budget rules to allow crime bill vote	N
Invoke cloture on lobbying disclosure and gift ban bill	N
Invoke cloture on California desert protection bill	N
Waive Senate budget rules to allow GATT vote	Y
Approve national education standards	N
Approve balanced-budget constitutional amendment	Y
End U.S. trade embargo on Vietnam	N

1993

Allow vote on Clinton's economic stimulus plan	N
Require unpaid family and medical leave	N
Provide incentives to limit campaign spending	N
Pass Clinton budget with new taxes and cuts	N
Authorize funds for the National Service program	N
Confirm Ruth Bader Ginsburg to the Supreme Court	Y
Allow the president to decide on gays in the military	N
Reduce spending for the anti-missile program	N
Bar higher grazing fees and other public land reforms	Y
Provide foreign aid with aid to Russia	Y
Allow federal abortion funding	N
Limit subpoena of Packwood diaries	Y
Ban certain semiautomatic assault weapons	N
Approve national "motor voter" registration bill	N
Approve five-day waiting period for handguns	N
Approve NAFTA	Y

Approve budget increasing taxes and reducing deficit	N

1992

Provide extended unemployment benefits	Y
Oppose deeper cuts in spending for SDI	Y
Reject stricter nuclear power licensing procedures	Y
Impose 9-month moratorium on nuclear testing	N
Override family and medical leave veto	N
Reduce enterprise zones and IRA deductions	Y
Allow abortion counseling at federally funded clinics	N
Provide $26.5 billion for foreign assistance	Y
Override veto of cable TV rate cap bill	N
Reauthorize water projects in Utah and California	Y
Approve school-choice pilot program	Y
Allow funds shift from defense to domestic programs	N
Reject lifting fetal tissue research ban	N
Override campaign finance reform veto	N

1991

Approve waiting period for handgun purchases	Y
Raise senators' pay and ban honoraria	Y
Tie China's trade status to human rights progress	N
Kill amendment to allow female combat pilots	N
Authorize use of force in Persian Gulf	Y
Confirm Clarence Thomas to Supreme Court	Y
Pass Civil Rights Act of 1991	Y

1990

Oppose prohibition of some semiautomatic weapons	N
Adopt constitutional amendment on flag desecration	Y
Oppose requiring parental notice for minors' abortion	N
Halt production of B-2 stealth bomber at 13 planes	N
Approve budget with spending cuts and taxes	Y
Pass civil rights bill over Bush veto	N

1989

Oppose reduction of SDI funding	Y
Oppose barring federal funds for "obscene" art	N
Allow vote on capital gains tax cut	Y

right hand to deflect handshakes, reaching out to grip proffered hands with his left. "I do try harder," Dole once said. "If I didn't, I'd be sitting in a rest home, in a rocker, drawing disability [benefits]."

Dole did not return to the University of Kansas, where before going to war he had been a track star with thoughts of medical school. Instead he went to Washburn University in Topeka, where he could finish his bachelor's degree and work toward a law degree at the same

time. He got both degrees magna cum laude in 1952, by which time he had also sought and won his first public office — a seat in the Kansas legislature.

He left that seat after one term to be county prosecutor back in his hometown of Russell, where his father had run a cafe, then a grain elevator and later a small creamery. Dole's mother had taken in sewing and sold Singer sewing machines door to door. The Doles had been Democrats, and their son admitted admiring President Franklin D. Roosevelt.

But western Kansas was Republican ground, and Dole entered public life in the GOP.

After three re-elections as prosecutor, he made his first bid for Congress in 1960. The Republican nomination was tantamount to election, and Dole won it by 982 votes.

Dole's four terms in the House were marked by a focus on the Agriculture Committee, where hard work and cooperation enabled a young member of the minority to have some effect. He voted

...On the Major Issues

1988

Enact omnibus trade bill over Reagan veto	N
Approve death penalty for drug-related murders	Y
Oppose workfare amendment to welfare overhaul bill	N

1987

Limit testing of anti-ballistic missiles in space	N
Confirm Supreme Court nominee Robert H. Bork	Y
Enact omnibus highway bill over Reagan veto	N

1986

Block chemical weapons production	N
Impose sanctions on South Africa	N
Aid Nicaraguan contras	Y

1985

Weaken gun control laws	Y
Produce MX missiles	Y
Limit textile imports	N

1984

Permit school prayer	Y
Cut military aid to El Salvador	N
Keep tax indexing	Y

1983

Overturn Supreme Court decision legalizing abortion	Y
Create Martin Luther King Jr. holiday	Y
Bar funding for MX missile	N

1982

Increase gasoline tax 5 cents per gallon	Y
Cut $1.2 billion for public works jobs	Y
Retain tobacco price supports	Y
Impose sanctions on South Africa	N
Aid Nicaraguan contras	Y

1981

Allow vote on anti-busing bill	Y
Disapprove sale of AWACS planes to Saudi Arabia	N
Index income tax rates against inflation	Y

1980

Block Justice Department busing suits	Y
End revenue sharing for state governments	Y
Approve military draft registration	N

1979

Guarantee loans for Chrysler Corp.	Y
Kill stronger windfall profits tax on oil companies	Y
Impose moratorium on nuclear power plant building	N

1978

Approve treaty giving Panama Canal to Panama	N
Raise mandatory federal retirement age from 65 to 70	Y
Approve airline deregulation bill	Y

1977

End federal price controls for onshore natural gas	Y
Kill plan to cap outside income at 15% of Senate pay	Y
Assert congressional authority on South Korea policy	Y

1976

Kill pristine-air rule from Clean Air Act amendments	Y
Authorize $2 billion for public works jobs	N
Limit higher-income persons' access to food stamps	Y

1975

Resume military aid to Turkey	N
Implement Arab-Israel peace accord monitoring Sinai	Y
Approve tax rebates and tax rate cuts for individuals	Y

1974

Impose death penalty for certain crimes	Y
Enact Freedom of Information Act over veto	N
Kill amendment to ban busing for desegregation	N

1973

Reduce land-based U.S. troops overseas by 40 percent	N
Require president to effect fuel rationing plan	N
Ban practices that circumvent caps on crop subsidies	N

1972

Equal Rights Amendment	Y
Antiballistic Missile Treaty with the Soviet Union	Y

---

with his party on nine out of 10 votes and usually took part in the conservative coalition of Republicans and Southern Democrats — except that he voted for both the Civil Rights Act of 1964 and the Voting Rights Act of 1965. He opposed the creation of Medicare in 1965, as did most Republicans, as well as the Equal Employment Opportunity Act of 1966.

In 1968, Dole sought the seat of a retiring GOP senator and easily defeated a former governor in the primary. It was a GOP year most everywhere, and Dole won that November with 60 percent of the vote.

Arriving in the Senate in 1969, the first year of Nixon's presidency, Dole soon found a role as a floor debater willing to defend his party's new president. His eagerness for such combat put off his party elders in the Senate, especially Minority Leader Hugh Scott of Pennsylvania, but it stood him in good stead with other Republicans.

Nixon tapped Dole to be chairman of the Republican National Committee in January 1971, and the same bulldog tendencies would lead to a spot on the 1976 national ticket.

President Gerald R. Ford was trailing Democratic challenger Jimmy Carter in the summer of 1976, and Dole seemed a good choice as his point man in the attack plan for that fall. Dole also had ties to the Western populist wing of the party, which was disappointed that the nomination had not gone to Ronald Reagan that year.

Dole ripped into Carter, while Ford stayed in the Rose Garden. The gap in the polls narrowed steadily, but not without cost. Dole's performance in his debate with Democrat Walter F. Mondale created a firestorm of criticism, not only for "Democrat wars" but for shots Dole took at Carter's Playboy interview and for Dole's weak defense of Ford's pardon of Nixon. When the Ford-Dole ticket lost, Dole got much of the blame for losing and little credit for making it close.

The bad press did not deter him from another national campaign just four years later. Although his own seat was up and the list of Republican aspirants was long, Dole entered the early presidential contests in 1980. But he had trouble getting out of Washington to campaign and wound up with an astonishingly negligible 597 votes in the New Hampshire primary (out of nearly 150,000 cast). He pulled out, endorsed Reagan and filed for re-election.

But once again, Dole's descent into a valley simply lead to a new peak. The GOP seized not only the White House but the Senate in 1980, and Dole, re-elected with 64 percent of the vote, became chairman of the Finance Committee. In that job he would win wide favor for passing Reagan's tax cuts in 1981 and a hail of disapproval for the tax increases he crafted in subsequent years to reduce the ballooning budget deficit. Gingrich, then a second-term back bencher in the House, labeled Dole "a tax collector for the welfare state" — a dart that stuck.

Nevertheless, Dole stepped up immediately when the majority leader job came open late in 1984. Four others ran, including three who are still in the Senate — Ted Stevens of Alaska, Pete V. Domenici of New Mexico and Richard G. Lugar of Indiana (now a rival bidder for the GOP presidential nomination). Dole survived to the final ballot with Stevens and narrowly prevailed, in part with the support of conservative gadfly Sen. Jesse Helms, R-N.C. — whose heavy use of floor privileges Dole pledged to preserve.

Dole's first tour as the Senate's ringmaster (1985-86) had its highs and lows. "You have to produce and you have to prove leadership," Dole would say, and he paid the price to do both.

Beyond the legislation that passed with his help — including a major tax code revision, a new immigration law, a five-year farm bill and aid to the Nicaraguan contras — he overcame the small groups of senators who had been

Interest Group Ratings

These ratings represent the percentage of votes Sen. Bob Dole, R-Kan., cast in agreement with each group's stated position on test votes selected by the groups. The groups are the liberal Americans for Democratic Action, the conservative Americans for Constitutional Action (1961-80), the American Conservative Union (1981-94), the AFL-CIO and the U.S. Chamber of Commerce (1965-94).

Year	ADA	ACA/ACU	AFL-CIO	USCC
1994	0	100	0	90
1993	10	88	0	100
1992	5	93	17	90
1991	5	86	17	80
1990	0	83	33	75
1989	5	86	0	88
1988	15	91	33	91
1987	5	77	20	83
1986	0	91	0	89
1985	0	91	10	90
1984	10	86	0	83
1983	5	64	19	56
1982	15	80	20	62
1981	5	76	11	100
1980	22	77	28	90
1979	21	64	21	75
1978	20	58	22	83
1977	5	70	11	88
1976	10	87	16	75
1975	17	67	24	75
1974	19	84	18	80
1973	10	82	27	78
1972	0	84	10	100
1971	4	71	17	100
1970	13	76	17	80
1969	0	64	18	80
House Service:				
1968	0	90	25	100
1967	7	96	9	100
1966	0	93	0	100
1965	0	89	0	100
1964	8	95	9	—
1963	0	100	9	—
1962	0	91	0	—
1961	0	92	0	—

bringing the chamber's business to a standstill. His success rested on the palpable sense of his will to use what power he had. During the floor consideration of South Africa sanctions in 1985, Dole had the official copy of the legislation locked in a safe, temporarily preventing further action. Bitterly denounced on another occasion by Democratic leader Robert C. Byrd of West Virginia, Dole shot back: "I did not become majority leader to lose."

The loss of the Senate majority in 1986 freed Dole to concentrate on what he privately called "the other thing," the

party's 1988 nomination for president. He spent more time on the road, but remained as the Republican leader in the Senate throughout the campaign cycle. Some believed this showed Dole's lack of confidence in his own chances, but for Dole, the issue was demonstrating his willingness and ability to lead.

Dole has made the same call in the current cycle. If the president can run for re-election while serving as president, he asks, why should the Senate leader not seek promotion while continuing to do his job? For Dole, wielding power — with all its risks and challenges — is the best audition there could be for all the power, risks and challenges of the presidency.

For those who view politics less as an ideological test and more as a confrontation between personalities, Dole will always be formidable. Those who measure first the man will be struck by how he has endured, rising repeatedly from the graves others have dug for him. The years have elevated him beyond regionalism, above his days as someone else's hit-man and beyond the usual definitions of liberal and conservative.

One Last Lesson

But all this could have been said of Dole the last time he ran for president. What is different now is that he has internalized one more great lesson: that he cannot win the nomination with the votes of those who appreciate his finer skills as a legislator.

The very qualities professionals appreciate most — such as his ability to reach in all directions in crafting a deal — arouse suspicion among the partisans who decide who gets the party nomination. Obviously mindful of this problem, Dole in the past 30 months has shown more fealty to party principle.

The game of the nomination is played with what Princeton's Greenstein calls "a deck full of wild cards." But for now, at least, Dole has more right than anyone to look to November 1996 and a presumed match-up with Clinton.

This raises yet a final difference between Dole's current circumstances and those of the 1988 campaign. In that era, Dole was running to succeed a personally popular president whose special qualities of charm and unifying, upbeat energy he could not hope to reproduce.

In this cycle, Dole has the great advantage of contrasting himself against a president of relative youth (24 years his junior) whose personal history from draft avoidance to vacillations in the Oval Office may well make Dole's age and gravitas more attractive than ever before.

House and Senate Candidacies

SENATE SERVICE

1992 General

Bob Dole (R)	**706,246 (62.7%)**
Gloria O'Dell (D)	349,525 (31%)
Others	70,676 (6.2%)

1992 Primary

Bob Dole (R)	**244,480 (80.4%)**
R. W. Rodewald (R)	59,589 (19.6%)

1986 General

Bob Dole (R)	**576,902 (70%)**
Guy MacDonald (D)	246,664 (30%)

1986 Primary

Bob Dole (R)	**228,301 (84%)**
S. J. Ashley Landis (R)	42,237 (16%)

1980 General

Bob Dole (R)	**598,686 (64%)**
John Simpson (D)	340,271 (36%)

1980 Primary

Bob Dole (R)	**201,484 (82%)**

1974 General

Bob Dole (R)	**403,983 (51%)**
William R. Roy (D)	390,451 (49%)

1968 General

Bob Dole (R)	**490,911 (60%)**
W. I. Robinson (D)	315,911 (39%)

HOUSE SERVICE

1966 General

Bob Dole (R)	**97,487 (69%)**
Berniece Henkel (D)	44,569 (31%)

1964 General

Bob Dole (R)	**113,212 (51%)**
Bill Bork (D)	108,086 (49%)

1962 General

Bob Dole (R)	**102,499 (56%)**
J. Floyd Breeding (D)	81,092 (44%)

1960 General

Bob Dole (R)	**62,335 (59%)**
William A. Davis (D)	42,869 (41%)

1960 Primary

Bob Dole (R)	**16,033 (45%)**
Keith Sebelius (R)	15,051 (42%)
Philip J. Doyle (R)	4,423 (12%)

CQ Vote Studies

Participation: The percentage of recorded votes for which Dole was present and voting.

Presidential support: The percentage of votes on which Bob Dole agreed with the public position of the president.

Party unity: The percentage of votes on which Dole agreed with the majority of Republicans voting against a majority of the opposing party.

Conservative coalition: The percentage of votes on which Dole stood with a majority of Republicans and Southern Democrats against a majority of Northern Democrats.

S — Supported
O — Opposed

Year	Voting Participation	Presidential Support		Party Unity		Conservative Coalition	
		S	O	S	O	S	O
Senate							
1994	99	35	65	95	4	97	3
1993	98	28	72	95	5	88	7
1992	99	88	12	94	6	92	8
1991	100	96	4	93	7	98	3
1990	100	80	20	86	14	95	5
1989	99	94	4	89	11	87	13
1988	86	68	19	70	12	86	5
1987	95	71	24	85	10	81	6
1986	99	92	8	92	7	95	4
1985	99	92	7	92	6	92	5
1984	97	90	9	90	8	96	2
1983	96	78	21	88	8	89	7
1982	98	86	13	91	8	85	10
1981	98	85	7	94	5	92	5
1980	96	48	49	72	24	77	20
1979	93	39	57	78	16	85	14
1978	95	32	65	77	19	83	14
1977	97	53	44	85	12	89	8
1976	78	66	17	71	12	77	6
1975	93	75	16	86	8	90	5
1974	89	63	33	71	21	76	17
1973	96	71	27	83	14	89	10
1972	92	87	4	87	3	88	1
1971	86	80	13	89	9	87	4
1970	94	81	15	88	8	86	7
1969	94	75	21	80	12	87	7
House							
1968	85	42	46	84	7	88	0
1967	94	40	53	90	10	91	4
1966	99	37	63	90	10	100	0
1965	99	34	63	91	7	98	2
1964	99	27	73	94	6	100	0
1963	99	23	76	100	0	93	7
1962	98	33	65	93	5	94	0
1961	99	15	83	88	12	100	0

CQ ROUNDTABLE

By Ronald D. Elving

Campaign Data Can Be Calculated Nonsense

After the 1988 election, veteran Chicago Tribune reporter Jon Margolis switched from following national politics to covering baseball. Asked why, he said he had never seen a story that read: "The Chicago Cubs defeated the St. Louis Cardinals today by a score of 2-1. The Cardinals denied it."

The world of politics has borrowed many of its metaphors and expressions from baseball, but only on Election Day is its scoring so clear-cut.

In baseball, statistics are used to dispute which hitter or pitcher is the greatest; they do not supplant the scoreboard. In politics, numbers games often become the game itself.

We are now deep into "spring training" for the presidential nomination fight of 1996, with all the attendant polling, fundraising and arguing about which numbers mean what.

Take the egregious example of the straw polls conducted in dozens of states. The putative winner is often a long shot whose actual standing with random samples of the general public is between minuscule and microscopic.

Even some statewide party events, such as the Iowa state GOP convention Aug. 19, feature straw polls. The preferences of thousands are expressed, but the sampling is no more scientific. The Iowa straw poll, for example, prompted candidates to import participants from other states, paying their entry fees and travel expenses.

Even if none of the candidates believes such measures have validity, none can afford to let another candidate engineer a result that could be marketed to gullible portions of the public via complicitous elements of the media.

The great prejudice of journalism is for a good story. And if an underdog candidate does well in a straw poll somewhere, the story has not only surprise and personal drama but also the illusion of precision and reliability that is peculiar to numbers.

When statistics are involved, the temptation to treat even a bogus event as meaningful can be all but irresistible.

To help us resist, Temple University Professor John Allen Paulos has written a succinct new book called "A Mathematician Reads the Newspaper." In it, he seeks greater respect for "the role of mathematics in understanding social issues" while urging "keener skepticism about its

> **When statistics are involved, the temptation to treat even a bogus event as meaningful can be all but irresistible.**

uses, non-uses, misuses and abuses."

The author's simple aphorism — "Always be smart; seldom be certain" — would reverse the regular order in Washington and on the campaign trail.

Paulos examines the larger journalistic enterprise, not sparing the sports page, the business section or even the recipes and horoscopes. But his critique has special bite when applied to public affairs, because in this arena the shortcomings have less to do with innocence or inadvertence and more to do with perspective and persuasion.

When it comes to politics, Paulos contends, journalists are too often in cahoots with those who spin fresh tales from the flimsiest numerical material.

"With primaries, caucuses, state conventions, a glut of rules on eligibility, incessant polling, media watches, and reams of punditry," he writes, "... candidates' spin doctors have ample material from which to fashion an argument that their man is the front-runner."

To illustrate, Paulos offers a caucus in mythical "Nebarkamassacalowa," where 55 delegates are asked to assign preference rankings to each of five presidential hopefuls. Candidate A is the first choice of 18 caucus participants, Candidate B of 12, Candidate C of 10 and so on.

Candidate A claims victory, but Candidate B demands a runoff and wins it handily because he is more often the participants' second or third choice than is Candidate A. Then Candidate C argues for additional rounds of voting, each time dropping the candidate with the fewest first-place votes in the previous round. By this method, Candidate C picks up strength in each round and surpasses Candidates A and B.

But even Candidates D and E could construct rules by which weighted voting or one-on-one matchups gave them a chance to come out ahead.

In 1992, Democratic Sen. Tom Harkin of Iowa won delegate events in Iowa, Minnesota and Idaho, leading his staff to call him the campaign leader for capturing more land mass than any rival. It was a joke, but just barely.

In the months ahead, the most expensive presidential campaign in American history will produce more news releases, audio and video feeds, fax transmissions and Internet messages than ever before.

Much of this outpouring will take numerical form. Discussion of the issues — from Medicare and welfare to affirmative action, immigration and crime — will bring a blizzard of conflicting statistics.

It will be hard to keep score. And numbers will once again be most seductive when most misleading. En garde. ∎

HOUSE CAMPAIGNS

GOP Freshmen Stocking Up For '96 Challenges

Most who won with less than 55 percent of vote already have raised $100,000

To scare off potential competitors or build a bankroll against fierce challengers in 1996, nearly two-thirds of the House freshmen elected by close margins in 1994 already have raised more than $100,000 each toward their re-election efforts.

A survey of midyear campaign finance reports filed with the Federal Election Commission shows that most of the 51 House freshmen elected with less than 55 percent of the vote — 43 Republicans and eight Democrats — are building formidable campaign accounts for 1996. The reports cover activity from Jan. 1 to June 30.

Conventional wisdom says freshmen are among the most vulnerable incumbents. But in addition to the typical problems freshmen face, those elected in close races have a longer way to go to sew up their bases in time for the 1996 elections.

"Anyone who got under 55 percent should be pushing," said Gary C. Jacobson, a political scientist at the University of California, San Diego, who specializes in House elections. "Every challenger will be looking at that vote margin."

The top 10 fundraisers in this group of freshmen are all Republicans.

"There has been a lot of enthusiasm in our freshman class on a number of fronts. Fundraising is one of them," said Craig Veith, communications director of the National Republican Congressional Committee.

Freshman Zach Wamp, R-Tenn., who was narrowly elected on his second try for the House, said fundraising is "the only barometer" many people have of the level of support a candidate enjoys. Though not in the top 10, Wamp said he exceeded his goal of $80,000 for the six-month period by more than $27,000, and some of that came from sources that didn't support him in 1992 or 1994.

CQ Weekly Report August 12, 1995

Ensign **Baldacci**

Given their fall from power after the 1994 elections, Democrats may feel the impact in their fundraising efforts. Groups that often gave to Democrats because they were in the majority may feel less inclined to do so now, Jacobson said.

Only three of the eight Democratic freshmen elected with less than 55 percent of the vote reached the $100,000 mark in total receipts, which include contributions, loans, transfers from other committees, refunds and rebates and interest payments. They are William P. "Bill" Luther of Minnesota, Ken Bentsen of Texas and Mike Ward of Kentucky.

Tricia Primrose, spokeswoman for the Democratic Congressional Campaign Committee, said she believes most of her party's freshmen "are doing well," even though their totals may be down slightly from years past.

While he may lag behind many of his GOP colleagues, John Baldacci, D-Maine, said he is satisfied with the pace of his fundraising. After being elected with 46 percent of the vote in a district held by Republicans for more than two decades, Baldacci said he realizes the need to get a leg up early.

"We're reaching the goals we've established," Baldacci said, but added, "I take nothing for granted."

In addition to the $48,296 he has raised for his 1996 re-election bid, he collected $46,541 through his 1994 campaign committee, which he applied toward a 1994 debt.

Several other freshmen, both Republicans and Democrats, also are raising money to retire debts from their previous campaigns.

For example, Patrick J. Kennedy, D-R.I., raised $169,461 under his 1994 campaign committee during the first six months of the year. Despite this, the committee closed the period with a debt of $326,245 and only $2,973 in cash on hand. Kennedy's 1996 committee raised $72,950 toward his re-election campaign and reported $30,242 in cash on hand.

And, while they are among the top five fundraisers, Greg Ganske, R-Iowa, and Frank A. Cremeans, R-Ohio, are still saddled with huge debts from their 1994 campaigns.

Ensign Is Top Fundraiser

The leading fundraiser among the House freshmen elected by close margins is Rep. John Ensign, R-Nev., who defeated Democratic Rep. James Bilbray with only 48 percent of the vote.

One of three freshmen to land spots on the House Ways and Means Committee, Ensign reported receipts of $448,698 and has more than $220,000 in cash on hand. Ensign is more than halfway to the amount he raised for the entire 1993-94 cycle, $735,800.

Ensign's tally includes $196,854 in contributions from political action committees, including several health-related PACs such as the American Hospital Association.

"As distasteful as fundraising is, you need it to get back [to Washington] ... and continue the revolution," said Ensign, who added that he expects opponents to pour a lot of money into a race against him.

The two other freshman members of the Ways and Means Committee also have been successful in building sizable bankrolls.

Jon Christensen, R-Neb., who

45

defeated Democratic incumbent Peter Hoagland with 50 percent of the vote, has raised $370,388 and has about $300,000 in cash on hand. Like Ensign, Christensen has had success raising PAC money, collecting $136,750 since the beginning of the year.

Phil English, R-Pa., the third freshman member on Ways and Means, raised $168,696, including $92,392 in PAC contributions.

Also listed among the top fundraisers are two freshman subcommittee chairmen.

David M. McIntosh, R-Ind., was elected with 54 percent of the vote, and after coming to Washington he was rewarded with the chairmanship of the Government Reform and Oversight Subcommittee on National Economic Growth, Natural Resources and Regulatory Affairs. McIntosh has collected $231,914, including nearly $100,000 in PAC money.

Thomas M. Davis III, R-Va., chairs the Government Reform District of Columbia Subcommittee. Davis, who represents a Northern Virginia suburb of Washington, raised $397,903. That is more than 10 times as much as Leslie L. Byrne, the Democratic incumbent Davis defeated in 1994, had raised at the same point in 1993.

Reporting the lowest total among the freshmen was John Hostettler, R-Ind., who raised only $4,111.

Top Five Fundraisers

The leading fundraisers among the House freshmen elected by close margins in 1994, based on money raised during the first six months of 1995:

	Total Receipts	Cash On Hand
1. John Ensign, R-Nev.	$448,698	$221,911
2. Thomas M. Davis III, R-Va.	397,903	156,401
3. Jon Christensen, R-Neb.	370,388	301,713
4. Greg Ganske, R-Iowa	292,684	155,515
5. Frank A. Cremeans, R-Ohio	267,102	28,333

SOURCE: Federal Election Commission

And George Nethercutt, R-Wash., who brought down Speaker of the House Thomas S. Foley in 1994, raised only $43,384 under his 1996 committee.

Still, as Jacobson and others note, it is early. Byrne went on to raise $1.1 million in total receipts for the 1993-94 cycle.

In addition, incumbents' fundraising needs depend on their district, said Christopher Klose, a Democratic political consultant.

A Step Ahead

Several of the freshman Republicans elected with less than 55 percent of the vote defeated incumbents in 1994 and, like Davis, generally have done a better job of raising money so far than the people they replaced had done at the same time two years ago.

For example, Daniel Frisa, R-N.Y.,

the only challenger to defeat a Republican incumbent, raised $224,455 during the first six months of 1995.

David Levy, the incumbent Frisa toppled in the 1994 Republican primary, had only raised $27,026 at the same point in 1993.

In Washington state, where Republicans picked up six Democrat-held seats in 1994, freshmen Randy Tate, Rick White and Richard "Doc" Hastings have raised more money than the freshman Democrats they ousted had raised at the same point in 1993.

Challengers Gearing Up

A freshman likely to have one of the toughest re-election bids is Michael Patrick Flanagan, R-Ill., who in 1994 defeated Democrat Dan Rostenkowski, the former chairman of the Ways and Means Committee and an institution in Chicago politics.

Flanagan's victory was due mostly to the fact that Rostenkowski was under indictment at the time of the election. Democrats already are gearing up to take him on in the traditionally Democratic district in 1996.

State Rep. Rod Blagojevich raised twice as much as Flanagan's 1996 committee through the end of June. The incumbent's 1996 campaign committee raised $96,003, while his 1994 committee still was saddled with a $58,591 debt. ■

COTTON LOBBY

King Cotton's Legions Get Ready For Battle Royal on Subsidies

Industry must compete not only with other farm interests but with nutrition programs that feed the hungry

GUNNISON, Miss. — Depending on your point of view, Kenneth Hood is either a comfortable millionaire or a calloused farmer teetering on the brink of financial ruin.

The veteran northwest Mississippi cotton grower and ginner has amassed millions of dollars in assets, thanks in part to the generosity of the government cotton program and skyrocketing demand for natural fibers. But, facing uncertain weather and growing overseas competition, he plows back most of his money into his 13,000-acre farm in a struggle to keep it in the black.

"Every year, me and my family put every penny on the line," he said.

About two hours north of Hood's farm, Gloria Mercier is involved in a very different daily struggle. The chief of nutrition for Shelby County, Tenn., Mercier's job is to make sure that low-income residents — especially children — get enough to eat.

"What bothers me is that when there is a shortage of food for the family, the children may not be able to get what they need," she said.

The competing demands of people like Mercier and Hood are creating a major conflict in Washington this year. With talk of a balanced budget dominating Capitol Hill, lawmakers will spend the next several months trying to cut $48.4 billion over seven years from the agriculture budget — which funds both crop subsidies and nutrition programs such as food stamps.

In past years, rural legislators and urban liberals came together in an unusual alliance that promoted funding for programs that benefited farmers and low-income residents alike. But this year is different, as rural conservatives say that nutrition programs should bear much of the cutting, and urban liberals in turn are trying to slash farm subsidies.

In addition to cutting spending, lawmakers also are planning to revamp agriculture policy as they begin work on reauthorizing the farm bill — a

CQ Weekly Report July 22, 1995

DAVID HOSANSKY

Cotton grower Kenneth Hood surveys his 13,000-acre Mississippi farm.

massive piece of legislation that governs policy on crop subsidies, soil conservation and nutrition programs. This is already setting off battles between various commodity groups over which should benefit most from the changes.

In both of these debates, Hood and his fellow cotton producers are finding themselves strongly protective of the farm subsidy system.

"Of all the major commodity organizations, the group that is most wedded to the status quo is the cotton growers, for obvious reasons," said Stu Hardy, a spokesman for a coalition of agribusinesses that opposes cotton on some farm bill provisions. "Their marketing loan program has worked very well. Demand is strong right now, the market is strong, so why change?"

By most measures, cotton would seem to face a daunting task when it comes to defending the status quo.

With an anti-government tide running high in Washington, a broad coalition of groups — including free-market conservatives, urban liberals, environmentalists and even some farmers — would like to revamp or entirely dismantle the six-decade-old farm system. Agriculture, they say, should compete in an open market.

"We're in a different world now," said Bill Barrett, R-Neb., chairman of the House Agriculture Subcommittee on General Farm Commodities. "The day may be coming when we don't have a farm program, certainly as we have it today."

But as farm bill markups begin this month, many backers of "King Cotton" are exuding confidence. After all, they were a big winner in the 1985 and 1990 farm bill fights, and are one of the most powerful political forces in the resurgent South.

"I feel confident," said Phillip C. Burnett, executive vice president of the National Cotton Council of America, "that we're going to continue to have good farm policy in this country."

Lobbying Powerhouse

The secret of the cotton lobby's power is so simple that it can be summarized in a single word: unity.

The National Cotton Council represents all seven segments of the domestic cotton industry — from farms to mills. While other industries such as peanuts and sugar are fractured by competing demands of farmers and manufacturers, representatives of each segment of the cotton industry hash out their differences in private board meetings, then come to Washington with a unified agenda.

This alliance began in 1938, just five years after the federal government began intervening in agricultural markets. At the time, leaders of the economically depressed cotton industry felt that they needed to present a united front to policy-makers in order to survive.

Today, their top legislative priority is to preserve the current farm subsidy system — including controversial provisions that allow large planters to collect hundreds of thousands of dollars in subsidies every year. Those provisions have come under attack by liberal Democrats such as Sen. Patrick J. Leahy, D-Vt., who say the money would be better spent on nutrition programs for the poor.

By coming together, the segments of the approximately $60 billion cotton industry enjoy access to lawmakers across a broad swath of the nation's Southern tier. Manufacturers in North Carolina and merchants in Tennessee back the legislative goals of farmers in Mississippi and Texas.

Cotton also wields power because of its economic impact. It costs about $350 an acre to grow cotton in the Mississippi Delta — more than quadruple the cost of growing wheat and soybeans — because cotton is a fragile plant that is grown with far more chemicals. The additional expenditures on labor, pesticides, herbicides and machinery mean that cotton pumps a considerable amount of money into local economies, giving it greater leverage in political deal-making.

"The cotton guys show up," said Chandler Keys, a National Cattlemen's Association lobbyist who has worked with cotton on various agricultural issues. "They're one of the best lobbies in Washington. . . . Anything the cotton council gets into and wants to be a player on, they're effective."

Cotton industry officials said it's a difficult task to keep up their alliance. Veteran shippers and manufacturers, as well as Cotton Council officials such as Senior Vice President Gaylon B. Booker, described arduous and sometimes contentious negotiations behind closed doors in order to arrive at a legislative proposal that will benefit every segment of the industry. In broad terms, that means keeping prices high enough to profit farmers, generating enough movement of cotton to benefit ginners, warehousemen, merchants and cooperatives, and ensuring a reliable and competitively priced supply of cotton for crushers and manufacturers.

Every segment gives a little in negotiations, they said. When the 1985 and 1990 farm bills were being crafted, for example, merchants expressed unhappiness with a provision that essentially would enable farmers to store cotton for up to 18 months instead of moving it into the market. They agreed to it, however, in return for a provision to allow cotton imports in certain situations where U.S. prices consistently exceeded world prices.

"We disagree a lot among ourselves," said James E. Echols, president of the Memphis, Tenn.-based cotton merchant company, Hohenberg Brothers. "But in the big-

The Land of Cotton

The land of cotton stretches from Virginia to California. In an average year, the crop covers more than 13 million acres or about 21,000 square miles. From this combined acreage, the nation's cotton farmers harvest approximately 19.4 million bales or 9.3 billion pounds of cotton. If all the cotton produced annually in the U.S. were used in making a single product, blue jeans, it would make 5 billion pairs.

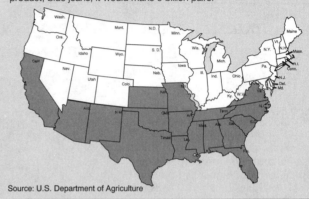

Source: U.S. Department of Agriculture

Commodity Credit Corporation Net Outlays for Upland Cotton
(in millions of dollars)

The Commodity Credit Corporation administers federal programs designed to stabilize the supply and price of farm commodities. Outlays below reflect a wide range of programs benefitting cotton. A negative number means that repayment of past loans exceeded government outlays.

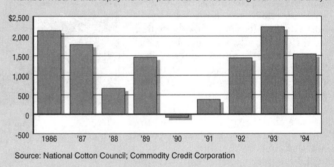

Source: National Cotton Council; Commodity Credit Corporation

MARILYN GATES-DAVIS

ger picture, we think it's better to work within the system than going our own way."

Most Successful Program

The cotton program generally resembles government programs for wheat, rice and feed grains such as corn. The concept behind each is to lend farmers money in advance of commodity sales, prop up prices by limiting supply and provide farmers with subsidies when market prices drop.

In each program, the government controls supply by encouraging farmers to idle acres. The government also effectively guarantees farmers a certain price for their commodities by, in general, paying them the difference between a government "target price" and the often lower market price.

But cotton gets some special benefits:

● Cotton growers can begin receiving increased government payments within three years of plowing additional land for cotton. Wheat and feed grain growers wait five years.

• The government sometimes pays cotton farmers for the costs of storing the commodity. It does not do this for other farmers.

• Cotton growers can take advantage of a "marketing loan" provision, allowing them to repay the government for less than the full amount of the loan when prices slump. Rice growers also have this option, but wheat and feed-grain producers, because of a different formula for calculating world prices, generally do not benefit from this provision.

• The government issues "marketing certificates" to cotton buyers to boost the sales of U.S. cotton when it greatly exceeds the world price. Some other commodities do not enjoy this benefit.

Partly because of these and other, more narrowly tailored provisions, cotton production in the United States has more than doubled in the past 10 years to about 19.5 million bales. Demand has kept pace with output, and U.S. cotton exports have also surged, earning about $2.1 billion in 1993, according to the Agriculture Department.

Cotton farms tend to be larger and more profitable than other farms. The average cotton producer earns $46,136 in annual net farm income, which is slightly higher than that of other producers, according to Agriculture Department statistics.

To industry officials, the program is one of the great success stories of government.

"This program we have is probably the most successful program for any agricultural commodity in U.S. history, if you define success as more of the plant being produced and more of the plant being consumed," said Woods Eastland, son of former Sen. James O. Eastland, D-Miss., and president of a Greenwood, Miss., cotton marketing cooperative, Staplcotn.

Asked about the progam's popularity, Sen. Thad Cochran, R-Miss., said half-jokingly that the only change his constituents would make to the farm bill is to replace "1990" with "1995."

Free-market conservatives and other critics, however, note that such a successful program doesn't come cheaply. On the contrary, it has cost taxpayers an average of $1.1 billion a year from 1986 to 1993.

A report by the General Accounting Office, released July 20, recommended that Congress consider doing away with the program because successful cotton producers no longer need government help.

"The cotton program has evolved over the past 60 years into a costly, complex maze of domestic and international price supports that benefit producers at great cost to the government and society," stated the report, written at the request of House Majority Leader Dick Armey, R-Texas, an opponent of farm programs.

Cotton lobbyists sharply disagree, saying that the program is helping to generate strong markets and boost prices, which makes it less of a burden on the government. They note that the program cost taxpayers just $260 million last year, according to preliminary Agriculture Department estimates, and may cost even less this year.

And if the program were greatly scaled back, cotton supporters worry that the economy of the rural South would suffer deeply.

"It would really be a lick," said Jim Buck Ross, Missis-

sippi commissioner of agriculture. "We'd probably build more casinos."

Sharecroppers and the Landed

The cotton plants, low and leafy, are less than 2 feet tall in the Mississippi Delta region in July, and won't mature until the early fall. At that time, the bolls will open and transform green fields into white, a Southern version of the change of seasons.

For residents of this economically struggling section of the country, where William Faulkner immortalized small-town tensions and Confederate cavalry Gen. Nathan Bedford Forrest is still revered, cotton is interwoven into the local culture. Families grow cotton because that is what their fathers and grandfathers did, and the crop dominates the low-lying fields on both sides of the Mississippi River from Missouri to Louisiana.

"Cotton's king down here," Ross said. "If that cotton [price] stays up there and our football team wins, we're going to have heaven."

In the view of farmers who work seven days a week and rely on government assistance to endure the grueling cycle of planting and harvesting, lawmakers who want to pare the cotton program are being unfair.

Farmers oppose a plan floated by some Democrats that would bar individual farmers from getting more than about $40,000 in annual "deficiency payments" — a government subsidy paid to farmers when the market slumps. "We're against any limitations whatsoever," said Robert A. Carson Jr., a cotton farmer in Marks, Miss.

Carson even opposes the current limit of $50,000 in deficiency payments per farmer and, like many other growers, has taken advantage of legal loopholes to exceed it. He subdivided his farm into five corporations and three individuals, thereby qualifying for up to $400,000 a year in subsidies.

Carson and other cotton farmers also oppose a Clinton administration proposal, which has some support in Congress, that would bar farmers who earn $100,000 or more a year in off-farm income from getting government subsidies. Carson worries that all the transfer payments within his operation could be construed as off-farm income, disqualifying him from subsidies.

"Personally, I think means-testing is discriminatory," he said. "Growers ought to be able to make any decision and not have to be restricted."

But it is also in this part of the country, long troubled by rural poverty, that the federal government began establishing nutrition programs in the 1960s. Advocates for the poor worry about the consequences if the federal budget ax spares subsidies for farmers of cotton and other commodities and guts the nutrition programs instead.

Mercier recalls the faces of malnourished children in rural Tennessee in 1965, when she helped launch a school breakfast program. Many of the children were listless then, with dark eyes and dry skin, she said — classic symptoms of malnutrition.

Now, hunger in rural America has largely been rolled back, she said.

"If they ... damage the national nutrition programs in favor of small, parochial commodity programs, that's a battle they're going to lose, and lose badly."

—Sen. Patrick J. Leahy, D-Vt.

Cotton's Integrated Strategy

Marketing Loans and Target Prices

Cotton farmers can get a marketing loan from the government that allows them to repay their loans at a lower rate when market prices drop. Congress sets a "target" price for major crops such as cotton, paying the farmer a deficiency payment to cover the difference between the target price and the average price received or the loan rate, whichever results in a lower payment. Only 85% of planted acreage is covered.

The seven sectors of the cotton industry — from farmers to manufacturers — generally work as a team on legislative issues. This gives the $60 billion industry considerable clout on farm bill issues.

PRODUCERS

Producers grow the fiber on some 35,000 farms in the U.S. Total revenues in 1994 were $4.6 billion.

Top 10 producers

North Carolina
Texas
South Carolina
California
Georgia
Tennessee
Mississippi
Alabama
Arkansas
Louisiana

GINNERS

Ginners separate the fiber from the seed. About 1,400 ginners had revenues of $657.9 million in 1994.

COOPERATIVES

Cooperatives process, handle or market cotton or cottonseed from their producer members.

1

Nonrecourse loan rate

A per-bale loan rate at which farmers can borrow money after harvest, so they can hold their crops for later sale. The crop is the collateral for the loan, and the farmer can either repay the loan and sell the crop or default on the loan and forfeit the crop to the government.

Target price

In 1994 the government guaranteed farmers 72.9¢ per pound of cotton.

3

68.3¢/LB

2

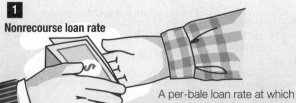

Average market price

Cotton sold for 68.3¢ per pound on the market in 1994.

4

Deficiency payment

The government paid the farmer the difference in price, 4.6¢ per pound. Total deficiency payments by the government in 1994, **$260 million.**

WAREHOUSE WORKERS

Warehouse workers store the ginned fiber, called lint, now pressed into bales weighing about 500 pounds each.

MERCHANTS

Growers or cooperatives sell their cotton to a local buyer or merchant, who in turn sells it to a textile mill in either the United States or a foreign country.

CRUSHERS

Crushers process the seed. After the linters (downy fuzz) are removed from the seeds, the seeds are crushed and the hulls are separated from the kernel. The linters are sold to the paper, batting and plastics industries. The seed is processssed into cottonseed oil used in vegetable oil, soap and paint. The hulls are used as feed for livestock.

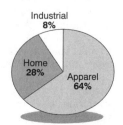

Industrial 8%

Home 28%

Apparel 64%

MANUFACTURERS

Manufacturers convert the fiber into yarn and fabric. Well known manufacturers are Burlington Industries, Collins & Aikman Corp., Cone Mills and Milliken & Co.

MARILYN GATES-DAVIS

"Why regress?" she asked. "Large cotton farmers don't need any help at all. . . . I'm afraid it [the cuts] will set us back to where we were in '65."

Cotton farmers respond that they need government assistance as much as the poor. In Gunnison, for example, Kenneth Hood worries that two or three consecutive years with low yields could drive him into bankruptcy.

He and other farmers also argue that cotton does more for the nation's economy than do nutrition programs.

"You've got to remember that a welfare recipient is not doing anything to help himself or his country, while the people who are willing to go out and work 18 hours a day are doing that much more for the country," he said.

Two-Tier Battle

As powerful as the cotton industry is, it may not be able to defeat both nutrition advocates and other commodity lobbies with competing agendas.

In the first stage of this two-tier battle, the cotton lobby is allied with other commodities in a campaign to minimize cuts to farm programs. If that is successful, in the second stage cotton will be embroiled in a complicated, and potentially drawn-out, technical battle over provisions within the farm bill.

The farm interests appeared to win the first round against supporters of nutrition programs, as Congress approved a non-binding provision in the budget resolution that could result in farm programs being cut by as little as about $9 billion over seven years, compared with as much as about $40 billion for nutrition programs.

But Leahy, the ranking member on the Senate Agriculture, Nutrition and Forestry Committee, said he would not allow nutrition programs to be cut deeply without a fight. He predicted that he could muster support on the Senate floor for amendments to the farm bill this fall that would restrict subsidies to wealthy farmers.

"If they [farm lobbies] are going to try to severely damage the national nutrition programs in favor of small, parochial commodity programs, that's a battle they're going to lose, and lose badly," he said.

At least part of Leahy's agenda is backed by a progressive group of organic and small farmers, The Campaign for Sustainable Agriculture, which favors tighter caps on the amount of subsidies that can go to each farm. Members of the group worry that the budget cuts otherwise will permit large operations to continue to receive hundreds of thousands of dollars a year, while shredding the safety net for smaller farmers.

Another problem for cotton and other commodity groups may be Senate Agriculture Committee Chairman Richard G. Lugar of Indiana, who has proposed cutting government target prices by 2 percent to 3 percent per year over five years. But Lugar has declined to specify how he

DAVID HOSANKSY

Cotton farmer Robert A. Carson Jr. of Marks, Miss., says he is opposed to any limitations whatsoever in the government's cotton program.

would apportion cuts between farm and nutrition programs. *(Weekly Report, p. 1167)*

Furthermore, a broad coalition of conservative Republicans and liberal Democrats in the House want to phase out all farm programs from the budget, regardless of what happens to nutrition programs.

"At a time when we must work within the constraints of a balanced budget, we have to eliminate all unnecessary spending," said Dick Zimmer, R-N.J., who cosponsored legislation to phase out farm programs over seven years. "If that means cutting agricultural subsidy programs favored by Republicans or urban projects protected by Democrats, so be it." *(Weekly Report, p. 1740)*

Even if cotton wins this first stage, minimizing cuts to farm programs, it will then grapple with other commodities over which parts of the farm bill to preserve.

In this second battle over technical aspects of federal farm programs, the cotton lobby wants to retain the current government restrictions on crop plantings.

By continuing policies that encourage corn farmers to keep planting corn and wheat farmers to keep planting wheat, the industry hopes to prevent cotton markets from becoming saturated.

But many corn and wheat farmers favor "decoupling" — a government policy to let farmers plant any crop they want and still collect federal payments.

Corn farmers also want to end the government policy of encouraging farmers to idle land. Cotton farmers want to retain that policy, arguing that it would cost billions of dollars for the government to relinquish that control, forcing deeper cuts in other farm programs.

It may be in this battle with other commodities that cotton interests face the longest odds. The most powerful rural lawmakers — including House Agriculture Committee Chairman Pat Roberts, R-Kan., and Senate Majority Leader Bob Dole, R-Kan. — represent Midwestern planters whose agenda is sometimes at odds with Southern cotton planters'.

Indeed, a three-page policy paper circulated by Republican staff members of the House Agriculture Committee in June recommended both the planting flexibility and elimination of land-idling policies favored by many Midwestern farmers. *(Weekly Report, p. 2060)*

In the end, cotton lobbyists say they would rather reach some accommodation with their fellow commodity representatives than try to persuade Congress to reject the competing proposals outright. They feel that commodity groups do better to work out their differences among themselves, just as the different sectors of the cotton industry try to do.

"I don't want to come across as a naysayer," said John Maguire, a Washington-based lobbyist for the National Cotton Council. "We can't draw lines." ∎

MEDICARE LOBBY

Spadework on Medicare Pays Off for GOP

Concessions and sweeteners keep constituent groups happy despite partisan rhetoric in Washington

Beyond the almost daily fireworks between congressional Republicans and Democrats over the GOP proposal to overhaul the Medicare system, there is a strange silence.

The elderly, doctors, hospitals, health insurers — all the groups that would be affected by the changes — are watching warily, but hardly manning the barricades and agitating for a veto from President Clinton. Most even have some praise for the proposal despite the massive reductions in Medicare spending that it would entail.

The groups' response stands in sharp contrast to the outcry last year that came after the release of Clinton's health care proposal. Of course, the Republican proposal is not yet complete, and some of the crucial details such as budget numbers and legislative language have yet to be made public. And some health and budget experts contend the proposal could cause some serious problems in the health care marketplace.

But interviews with representatives of Medicare beneficiaries and providers suggest it is no accident that such a truly revolutionary proposal is being met with such equanimity. The Republican strategy from early in the year was to work closely with every group, figure out what everybody needed and include enough sweeteners to make the spending reductions tolerable.

"The speaker has done a superb job of figuring out what was important to all of the health care groups and

SCOTT J. FERRELL

Arthur Flemming of "Save Our Security," led a Medicare protest in Washington Sept. 19, but it was more the exception than the rule.

what it would take for them to support it given some of the less attractive parts of the plan," said Pam G. Bailey, president of the Healthcare Leadership Council, a group that represents the 50 largest health care companies nationwide.

Thomas A. Scully, a former budget aide to President George Bush, and now president of the Federation of American Health Systems, which represents for-profit hospitals, said, "We had put together a multimillion-dollar ad campaign [against the plan] and we're not going to launch it, given how much Newt [Gingrich] and the leadership has worked with us. We're not thrilled, but at least we're neutral."

Even the redoubtable American Association of Retired Persons (AARP) is holding its fire. In testimony before the House Ways and Means Committee on Sept. 22, Eugene Lehrmann, the organization's president, voiced many criticisms, but also applauded several key elements.

"We are pleased to see the House leadership take the important step to

limit direct increases in beneficiary out-of-pocket costs," he said, referring to a key selling point of the GOP plan: The elderly would pay only incrementally more for the doctor portion of Medicare (Part B) than they do today — in 2002 it would be about $90 to $93 a month — but they would not face additional out-of-pocket payments for services such as lab tests or home health care.

Not surprisingly, Republican leaders in Congress heralded the plan as an innovative approach that would save money and ultimately offer the elderly a better deal.

"The premise is very simple," said House Speaker Newt Gingrich, R-Ga. "Medicare today is a 1964 Blue Cross insurance plan codified into law by Lyndon Johnson. For the last 31 years, the private sector has been evolving a series of solutions to health care, which are other options, many of which are less expensive, some of which are more convenient."

Democrats were having none of it. For much of the week they complained bitterly that Republicans were rushing the Medicare overhaul, leaving no time for analysis and public comment, and they warned of the plan's dire effects. They were particularly infuriated that on Sept. 22, the one day of scheduled hearings, only an outline of the legislation was available.

"We have no estimate as to what all of this will do in terms of money, in terms of the pockets of the elderly, in terms of the taxpayers," said Rep. Sam M. Gibbons, D-Fla., one of the handful of members who was in Congress when the original Medicare plan passed in 1965.

The White House launched a full-scale attack, saying that the proposal would take so much money out of the Medicare system that it would drive up beneficiaries' premiums and limit their access to care. "There is no way you can take that much money out of the Medicare system and expect average working people not to pay substantially higher premiums than they would otherwise pay when they retire," said Labor Secretary Robert B. Reich, the lead witness at the unorthodox, "alternative" hearing held by Democrats on the Capitol lawn while the Republicans were holding their hearing.

The Republican proposal essentially envisions a new Medicare marketplace in which the elderly can choose the type of Medicare plan they want — either traditional Medicare or a "Medicareplus," which could consist of either a managed care plan or medical savings account. The government would cap the amount that is spent annually on the program, forcing doctors, hospitals and other health care providers to find a way to deliver the services at a lower cost. The total savings would be $270 billion over seven years.

The key to the plan's budget credibility is its "fail safe" mechanism, which would strictly restrain the growth in spending in the traditional fee-for-service Medicare program. The mechanism essentially would gradually reduce the amounts that doctors and hospitals are reimbursed annually to ensure they meet the budget targets. If they miss the targets, the secretary of Health and Human Services can reduce future payments to the sectors of the industry responsible.

Sweeteners for Everyone

The key to its political salability is its attention to the needs of every group in the health care industry. Managed care companies, for example, would be getting access to a vast new pool of insured patients. While many of those patients are older and less healthy than most current HMO subscribers, managed care companies are gambling that government premiums for healthy patients will be enough to offset the additional costs of those with expensive illnesses.

Along with insurers and new organizations called provider-sponsored networks, managed care companies have been clamoring to get into the Medicare marketplace — projected to be worth $174 billion in 1996. Some health economists see this as a much

needed change and a step toward making Medicare more efficient.

A key to winning the support of hospitals and doctors was the Republican decision to allow provider-sponsored networks to contract with Medicare and compete for patients along side of managed care companies and insurers. These networks — put together by doctors and hospitals — are similar to managed care plans but have somewhat different financial structures. Still to be

SCOTT J. FERRELL

Crane, Archer and Gibbons listen to testimony during Ways and Means Committee hearing on Medicare on Sept. 22.

decided is exactly how they will be regulated. "They've been very receptive to our ideas; we send them [legislative] language, they send us language, we send them language," said Michael Rock, a lobbyist for the American Hospital Association.

There are other goodies in the plan that will help the hospitals and doctors as well. For instance the plan would relax antitrust rules, encouraging cooperation between hospitals, doctors and other community care facilities. It also includes strict medical malpractice provisions that would make it much harder to sue doctors and hospitals. The bill puts tight limits on damages for pain and suffering and punitive damages.

"We've been very concerned about malpractice relief and we're getting that," said James H. Stacey, a spokesman for the American Medical Association.

Achilles Heel

Despite the sweeteners, hospitals, doctors and insurers say they are un-

easy about some aspects of the plan, notably the fail-safe mechanism. According to Robert D. Reischauer, a fellow at the Brookings Institution and a former director of the Congressional Budget Office, the fail safe mechanism would work, but there would be tremendous political pressure both on the administration and Congress not to implement it because it would hit the health system so hard.

He also contends that it is problematic that the overall financing structure would tilt the playing field so much toward managed care.

Managed care organizations would receive set amounts that are likely to be higher than the actual cost of caring for most elderly people. Caring for about 90 percent of the elderly costs just $1,340 per person a year, according to a study based on data from the Health Care Financing Administration. The amount that managed care companies are expected to receive under the Republican plan is expected to be close to the fee-for-service plan costs of $4,800 to $6,700 per person over the seven year period.

The result would be that some managed care plans could receive a windfall and there would be no way to recapture that money and put it back into the fee-for-service system, he said.

"This means we're . . . leaving too little in the budget of the traditional fee for service sector and we're having to reduce traditional provider payments more than an equitable amount," said Reischauer. ■

GOVERNMENT INSTITUTIONS

The outcome of the 1994 midterm elections affected not only the issue agenda in Washington but the institutions themselves and the relationships within and among them. In Congress, the transition from Democratic to Republican control wiped clean the relationships that had evolved between the congressional leadership and the committee and subcommittee chairmen. Well-entrenched Democratic chairmen, who had built their committees into formidable power centers that could at times defy the wishes of the leadership, found themselves in the minority. In the vacuum, an assertive House Speaker, Newt Gingrich, and Senate Majority Leader Robert Dole took steps to strengthen the authority of the new Republican leadership over the committees.

Despite strengthened leadership, the GOP is facing the same problem in passing legislation that the Democrats frequently wrestled with: fractious intraparty squabbles. Republican-sponsored legislation must satisfy the party's tax cutters as well as its deficit hawks, its conservatives as well as its moderates. And Republican priorities and legislation are under increasingly effective assaults from Democrats, who are learning to battle from the minority ramparts.

The Democrats' chances of regaining the Senate in 1996 suffered a blow in October, when Sam Nunn of Georgia became the eighth Senate Democrat to announce he would not seek reelection. Nunn's departure after twenty-four years in the institution could greatly affect the workings of the Armed Services Committee.

The next two articles in this section focus on the appropriations process. In theory, policy changes are made through authorizing legislation, but legislators are now frequently attaching legislative riders to appropriations bills, which move through Congress more quickly. The second article addresses the enduring practice by appropriators of adding their pet projects to bills. Despite railing against the practice while in the minority, many Republicans have embraced the opportunity that majority-status affords them.

CQ editors then turn to the powers of the presidency. Now that Congress and the legislative agenda are in Republican hands, the Democratic president no longer has much influence over the definition of issues. The president's only remaining tools are persuasion and the veto, which is a blunt instrument.

In the concluding article, CQ editors look at the judiciary and the role it has played in confusing the issue of majority-minority congressional districts.

HOUSE LEADERSHIP

Gingrich Puts More Power Into Speaker's Hands

Chairmen put aside objections over shift in hopes of keeping control of Congress

When it came time to make politically risky changes in Medicare, House Speaker Newt Gingrich, R-Ga., looked around for the person he thought was best qualified to handle the job and picked Newt Gingrich.

Then he called the chairmen of the Commerce and Ways and Means committees into his office and proposed that he lead an ad hoc group on Medicare. Thomas J. Bliley Jr. of Virginia and Bill Archer of Texas, two senior Republicans with a combined tenure of 30 years on their committees, raised concerns about the panels' loss of jurisdiction. Gingrich assured the chairmen they would have important roles in rewriting Medicare, but that he would be in charge.

The scene in the Speaker's office typifies Gingrich's style over the past nine months. In matters deemed important to the party or of personal interest to him, he has not hesitated to take control. Maximizing both the formal and informal powers at his disposal, Gingrich is using his position to consolidate power like no Speaker since Joseph Cannon of Illinois in the early part of this century, often at the expense of the committee chairmen.

Gone are power centers like those dominated by former Ways and Means Chairman Dan Rostenkowski of Illinois and former Energy and Commerce Chairman John D. Dingell of Michigan, the last of the old-time committee barons. *(Box, p. 58)*

CQ Weekly Report October 7, 1995

Speaker Gingrich has increased the power of his office, often at the expense of committee chairmen such as (clockwise from left) Bliley, Livingston, Archer and Hyde.

Over several months, Gingrich has stepped in and overruled committee chairmen on a range of significant legislation, including appropriations, tax policy and telecommunications law.

The loss of autonomy for chairmen and the potential long-range effects of the shift in power to the Speaker's office is a worry for some of them, but so far they are putting up little protest. They say their overriding concern is ensuring that their majority status is not a one-Congress fluke.

Archer, who spent five years as ranking minority member of Ways and Means under Rostenkowski, acknowledged that he enjoys less freedom than the chairmen of yore. "But I accept that," he said. "Because that's

part of making something happen. In the end, you have to be part of the process. You don't run out there like the Lone Ranger and do whatever you want to do."

The chairmen "are willing to give up some independence and some of their prerogatives because they know if Newt doesn't succeed, they won't be chairmen much longer," said John Motley, executive vice president of the Air Transport Association and a longtime observer of Congress.

Power Centralization

In their first year in the majority, House Republicans have benefited in a big way from the Speaker's centralization of power. Even Democrats speak admiringly of the Republicans' success in passing major portions of their agenda and of their ability to stick together despite the tensions between moderates and conservatives.

In many cases, the committee chairmen have submerged their own policy goals to the collective agenda as defined by Gingrich. First came the imperative of passing planks of the "Contract with America." Now Gingrich is leading efforts to pass a reconciliation bill, a budget-balancing measure that attempts to reconcile tax and spending policy with deficit-reduction targets.

Henry J. Hyde of Illinois, who became chairman of the Judiciary Committee after 20 years as a minority member, said he willingly set aside his priorities to focus on contract legislation — even a measure he adamantly opposed, a constitutional amendment imposing congressional term limits.

"There has not been time to implement items of my personal agenda," Hyde said. "But they are small potatoes. I'm fully in accord with the priorities of this leadership. . . . On the whole, it is a salutary way to proceed, because we have focus and direction, not drift."

In April, while House Republicans celebrated their 100-days victory in passing major portions of the contract, Gingrich was looking ahead to the end-of-the-year fiscal battle. Republicans were about to take on Medicare, a program with wide support among the elderly and the middle class, and the issue had to be handled deftly.

Gingrich, who had developed an expertise in federal health care policy while in the minority, felt the issue needed to be communicated in just the right way or the party would lose the war of rhetoric to the Democrats, who were eager to link painful reductions in Medicare to the GOP's tax break.

"He realizes he's the best communicator the Republicans have," said an aide to the Speaker. "Newt could hold the press conferences. He could drive the national story. He was being covered like the president."

Gingrich seized on the annual report from the Medicare board of trustees, which warned of the potential for bankruptcy. Though the findings were nothing new — Congress frequently tinkered with the fund in response to the trustees' warnings — Gingrich decided to use the report to define the problem with Medicare, setting the stage for Republicans to define the solution.

Before long, every Republican from Majority Leader Dick Armey of Texas on down was talking about the need to save Medicare from bankruptcy.

Gingrich formed what became known as the design team on Medicare, a group consisting of eight members from the leadership and from the Ways and Means and Commerce committees. It worked out of the Speaker's conference room over four months, sometimes meeting daily to write the Medicare proposal that was unveiled on Sept. 21.

In the process, subcommittees became the eunuchs of Medicare policy, relegated to holding hearings without a legislative proposal.

"In the Commerce Committee, the subcommittees are practically irrelevant," said Henry A. Waxman of California, a senior Democrat on the committee.

Still, with top-down management the Republicans have avoided the kind of disaster that destroyed the Democrats' chances last year of reforming health care in the United States. Though they held both the White House and a majority in both houses of Congress, they never could

SCOTT J. FERRELL

Gingrich chats with Bill Archer, R-Texas, who took over the chairmanship of the Ways and Means Committee when the Republicans captured Congress.

agree on an approach. The committees bogged down with competing proposals; and the Commerce Committee threw in the towel after it became hopelessly deadlocked.

Maintaining Discipline

Though Gingrich's involvement at the committee level has worked well for the Republican conference as a whole, it has raised questions about the ability of individual chairmen to maintain discipline and to exercise the policy expertise that is found only at the committee and subcommittee levels.

Late last month, the House Appropriations Subcommittee on the District of Columbia passed a bill that would bring the city under tighter federal control. Gingrich, who has taken a personal interest in the District's finances, set the bill aside and ordered the appropriators to sit down with city officials, who oppose the measure, and a special financial control board created by Congress to hash out a

compromise.

"He brings an awful lot to the table, so you may have resources, financial and otherwise, that you didn't know you had," said subcommittee Chairman James T. Walsh, R-N.Y. "The down side is, you do your best to put a bill together going through the normal process and all of a sudden it's not the normal process anymore."

While the Speaker assured Walsh he did not want to undercut his authority, Walsh said it is not yet clear to him that that will be avoided.

After the Ways and Means Committee led by Archer eliminated nearly $1.8 billion in tax breaks for the ethanol industry last month, Gingrich on Sept. 28 met with ethanol-producing state lawmakers who opposed Archer. They were told that if they could demonstrate support for their position in the conference, they could then ask the Rules Committee, which is controlled by the Speaker, to overrule Ways and Means and reinstate the ethanol tax break, said Chris Hull, spokesman for one of the lawmakers, Jon Christensen, R-Neb.

The tax break benefits agribusiness giant Archer Daniels Midland, a major political contributor to both Republicans and Democrats. And it is adamantly opposed by oil and gas interests in Archer's home state of Texas, which compete with the ethanol industry.

In another instance, Archer refused to end preferential tax treatment for corporations over the objections of fellow Republicans who worried about a spate of negative media coverage. When Gingrich suggested he reconsider, Archer did.

Commerce Chairman Bliley in May painstakingly stitched together a consensus on a major telecommunications bill. The panel approved the bill overwhelmingly. But Gingrich stepped in and ordered changes that favored the regional Bell companies' quest to enter the lucrative long-distance market.

"It was pretty remarkable," said one committee Democrat, "for the chairman who advocated one position and won in committee to have to do a flip-flop before the bill reached the floor." *(Weekly Report, p. 2347)*

When Appropriations Chairman Robert L. Livingston of Louisiana objected earlier this year to the number

Committee Barons Since the 1940s

Below are House committee chairmen considered to be the most powerful of their breed in recent decades. They served in the House after 1946, when the committee system was updated by the Legislative Reorganization Act.

Their names were selected through an informal poll by Congressional Quarterly. Three congressional scholars —

Roger H. Davidson at the University of Maryland, Steven S. Smith at the University of Minnesota and Barbara Sinclair at the University of California, Riverside — were asked to suggest names of the most powerful chairmen since 1946. These are the chairmen who appeared on at least two of the three lists:

Carl Vinson

Chairman, Naval Affairs Committee, 1931-1947;
Armed Services Committee, 1949-1953, 1955-1965
(D-Ga.; House 1914-1965)

A forceful personality and a whiz at bill-writing, Vinson left his imprint on national defense policy during five decades in the House. Vinson coordinated efforts with President Franklin D. Roosevelt, who shared his passion for the Navy, to build the largest naval fleet in the world by the end of World War II.

Vinson, nicknamed the "Swamp Fox" for his parliamentary maneuvering, was a defender of spending for new hardware and fiercely resisted any effort to rein in the Navy. Serving as a paternal advisor to younger presidents, Vinson also exerted influence on domestic issues in the turbulent 1960s. Vinson was a great-uncle of Sen. Sam Nunn, D-Ga., former chairman of the Senate Armed Services Committee. Vinson retired in 1965. He died in 1981.

Clarence Cannon

Chairman, Appropriations Committee, 1941-1947, 1949-1953, 1955-1964
(D-Mo.; House 1922-1964)

From his stronghold on the Appropriations Committee, Cannon marshaled the power of his committee in a campaign against the Senate Appropriations Committee, chaired by Carl Hayden, D-Ariz., to assert House control over the appropriations process. True to his reputation for stubbornness, Cannon resisted efforts to curb the power of subcommittee chairmen and gained the loyalty of committee members.

Cannon's committee produced budget-conscious appropriations bills for both Democratic and Republican administrations. Cannon maintained a resolute hand on the committee into his 80s. He died in 1964.

Howard W. Smith

Chairman, Rules Committee, 1955-1967
(D-Va.; House 1931-1967)

Brashly asserting the power of his committee, Smith bottled up civil rights, education aid, minimum wage and labor rights legislation in his pliant committee. One of his tactics was retreating to his farm and refusing to convene the panel. Once, when civil rights legislation was pending, Smith said he could not come to the Capitol because his barn had burned down.

Finally, in 1961, Speaker Sam Rayburn, D-Texas, outmaneuvered Smith by expanding the size of the committee and adding more liberal Democrats. In 1965, the House adopted a rule allowing members to spring a bill from committee after 21 days. The rule was rescinded two years later, after Smith was defeated in a primary race by a moderate Democrat. He died in 1976.

Wilbur D. Mills
Chairman, Ways and Means Committee, 1958-1975
(D-Ark.; House 1938-1977)

Folksy, Harvard-educated Mills stacked his committee with loyalists and dominated the House with his power over assignments to other committees. The House only infrequently balked at decisions by his committee, allowing Mills to place his stamp on tax reform and health care legislation.

Mills' autocratic manner and his increasingly lax management, however, prompted drastic cuts in the committee's power when the post-Watergate generation came to Congress. The committee no longer dictated membership on other committees. After a scandal involving Mills' relationship with stripper Fanne Foxe, the Democratic Caucus failed to return him as chairman, and he decided not to run for re-election in 1976. He died in 1992.

Richard Bolling
Chairman, Rules Committee, 1979-1983
(D-Mo.; House 1949-1983)

After failing to break into the House leadership, Bolling assumed the chairmanship of a committee that had been dominated by Southern conservatives for decades. He cooperated with the House leadership and oversaw an expansion of the committee's staff and budget.

A partisan Democrat, Bolling fought President Ronald Reagan's budget and spending cut proposals. Before he became chairman, Bolling had forged a coalition to pass the 1964 Civil Rights Act, designed a new federal budget process and pushed for changes in committee structure. He resigned at the end of his term in 1982. Bolling died in 1991.

Dan Rostenkowski
Chairman, Ways and Means Committee, 1981-94
(D-Ill.; House 1959-1995)

Running his committee like a big-city ward, where personal loyalty supersedes ideology, Rostenkowski restored the power of Ways and Means after a period of weak rule by predecessor Al Ullman, D-Ore. A proud Democrat forced to work mostly under Republican administrations, Rostenkowski nevertheless was able to produce legislation acceptable to both parties.

The 1985-1986 overhaul of the federal tax code was his proudest accomplishment, but he was also a major figure on trade, budget and health care issues. He and John D. Dingell, D-Mich., former chairman of the Energy and Commerce Committee, were considered the last of a breed of powerful committee chairmen.

His downfall was an indictment on charges of embezzlement and fraud in connection with the House Post Office scandal. He lost his bid for re-election in 1994.

John D. Dingell
Chairman, Energy and Commerce Committee, 1981-1995
(D-Mich.; House 1955-present)

An aggressive and ambitious chairman, Dingell ruled his committee with an iron gavel, punishing those who crossed him, rewarding loyalists and fiercely defending his committee's turf.

Dingell pushed through his committee industry-friendly environmental initiatives, and shepherded telecommunications legislation through the House. One of his landmark accomplishments was the 1990 Clean Air Act reauthorization, which was acceptable to industry after years of resistance to harsher versions of the legislation.

Dingell's rule ended when Republicans took over the House this year. He is now ranking minority member.

of controversial policy initiatives being tacked onto his spending bills, Gingrich overruled him, and the riders stayed in.

Livingston said he didn't object to the policies themselves, many of which were sponsored by conservatives like himself. But like appropriations chairmen before him, his main concern is getting his bills through Congress.

"There comes a time when the burden of outside legislation becomes so onerous that the bills cease to have a chance of passage," Livingston said.

rassing internal GOP memorandum that quoted Gingrich laying out several options for dealing with the rebels. He suggested that he first could try persuasion, but failing that, he could threaten to strip Combest of his Intelligence Committee chairmanship and deny Emerson the chance to succeed Roberts as chairman if Roberts ran for the Senate.

On Sept. 27, the day the memo circulated, Gingrich summoned Combest and Emerson to his office, told them that he had no intention of threatening them and offered to help

the Speaker of the House. And I would very much resent someone telling me how to run my committee."

Making Maximum Use of Powers

Gingrich astutely has called on all of the formal and informal powers at his disposal.

When he became Speaker in January, he began to build on the institutional reforms of the 1970s that began shifting power from the committee barons to the Speaker. Under Gingrich, the House further restricted the powers of the chairmen by imposing six-year term limits and by ending proxy voting, which allowed them to walk into markups with blocs of proxy votes. Gingrich also hand-picked the committee chairmen, in some cases overlooking seniority to select loyalists.

Like two powerful Speakers who preceded him, Democrats Tip O'Neill of Massachusetts and Jim Wright of Texas, Gingrich uses such procedural devices as scheduling. He keeps tight control of the legislative schedule, which puts pressure on chairmen to move legislation.

Outside of his formal powers, Gingrich is reaping the benefits of masterminding and helping to finance through the political action committee, GOPAC, the Republican revolution in Congress.

"There is a personal loyalty to him that is without precedent in recent history," said Bill Gradison, a former Republican House member from Ohio. "I don't think anyone ever felt they owed their seat to Jim Wright, Tom Foley or Tip O'Neill."

But ultimately the collective satisfaction with centralized authority will depend on how the public perceives the Republican agenda once its full effects are felt.

"If the party begins to show some internal divisions on some key issues like Medicare, then I think we'll begin to see some Republicans questioning the wisdom of centralizing power so much in the House," said Steven S. Smith, a University of Minnesota political scientist who has written extensively on the committee system. "Individual members will be resentful if they have their arms twisted to the point that it gets them in trouble at home."

No matter what lies ahead, Gingrich will leave a lasting mark on the relationship between the Speaker and the chairmen. Barbara Sinclair, a congressional scholar at the University of California, said, "Whatever happens, there is going to be a ratcheting effect. It won't go back completely to the way it was." ∎

SCOTT J. FERRELL

One of the most powerful of the old-time chairmen, Dingell, right, is now ranking Democrat on the Commerce Committee. Bliley, chairman of the committee, was recently told by Gingrich that the Speaker would lead an ad hoc committee on Medicare.

The danger for the chairmen is that over time, their authority will be questioned by members and by outside groups interested in legislative business. While they would dismiss the likes of Archer or Bliley or Livingston at their peril, they may be tempted to go around the chairmen directly to the Speaker if it is perceived that that is where decisions are made.

Two Republican members of the Agriculture Committee discovered advantages in taking their case to Gingrich.

Larry Combest of Texas and Bill Emerson of Missouri were leading an effort in the Agriculture Committee to change a farm subsidy reform bill that had the backing of the leadership and of Chairman Pat Roberts, R-Kan.

Gingrich and Armey, who long has advocated dismantling subsidy programs, at first stood firm with Roberts against changes in the bill.

Then Democrats leaked an embar-

broker a compromise with the committee chairman.

Some House members fear that the policy expertise of the committees has been sacrificed to central authority. The House traditionally has fostered policy specialists whose influence is rooted in years of devotion to an issue. Roger H. Davidson, a congressional scholar at the University of Maryland, said the House historically has worked best when the leadership has orchestrated the workings of the committees while making maximum use of their expertise.

"Whether Gingrich has gone over the line in emasculating the committees and failing to take adequate account of their expertise, I think that's an open question," Davidson said.

Rep. Gene Taylor, a conservative Democrat from Mississippi who serves on the National Security Committee, said, "I hope to be chairman of Armed Services one day. By the time I get there, I fully expect to know more about the armed services of this country than

GOP Senators Limit Chairmen To Six Years Heading Panel

*Seniority system remains in force,
but loyalty is easier to test*

Senate Republicans voted July 19 to impose six-year term limits on committee chairmanships beginning in 1997 as part of a package of rules changes intended to make senior members more beholden to the party.

But chairmen and other senior members succeeded in moderating some changes in a dogged effort to defend the clout and independence that come with years of Senate service. As a whole, the changes leave the seniority system largely intact but provide more tools to enforce party loyalty.

For example, the GOP will now adopt a formal legislative agenda at the start of each Congress, with positions on issues determined by a three-fourths vote of the Republican senators. Badly outnumbered by conservatives, moderates in the party tried to defeat the new rule, complaining about ideological litmus tests, but it passed overwhelmingly.

The rules were debated in a closed-door meeting of the Republican Conference, the caucus of all 54 GOP senators. Majority Leader Bob Dole, R-Kan., formed a task force to consider changes in March after the uproar caused when Appropriations Committee Chairman Mark O. Hatfield, R-Ore., voted against the balanced-budget amendment. *(Weekly Report, p. 729)*

The caucus is split along generational lines, with impatient junior members who are more ideologically driven pitted against senior members who treasure the slow-moving Senate and its traditional respect for the diversity of its members' views.

Connie Mack, R-Fla., who chaired the task force, pronounced himself generally satisfied with the outcome, describing the new rules as "helpful" in promoting party unity and expanding the power of the leadership. *(Weekly Report, p. 1392)*

Not every senator appeared pleased. "Whatever they want to do,"

Connie Mack   **Bob Dole**

said a nonplussed Orrin G. Hatch, R-Utah, chairman of the Judiciary Committee. Hatfield seemed to have little fondness for the term limits, but he pointed out that six years is a long way off. "I would be 80," he said.

Another moderate, John H. Chafee, R-R.I., the Environment and Public Works Committee chairman, had sought to fend off the term limits by proposing that they apply to leadership. In the end, the conference voted to require rotation every six years in all leadership positions except the top jobs, the GOP leader and the largely ceremonial president pro tempore.

All other leadership jobs, including the whip and the conference secretary, would rotate. None of the changes apply to Democrats.

Several senators said the decision to exempt the leader was not at Dole's request but was suggested by more junior members, who said the party should not hamstring itself by pushing aside a leader who might be effective. Dole, the front-runner for the GOP presidential nomination, joked that he hoped to be in a new job after next year, anyway.

The new rules would apply even if the Republicans are in the minority. A member who had served six years as chairman could continue another six years as ranking minority member.

A key disagreement was over who would have primary responsibility for selecting committee chairmen. Currently committee members nominate their chairman, following seniority in almost every case. The choice is later

ratified by the conference and the full Senate. But Mack's task force proposed giving the leader authority to nominate the chairman, subject to ratification by the conference in secret balloting.

Mack said the leader would be expected to follow seniority, except in extraordinary cases, but that the plan was to make chairmen more responsive.

Yet it drew resentment from senior members as an assault on the seniority system and a weapon that could be used by the leadership to weaken their power. Budget Committee Chairman Pete V. Domenici, R-N.M., led the opposition. "The committee members have to get along. The committee has to function. And the conference can't be imposing . . . a chairman," he said afterward.

Domenici and others succeeded in defeating the proposal, but they had to accept a requirement that the committee vote on the chairman by secret ballot. Supporters say that requirement is designed to give junior members the opportunity to put forward another candidate without fear of retribution if the effort should fail.

The full Conference would vote on the committee choice, also by secret ballot. If the choice is rejected, then the leader would nominate a new chairman.

"It didn't go as far as I wanted, but we got the secret ballot," said John McCain, R-Ariz. McCain sponsored a proposal to allow a choice of nominees for chairmanships — one from the committee and one from the conference.

Republicans also voted to require a chairman to step aside if indicted for a felony until the case was resolved. If convicted, the member would lose his spot. The conference dropped a requirement that a member vacate a chairmanship if indicted on a misdemeanor "relating to conduct of official Senate business." Members said they feared that would invite politically inspired charges to force chairmen to step down. This is the only rules change that takes effect immediately. The others begin in 1997.

In addition, a new rule prevents a member who leaves a committee and returns from reclaiming his position on the seniority ladder.

Two proposals Mack had offered were not considered: a limit to prevent committee chairmen from running another committee or subcommittee (Appropriations subcommittees were exempt); and a proposal to let the leader fill one vacancy on top committees when there were two or more openings. Currently, a special panel handles appointments. The conference will consider those proposals later. ■

CQ Weekly Report July 22, 1995

GOP Leaders Tell the Troops, It's Time To Lock Hands

Internal differences, external battles continue to stall several proposals

Never timid in its quest to re-make government, the Republican majority in Congress has vowed to deliver to President Clinton by Christmas a bill that cuts taxes, saves Medicare, reinvents Medicaid, pares farm programs and, above all, balances the budget in seven years.

To do that, Republicans will have to bridge internal differences that so far have prevented them from enacting even the minor portions of their ambitious legislative agenda. Their track record shows that the best laid plans in the House can be easily undone in the Senate.

Major initiatives that were part of the House GOP's "Contract With America" are stalled or have been watered down by the Senate. Of the legislative proposals that grew out of the contract, only three have been signed into law.

Completion of the GOP's agenda has been inhibited by the countervailing goals of conservatives and moderates and tax-cutters and deficit hawks, and by the clashing ambitions of candidates for the Republican presidential nomination. Republicans now face their raison d'etre; most are increasingly determined to find a way to bridge their differences.

"Let me tell you what I think the real challenge to us in the next 60 days is," House Speaker Newt Gingrich, R-Ga., told House and Senate Republi-

SCOTT J. FERRELL

Speaker Gingrich addresses House and Senate Republicans on Sept. 14.

cans on Sept. 14. "It isn't the left. It isn't the Democrats. It's us."

Though the task is herculean given the time frame, the philosophical allure of balancing the budget while cutting taxes and reordering major domestic programs borders on the sublime among Republicans, especially in the empowered conservative majority. It is what they say they were sent to Washington to do. Contract initiatives like regulatory reform and the line-item veto, which are among the bills in limbo, pale in contrast.

Most Republicans cannot imagine facing re-election without clearing a deficit reduction package. Some contend that the GOP majority must also produce a bill that Clinton will sign.

"Not only do we want to gain politically, we want to prove to the American people that we can govern," said Sherwood Boehlert, R-N.Y. Adds Senate Majority Whip Trent Lott, R-

Miss.: "If we do it, everybody wins. If we don't do it, we're all going to lose."

The Crucial Period

For now, Gingrich and Senate Majority Leader Bob Dole, R-Kan., have to worry about just getting a bill through Congress.

The two leaders must make sure the budget-reconciliation bill — the technical term for reconciling tax and spending policy with deficit-reduction targets — does not go the way of many of the contract bills that sprang from campaign promises.

Major House-passed initiatives have either bogged down in the Senate or are idling in pre-conference limbo. Senate resistance has stymied efforts to rewrite the 1994 anti-crime law, ease clean water act regulations, make it harder to impose new federal regulations, and give the president the line-item veto.

Also, a number of spending cuts made by House appropriators were restored in the Senate the week of Sept. 11, including funding for Clinton's Goals 2000 education program and $2.6 billion in housing, environmental programs and energy assistance for the poor.

The GOP's intraparty strife has been evident in efforts to reform welfare as well, which has a direct bearing on reconciliation — it is one of the four major elements.

Moderate Republicans joined with Senate Democrats on Sept. 13 to kill a conservative proposal that would have denied additional benefits to welfare mothers who have more children. The drive to delete the provision was led not by a Democrat but by Republican Sen. Pete V. Domenici, of New Mexico, chairman of the Budget Committee.

In addition to welfare reform, the budget-reconciliation package will sweep in changes in Medicare and Medicaid, the twin health care entitlement programs, and tax cuts for families and business.

The danger is that given the unyielding posture of House conservatives, the final bill will contain a lot that Senate moderates find objectionable.

But the sheer breadth of the package may help produce a GOP majority, even if a final bill does not satisfy everyone.

"You end up with a huge bill, and there are going to be things that people don't like. But is Pete Domenici really going to vote against reconciliation because the family cap is back in?" said a Senate leadership aide.

Also working in favor of consensus is a recent effort by the leadership to improve their bicameral relationships. Contacts between House and Senate leaders and their staffs have strengthened in recent months, and, for all the bluster from the House about no compromises, leaders there know they are going to have to be flexible to help the Senate finish the job. "Mainly, it's a question of communication, working the issues across the Capitol, instead of just across the aisle," Lott said.

Walking a Great Dane

Success also hinges on whether Gingrich and Dole can resolve problems unique to each chamber.

For Gingrich, keeping the energetic freshmen in line on budget reconciliation will be like walking a Great Dane. In the past, Gingrich has been able to harness them with varying degrees, of success and it has sometimes been difficult to tell who is leading whom. His challenge is keeping the freshmen on board with whatever deal is worked out.

"Anybody that thinks the House Republican freshmen won't bring this place to a grinding halt has been out of the country for the last eight months," said Ed Gillespie, an aide to House Majority Leader Dick Armey, R-Texas.

House freshmen are particularly fond of the $245 billion in tax cuts to be included in the deficit-reduction package. Altough the size of the tax

cuts was negotiated in June, GOP deficit hawks remain uneasy about their impact on the deficit.

"We have a division within our own caucus over tax cuts," said Rep. Fred Upton, R-Mich., who supports scaling them back to target lower-income families. "Until the president signs off on them, we don't have the votes to override it. And I don't see the Senate necessarily getting on board either."

"Let me tell you what I think the real challenge to us in the next 60 days is.... It's us."

—Speaker Newt Gingrich

The freshmen feel they gave a lot of ground on the issue in reaching agreement with the Senate in June, and they are not anxious to compromise further.

Boehlert, a leading House moderate, said, "To tell some of these freshmen they have to come more toward the middle is like telling them they have to shoot their daughters. So you've got to phrase it a different way."

Dole is caught between the need to hew closely to the conservative approach dictated by the House and the necessity of getting the votes of a small group of moderates. Dole is also not anxious to alienate conservatives, whose support he needs for the GOP presidential nomination.

Still, Senate moderates do not intend to vote for reconciliation without an effort to tone down the bill. "We have an obligation to reach a middle ground, even if it means bucking our leadership," said Sen. James M. Jeffords, R-Vt.

Senate leaders have urged restraint, telling conservatives and moderates that both sides must give for the party to succeed. The important thing, they stress, is to avoid getting bogged down in intraparty negotiations.

The Fall Team

In blunt talk to a rare joint House-Senate meeting of Republicans, Gingrich warned that intraparty divisiveness imperils the fall agenda, and he urged members to submerge individual goals for the sake of passing a bill. "Every one of us, including Bob

Dole and me, are going to have good tactical reasons to vote no," he said.

Boehlert predicted that hard-liners will fall into line if the alternative is going into an election year without balanced-budget legislation.

"The last time I checked, every single Republican enjoyed being in the majority," Boehlert said. "So I think that's going to weigh heavily on the minds of some people who might be cantankerous and find the plan unacceptable for one, two or three reasons."

If they can achieve unity, the leadership in Congress can also count on the unique protective devices built into the budget-reconciliation process to insulate the bill from all but the most determined political forces. Debate is limited to 20 hours in each chamber, making a Senate filibuster impossible, and strict rules discourage non-germane amendments.

"It only takes 50 votes," said Lott with a smile. Normally, it takes 60 votes to break a filibuster, and the Republicans have only a 54-46 edge in the Senate.

Republicans insist they are serious about coming up with a bill that is within striking distance of a deal with the White House rather than writing a political manifesto to run on in 1996.

The president arguably took the first step toward a deal in June, when he abandoned a strategy of attacking the Republican-backed plan and unveiled a counterproposal to balance the budget.

Though the two sides are far apart — Clinton would set the books straight in 10 years, not seven, and would impose smaller spending cuts and smaller tax cuts — the president's plan embraces similar principles. *(Weekly Report, p. 1715)*

"The question is, can we work out the details?" asked Tony Blankley, Gingrich's spokesman.

The congressional leadership has threatened to force Clinton's hand by attaching to the bill a must-pass measure to raise the federal government's debt limit. But that option has receded as the potential for a deal has grown.

"We're optimistic that by mid-November we'll have things worked out and that won't be necessary," said a House leadership source. "A lot of us think that when all is said and done, there will be legislation. The down side if there's not is people will be frustrated. And you're in a blame game." ∎

Democrats Find Their Footing In Minority Party Trenches

Party finds unity in bringing chamber to a halt to protest adding GOP seat to Ways and Means

As House Democrats continue their metamorphosis into the minority party, they are finding themselves most effective when they feel themselves most abused.

Showing unity they have rarely exhibited this year, House Democrats brought the chamber to a crawl the week of June 26, demanding repeated roll call votes and forcing the House into its first all-night session of the year. But their unity was the product of a discouraging blow — the defection of another of their members to the Republican Party.

Rep. Greg Laughlin of Texas announced June 26 that he is joining the Republican Party. Before he agreed to switch, Laughlin had negotiated with GOP leaders for a seat on the powerful Ways and Means Committee. The agreement enraged Democrats when they learned that the committee would be expanded for Laughlin, bringing its total to 37 members, but that no room would be made for another Democrat.

The Democrats' complaints and delaying tactics are a classic example of how the minority can make life difficult for the party running the House. The GOP perfected such tactics when they were in the minority, often crippling the institution for days because of perceived and real procedural slights.

Six months into the 104th Congress, Democrats appear to be finally getting the hang of it.

Democratic leaders held a news conference June 29 to denounce Laughlin's seating on Ways and Means, charging that Republicans were packing the committee that will have responsibility for Medicare cutbacks and tax cuts the GOP is proposing. Adding a seat pushes the committee partisan split to 22-15

Gingrich

Armey

Gephardt

Bonior

members, a 59 percent-41 percent ratio, higher than the 53-47 ratio of Republicans to Democrats now in the full House.

"This is not democracy — it's autocracy. And it's a shameless attempt to stack the deck on House committees," said Minority Leader Richard A. Gephardt, D-Mo.

But House Speaker Newt Gingrich, R-Ga., dismissed such complaints and said he would continue to woo Democrats with offers of prime committee slots. "We want to attract people who agree with us," he said. "The Democrats look more and more like hard-line left wingers who are nasty."

Still, Gingrich was not without a small measure of admiration for the minority's tactics — maneuvers he raised to a high art when he was in the minority. "The liberal Democrats are

allowed one temper tantrum per month, and this is a perfectly appropriate temper tantrum," Gingrich said.

When the Democrats controlled the committee system, they stacked Ways and Means even more to their benefit than the Republicans have done so far. Democrats contend that this was justified because they have traditionally enjoyed a stronger margin of control in the overall House than have the Republicans. *(Chart, p. 65)*

In response to the Democrat's near-filibuster of the foreign operations spending bill (HR 1868), Majority Leader Dick Armey, R-Texas, kept the House in session all night June 28-29 and warned that he would delay the start of the July Fourth recess until action on that bill and several others was completed. The Democrats remained obstinate, disrupting committee meetings and delaying adjournment, through the end of the week. In the end, the Republican leadership deferred final action on the foreign aid bill and allowed the House to adjourn for the July Fourth recess.

The uproar did cause GOP leaders to rethink their commitment to bringing spending bills to the floor completely open to amendment — a procedure called an open rule.

One of the reasons Democrats were able to delay the foreign aid bill was because of the unrestricted amendment process, although the overwhelming number of amendments were offered by Republicans seeking to cut foreign aid funding. Nonetheless, Rules Committee Chairman Gerald B. H. Solomon, R-N.Y., warned that amendment limits on appropriations bills would be necessary if the Democrats continued their dilatory tactics. "We can't afford to fall behind schedule," he said.

The GOP leadership, however, has

not been deaf to complaints from the minority. For example, Gingrich permitted the House to revote on an amendment to the legislative appropriations bill (HR 1854) on June 22, after Democrats protested that the initial roll call was cut short before two Democrats were allowed to cast their votes. *(Weekly Report, p. 1804)*

The Minority Marathon

Even senior members of the party concede that House Democrats have a long way to go in making themselves a cohesive and effective opposition. But Democrats appear to have accepted that their influence on the legislative process will be minimal.

"Being in the minority, we need events to inspire and mobilize us," said Richard J. Durbin, D-Ill. "We've just caught a second wind. But this is a marathon, not a sprint."

Democrats say their strategy is to question the way the Republicans are running the House, hoping that their criticism of the GOP's wooing of Democrats and close collaborations with business lobbyists in crafting bills will magnify doubts and fears in voters' minds about the GOP's legislative agenda.

Most responsible for pushing this approach in the leadership is Minority Whip David E. Bonior, D-Mich. "The whole place is up for sale," Bonior claimed June 29.

Bonior argues that Democrats will regain their bearings only if they fight for their longtime constituencies — blue-collar workers, the elderly and minorities — rather than seeking to build bridges to conservatives who rarely vote the party line anyway.

On the other hand, conservatives say, Gephardt has tried with some success to play the role of conciliator in the party.

Bonior's slashing style works well when incidents such as Laughlin's defection galvanize the Democrats. But such tactics often leave the Democrats lacking a unified message on policy and legislation moving through the House.

"We in the caucus are floundering a little bit. We're not at our best yet at defining our message," said Gary A. Condit, Calif., another conservative Democrat who has occasionally clashed with the leadership.

A New Deal

Republican Conference Chairman

Party Ratios

Established as a standing committee in 1802, the House Ways and Means Committee is the oldest in Congress. Its jurisdiction includes taxes and international trade, major portions of Social Security and disbursement of the budget. Following are the party ratios for the committee since 1947, compared with the overall party ratios in the full House.

Congress	Committee Majority Percentage	Full House Majority Percentage
Republican Majority		
104th (1995)	59 [1]	53 [2]
	58	53 [3]
83rd (1953)	60	51
80th (1947)	60	57
Democratic Majority		
103rd (1993)	63	59
102nd (1991)	64	61
101st (1989)	64	60
100th (1987)	64	59
99th (1985)	64	58
98th (1983)	66	62
97th (1981)	66	56
96th (1979)	67	64
95th (1977)	68	67
94th (1975)	68	67
93rd (1973)	60	56
92nd (1971)	60	59
91st (1969)	60	56
90th (1967)	60	57
89th (1965)	68	68
88th (1963)	60	59
87th (1961)	60	60
86th (1959)	60	65
85th (1957)	60	54
84th (1955)	60	53
82nd (1951)	60	54
81st (1949)	55	60

[1] *Includes addition of Greg Laughlin, D-Texas, to the committee.*
[2] *As of June 30*
[3] *At beginning of 104th Congress*

John A. Boehner of Ohio labeled the Democrats' procedural disruptions as an attempt to divert public attention from their dwindling ranks. "What they're doing is trying to hide the fact that people are leaving their party, and using it to unify the rest of their party," he said.

Indeed, Laughlin's defection comes two months after Nathan Deal, Ga., switched to the GOP, saying his conservative principles were no longer welcome in the Democratic Party. Deal, too, received a choice committee seat — on the Commerce Committee — from the Republicans. *(Weekly Report, p. 1612)*

While Democrats have been quick to brand the party-switchers as opportun-

---

ists, the departures are emblematic of the difficulty Democrats are having making conservative members feel included when party leaders are struggling to differentiate themselves from the GOP's conservative agenda.

Laughlin had recently denied that he was on the verge of switching. But he and three other conservative Democrats — W. J. "Billy" Tauzin and Jimmy Hayes of Louisiana and Mike Parker of Mississippi — resigned from the Democratic Congressional Campaign Committee to protest a mailing lampooning congressional efforts to rewrite environmental laws. All four had been involved in crafting the revisions, which were backed primarily by House Republicans. *(Weekly Report, p. 1770)*

This move, along with their support for most of the "Contract With America," items has fed speculation that the remaining three, as well as several other Democrats, might follow Laughlin across the aisle. Tauzin said earlier that he would give House Democratic leaders until the end of the year to show that they can be more tolerant and inclusive of the conservative members.

But irate over the comments of Democratic leaders about other potential defectors, Tauzin said June 29 that he might reconsider that timetable, given the leaders' reaction to Laughlin's party switch and their insistence that they have tried to accommodate the party's more conservative members. "I would desperately hope my leadership would come to its senses and stop attacking their own members," he said.

Parker, who has hinted several times that he may switch, said, "If I were Dick Gephardt, I'd kick me out of the caucus in a heartbeat. Sam Rayburn never would've put up with a sucker like me."

Hayes "has no intention to switch parties," said his spokesman, Gordon Taylor. He added, however, that Hayes hopes Democratic leaders "will closely read" the reasons why Deal and Laughlin left the party. ∎

Nunn Will Be Difficult To Replace As Defense Coalition Builder

Effectiveness of Armed Services' next top Democrat depends on the changing temper of Congress and world events

The question of who — if anyone — will assume Sam Nunn's dominant role in Senate defense debates begs another question: Is the Senate evolving in a direction that will make it harder to forge the kind of bipartisan coalitions that are Nunn's forte?

Others possess the cardinal legislative virtues that the retiring four-term Georgia Democrat has plied so well: intelligence, diligence, trustworthiness and a keen sense of timing.

But Nunn's impact on defense policy also results from the neatness with which he fits a specialized niche in American politics that opened only a few years before his 1972 election to the Senate.

In the wake of the Vietnam War, most Democrats took a skeptical view of the utility of military force, while the Republican Party moved toward a harder line in dealing with the Soviet Union. For all but six years since 1972, neither party controlled all three centers of political authority — the White House, the Senate and the House. So small, bipartisan groups rallying under Nunn's expert leadership had leverage well out of proportion to their numbers.

Because Nunn's clout rests not merely on his aptitude but also on his position in the political spectrum, the question of who will fill his role is complicated. Not many Senate Democrats of Nunn's conservative stripe remain. And the ranks of GOP moderates, who have been among Nunn's key allies, also are thinning.

Nunn's departure brings the issue to a head because Michigan's Carl Levin — in line to succeed Nunn as senior Democrat on Armed Services — is not in Nunn's centrist mold. While Levin can boast of impressive legislative achievements, his overall record is well to the left of Nunn.

CQ Weekly Report October 14, 1995

SCOTT J. FERRELL

"When you're basically trying to put coalitions together . . . over and over again, it's a tougher job than simply making a speech and taking a rigid position and voting that way," Nunn says.

So, when Levin tries to forge bipartisan compromises, will his considerable legislative prowess be undermined by his liberalism? In other words, can Levin ever hope to become Nunn?

Or, with the Soviet military threat gone and the budget deficit and social decay overshadowing security issues on the national agenda, is the post-Vietnam political spectrum of "left-right" losing its relevance to future debates over U.S. defense policy? In other words, can Levin succeed without trying to be Nunn?

Or, as party lines harden, will it simply become impossible to forge the kind of coalitions that Nunn so often

has masterminded? In other words, if he stayed in the Senate, could even Nunn still be Nunn?

Nunn said that doing the job his way has taken its toll. "When you're basically trying to put coalitions together on defense and foreign policy over and over and over again, it's a tougher job than simply making a speech and taking a rigid position and voting that way," he said in an interview two days after he announced Oct. 9 in Atlanta that he would not seek re-election.

The Nunn Model

His colleagues' encomia to Nunn read like civics-text boilerplate.

"Thoughtful . . . thorough . . . decent . . . open to different ideas. . . . He takes the subject seriously and immerses himself in it," Levin said after Nunn's announcement.

That assessment of Nunn's strengths is typical, particularly in that "thoughtful" leads the list.

"An essential ingredient around here, if you want to influence an issue, is to know more than anyone else," said Armed Services member John McCain, R-Ariz. Nunn routinely cleared that bar, McCain said, "and he was generally right."

Nunn's sheer intellectual horsepower is tempered by an impressive discipline:

● He rarely makes statements on issues he has not thought through to his meticulous standards. "You have to be willing to let some issues go by without having a significant impact on them in order to do a thorough job and to have real credibility on those things you address," Nunn said in the Oct. 11 interview.

● He focuses on fundamentals rather than the details of specific programs. Nunn credits former Armed Services Chairman John C. Stennis, D-Miss., with teaching him "not to get bogged down in weapons-system analysis.

[Stennis] said, 'Your job is to make sure the military does that,'" Nunn said.

● And he has what Armed Services member Jeff Bingaman, D-N.M., calls "a real instinct for finding the common ground" — hammering out with other members of both parties a compromise that is not merely a lowest common denominator but a coherent policy.

Only a few weeks before Nunn's retirement announcement, a Senate deadlock over anti-missile defense policy was broken by a deal that was vintage Nunn. The stage was set when the Clinton administration issued a veto threat against provisions of the fiscal 1996 defense authorization bill (S 1026) that it considered to be a back-door attempt by GOP conservatives to slip U.S. anti-missile work past the limits set by the 1972 Anti-Ballistic Missile (ABM) Treaty.

Nunn, Levin and two Armed Services Republicans with whom Nunn has often collaborated — William S. Cohen of Maine and John W. Warner of Virginia — worked out a compromise that would allow the Pentagon to develop a more extensive anti-missile system than the treaty would allow, but that would bar its deployment pending a full-blown debate on whether to amend or abrogate the ABM Treaty. *(Weekly Report, p. 2731)*

Levin: 'A Diligent Guy'

In three Senate terms, Levin has racked up a solid record of achievement, many of the high points of which are the fruit of bipartisan collaboration.

For more than a decade, he and Cohen — senior Democrat and Republican, respectively, on a Governmental Affairs subcommittee that oversees federal procurement — have played key roles in crafting legislation intended to make government purchasing agents rely more on competitive bidding and other commercial practices.

A leading opponent of many nuclear weapons proposed by the Reagan and Bush administrations, Levin typically favored arms-control agreements as a more reliable means of heading off potential new Soviet threats rather than trying to counterbalance new Soviet weapons with new U.S. arms.

But during that same period, he pressed hard — and often successfully — to add more funds for conventional weapons to the GOP defense budgets.

Levin gets high marks for legislative skill from Democrats well to his right, such as Joseph I. Lieberman of Connecticut. A member of Armed Ser-

vices, Lieberman currently chairs the Democratic Leadership Council, formed by Nunn and others to pull the party toward the political center.

"What Carl has in his favor is that he's absolutely honorable, he's very smart, and he's a very effective legislator," Lieberman said. "He has great legislative patience. . . . He'll hang in there."

Nunn, too, is bullish on Levin's legislative talent: "He's been a very valuable member coming from a pro-defense but questioning and probing and skeptical point of view, and that's been a very healthy role."

As for building bipartisan, centrist coalitions, Nunn said, "I've played that role; [Levin] hasn't had to. When the time comes for him to play it, he will be able to. . . . He's a diligent guy."

More Partisan, or Less

Levin contends that personal relationships often are a larger factor in a member's effectiveness than his philosophical positions, especially since many of the ideological lines on defense are blurry. "Personal style is really what's more critical, in the Senate particularly, than where you can label someone on a spectrum," he said.

The Armed Services Committee's bill offers one eloquent bit of evidence that at least some of the old left-right lines are fading. An effort to add money to resume production of the B-2 "stealth" bomber was rejected by a bipartisan coalition, including nine Democrats and four Republicans. Levin was a keystone of the anti-B-2 majority, while Nunn was the only Democrat on the losing side.

On the other hand, Bingaman and others, citing the more partisan tone that has pervaded Capitol Hill since last November's election, speculate that centrist coalitions may be harder to come by. "The more polarized the environment, the more difficult it is to find the center," Bingaman said.

As evidence that defense is not immune from that process, Bingaman cites provisions in the Armed Services Committee's bill relating to anti-missile defense and nuclear weapons testing. Drafted to embody the views of GOP conservatives, both sections had to be substantially redrawn on the Senate floor — an event which some committee members fear could erode the committee's authority.

While acknowledging that current partisan tensions make bipartisan leadership more difficult, Levin predicts that, at least on the Armed Ser-

vices Committee, the situation will ease. "I think there is, actually, a learning experience going on. I would predict that in next year's bill, you're going to find a much greater effort to work out problems in advance."

The acid test of the vaunted desire for bipartisanship in national security policy may come after Nunn's departure — if, in the 1996 elections, Re-

SCOTT J. FERRELL

> "A Republican president would have to deal with the real world, not some right-wing think tank's vision."
>
> —Sen. Sam Nunn

publicans regain the White House while retaining control of Congress.

Even in that case, Nunn contends, a GOP president would need Democratic support to offset the views of some of the new breed of Republicans.

"A Republican president would have to deal with the real world, not some right-wing think tank's vision of . . . what we can say to the Russians to *make* them quit selling reactors to Iran, and what we can *require* the British to do," Nunn said disdainfully. "So they'd need support up here, and there will be Democrats who would be able to play a constructive role." ■

As They Cut, Appropriators Add a Stiff Dose of Policy

This year's spending bills are laden with legislative riders, but their conservative tilt threatens the GOP's unity

In GOP Rep. Joe Knollenberg's Detroit-area district, where the auto industry is a major presence, the word CAFE does not mean a homey place to eat. Instead, it connotes the kind of annoying federal regulation that helped elect this second-term House member on government-reform promises back in 1992.

Since the 1970s, "corporate average fuel economy" (CAFE) standards have required motor vehicles to meet gasoline mileage requirements to promote energy conservation. Automakers complain that CAFE standards put them at a competitive disadvantage to the Japanese, but the industry and its allies have been unable to do much about them.

Until now. Buried in the report accompanying the Transportation appropriations bill (HR 2002) the House passed July 25 is Knollenberg language that would reduce Department of Transportation funding by $2 million — money that CAFE foes feared would have gone to help tighten mileage standards for vans and light trucks.

In the bill itself, House Majority Whip Tom DeLay, R-Texas, inserted a provision to provide the right hook for Knollenberg's left jab: language that flatly bars any further tightening of CAFE requirements for cars or trucks. CAFE would survive, but in a frozen state.

"I've always felt very strongly that there was too much zeal about CAFE standards," Knollenberg said. "This was the first opportunity we had to do this."

CQ Weekly Report July 29, 1995

APPROPRIATIONS BILLS

live U.S. HOUSE C-SPAN

The Knollenberg-DeLay action is a tiny but increasingly typical example of the way House Republicans are using appropriations bills to make policy this year, combining funding cuts with smothering legislative language to hobble agencies large and small.

Bigger targets include:

• The National Labor Relations Board (NLRB), with a 30 percent funding cut and language that makes it tougher for the board to seek injunctions in unfair labor practices cases.

• The Occupational Safety and Health Administration, with a 16 percent cut in funding and language that sharply limits the agency's regulatory reach.

• The Environmental Protection Agency (EPA), with a 32 percent funding cut and 17 separate riders that would radically restrict EPA's ability to regulate specific types of pollution. The House rebelled July 28 and struck out all the restrictive riders, but leaders promised an attempt to restore most of them the week of July 31.

Despite that setback, GOP conservatives bent on reshaping government have found that spending bills are the handiest way to restrict, cut, remake and in some cases simply eliminate federal programs and agencies that have irritated them for years.

Unlike the authorization bills Congress usually uses to make such policy changes, appropriations measures move quickly and must eventually pass in some form. Even if the president vetoes them, chances are that an eventual compromise could carry at least some of the legislative changes.

Targeting Regulatory Powers

As they speeded up to pass as many bills as possible before the August recess, House appropriators paused long enough to tote up 209 programs they had killed so far, from the $128,000-a-year President's Advisory Commission on Historically Black Colleges and Universities to the Low Income Home Energy Assistance Program, which spends $1 billion or more a year.

Riding along with the billions in spending reductions were scores of legislative provisions like DeLay's that wrapped surviving agencies in new restrictions designed to sharply limit the government's regulatory activity.

"This is an extraordinary achievement," exulted House Speaker Newt Gingrich, R-Ga., as House leaders and senior appropriators celebrated completion of all but one full committee markup (the District of Columbia spending bill was postponed to September). "The amount of change they are managing this year is, I think, without

Fighting Crime at All Costs

Fighting crime is high on Texas Republican Sen. Phil Gramm's list of legislative priorities. As the new chairman of the Senate Appropriations subcommitte on Commerce, Justice and State, Gramm hopes to use his post to advance an anti-crime agenda.

In a year when House appropriators are increasingly using spending bills to achieve their policy goals, Gramm hardly stands out. However, it remains to be seen how successful he will be in corralling his independent-minded subcommittee members into sharing his aims.

Although he hasn't drafted his chairman's mark yet, Gramm has a clear idea of what he wants to accomplish in his spending bill. For example, he says he is inclined to sacrifice programs such as Legal Services and the capital budget for the Public Broadcasting Service (PBS) in order to fully fund administration requests for the Drug Enforcement Agency (DEA), FBI and border patrol.

"I'm going to provide full funding for the Justice Department," says Gramm.

'My Inclination Is To Eliminate Programs'

Gramm's focus on crime will come at the expense of other accounts, but he is prepared to make those trade-offs in order to find the money for what he wants.

"With a budget like this, is it better to eliminate programs or spread the pain around and hurt others that are more worthwhile?" Gramm asks rhetorically. His answer: "My inclination is to eliminate programs."

That conflicts with what the House has done. Appropriators there took smaller nicks out of more programs, spreading the pain around. The House cut back spending in several areas Gramm considers essential, such as the FBI, the DEA and border patrol.

RICHARD ELLIS

Gramm aims to fully fund the FBI and DEA, though his subcommittee may not like the sacrifices that would entail.

"There's no way I'm going to do what the House did," he says. "I told my chairman when we were given such a low allocation that there's no way I can support a bill that doesn't fully support DEA and FBI."

To help fund his crime agenda, Gramm is targeting the Commerce Department. He wants to eliminate a bunch of "little programs in the Commerce Department that are nothing but industrial policy. Obviously the [Clinton] administration believes the government should play a bigger role in picking economic winners. I believe the market should."

But the Clinton administration is not the only place Gramm is likely to find resistance to his policy agenda. His preference for giving money to fight crime at the expense of State and Commerce Department accounts may find resistance from Republicans on his own panel as well.

"I don't have a subcommittee that is particularly sympathetic to my views," he admits. He expects no help from Democrats and correctly predicts that Republicans on his panel may not back his priorities either.

New Hampshire Republican Judd Gregg acknowledges as much. Although agreeing with Gramm philosophically, Gregg says, "I may not be as aggressive in some accounts like PBS and Legal Services."

If Gregg were Gramm's only problem on the subcommittee, he would have an easier time. But his panel is loaded with GOP heavyweights such as full committee Chairman Mark O. Hatfield of Oregon, Alaskan Ted Stevens and Budget Committee Chairman Pete V. Domenici of New Mexico.

Gramm will not be successful unless he can get the Republicans on his panel to support him, something many — including Gramm himself — are skeptical about.

---

precedent going back to 1933."

The pressure of producing all that change was beginning to show, however, as Republican leaders scrambled throughout the week of July 24 to hold on to a majority that was increasingly threatened by the widening gap between the party's moderate and conservative wings.

Although conservatives had aggressively driven the agenda and easily overridden most challenges, frustration had built to the breaking point by July 28, when Republican moderates combined with Democrats to pro-

duce enough votes to knock the EPA riders off the VA-HUD measure.

But that just made conservatives angry, and a key bloc of farm-state legislators suddenly threatened to bolt. Caught between wings headed in opposite directions, party leaders put the VA-HUD measure on hold to give themselves time to work out a compromise.

That in turn seemed to raise the stakes for the Labor-HHS spending bill, which already had been touted as the likeliest candidate to collapse when it comes to the floor the week of

July 31.

After conservatives forced several social policy amendments onto the Labor-HHS spending bill, subcommittee Chairman John Edward Porter, R-Ill., warned that the riders' combined weight "is going to bring this bill down."

'A Lot of Hungry Republicans'

Appropriators have never been shy about legislating on their bills — the Interior bill typically has carried numerous riders on controversial environmental and arts-funding issues, for example. But fierce opposition from authorizers has helped keep the volume down in the past, as has the fear that loading up bills with controversial legislation simply complicates the already difficult process of passing 13 spending bills.

House Appropriations Chairman Robert L. Livingston, D-La., has said this year that he worries about endangering passage of his bills by allowing legislative riders, but he has bowed to reality. "After 60 years of unfettered Democratic rule, there are a lot of things that folks would like to change," he said. "You've got to understand — there are a lot of hungry Republicans here."

House Democrats are furious, but there is little they can do. "They're trying to bury all these policy issues so their [authorizing] chairmen don't have to take these issues on frontally," said Rep. David R. Obey of Wisconsin, ranking Democrat on the House Appropriations Committee.

Slipping broad legislative changes through on spending bills means Republicans can change policy without holding hearings or otherwise subjecting the changes to a public airing. "If you're going to hang somebody, it'd be nice if the person who's going to get hung gets a chance to comment," Obey said.

"The paradox of 1995 is that in some ways, the Appropriations committees are weaker in money matters and stronger in legislative matters, which is exactly the opposite of what it's supposed to be," said Allen Schick, a Brookings Institution expert on the budget and appropriations process.

With money tight and congressional leaders aggressively setting budget priorities, appropriators have lost much of the latitude they used to have in funding decisions, Schick said. On the other hand, they have sharply expanded their reach into the authorizing committees' policy-making turf.

"Appropriations committees know that if they venture too far in this direction, they'll have their teeth handed to them" by turf-conscious authorizers, Schick added.

But the fact is that this year there has not been much confrontation between the usually warring authorizers and appropriators, and authorizers are so far keeping their hands off most of the aggressive legislating appropriators are doing.

"A lot of it is time," said House Commerce Committee Chairman Thomas J. Bliley Jr., R-Va., explaining that authorizers have not had

SCOTT J. FERRELL

Livingston, right, looks on July 26 as Lewis hands a poster to Gingrich, who praised appropriators' "extraordinary achievement." Rep. C. W. Bill Young is behind Gingrich.

enough time to make the legislative changes that can get through right now on fast-moving appropriations bills. Changes made via spending bills apply for just one year, he noted, which "buys a pause" that will allow authorizers to "do it the way it ought to be done" later on, Bliley added.

Bliley worked with VA-HUD Appropriations Subcommittee Chairman Jerry Lewis, R-Calif., to craft the EPA restrictions in that spending bill, but both men stressed that they do not plan to work this way much longer. "Next year, frankly, I'm not going to carry this kind of burden," Lewis said.

Opponents of the GOP's legislative riders are looking to the Senate's more moderate appropriators to sharply limit the practice there and strip off much of what the House has added. Indeed, Senate Appropriations Committee Chairman Mark O. Hatfield, R-Ore., told his colleagues at a markup session July 27 that he wants them to "clean up" the House bills. "Let's keep them as lean and mean as we can as far as the dollars and the policy issues," he said.

Putting Out Fires

The revolt over the EPA riders and the immediate counter-revolt by conservatives showed that House leaders already have their hands full without worrying about the Senate.

Balancing the intraparty forces presented a challenge for Gingrich and company on several fronts:

● **Commerce Department phaseout.** Conservatives were unhappy

when the compromise House-Senate budget resolution cut the list of Cabinet departments to be killed from three to one, targeting Commerce but sparing Energy and Education. And when the Commerce, Justice, State appropriations bill (HR 2076) cut the Commerce Department by 17 percent but did not move to shut it down, conservatives threatened to abandon the measure. Gingrich and Majority Leader Dick Armey, R-Texas, quickly fired off a letter promising "our firm commitment to incorporate the dismantling legislation" for Commerce in the massive deficit-reduction bill Congress will produce this fall. Leaders indicated they had a "clear understanding" that the Senate would go along.

● **"Lockbox."** Bowing to the demands of hard-line deficit hawks who refused to wait until September to take up the matter, leaders agreed to allow conservatives to offer a "deficit-reduction lockbox" amendment when the Labor-HHS appropriations bill comes up the week of July 31. The mechanism would take the average of spending cuts made during floor debate in the House and Senate and "lock" the money away in an attempt to prevent it from simply being reallocated to other programs in a House-Senate conference. The House will also take up a free-standing lockbox bill in September. *(Weekly Report, p. 2167)*

Even Republican appropriators oppose the lockbox idea (Livingston said it would hamper House-Senate negotiations), which put leaders squarely in the

Medicare Vote Will Be Tight

Democrats who think they can sit tight waiting for Republicans to choke on the huge spending cuts they have promised to make this year got a glimmer of hope July 27 when Senate Finance Committee Chairman Bob Packwood, R-Ore., conceded his panel might have difficulty meeting its Medicare target.

Packwood predicted his committee ultimately would get within $10 billion to $15 billion of the $270 billion in Medicare cuts the GOP-passed budget-balancing plan requires between now and 2002. But under close questioning from reporters, he signaled it is no sure thing.

Packwood said he will convene a members-only meeting of his committee the week of July 31 to see if there is any hope of a bipartisan deal. If Democrats will help, he said, "we can do it." If not, he said, he might face difficulty getting his GOP colleagues to back a strictly partisan package of Medicare cuts.

"Whether I can hold everybody or not, I don't know," he said at a breakfast with reporters. If Finance fails, it would be up to the Budget Committee to step in and do the job, or to Senate GOP leaders to cobble together a package on the floor. But Packwood warned that is unlikely.

"My fear would be, my guess would be, if I don't have the votes to do it in Finance, Budget doesn't have the votes in Budget to do it, and there aren't the votes on the floor to do it," he said.

Packwood said at least two Finance Democrats have

> ## "Whether I can hold everybody or not, I don't know."
>
> —Bob Packwood, chairman
> Senate Finance Committee

told him they would be interested in helping reach an agreement on Medicare cuts. But Senate Minority Leader Tom Daschle, D-S.D., said Democrats would contribute only if Republicans pledged not to use the proceeds to "pay for tax cuts for those who don't need them." Translated, that means Republicans would have to agree to Democratic demands that they target any tax cuts this year to middle- or low-income families, a condition GOP hard-liners adamantly reject.

Packwood also signaled that he would be willing to talk to the White House about a compromise Medicare number somewhere between $160 billion (the rough minimum required to keep the Medicare trust fund solvent) and $270 billion over seven years. But that is conditioned on an agreement by Clinton to measure his cuts from the same "baseline" (projection of future spending) congressional Republicans are using — a notion that essentially means Clinton would have to agree to much deeper cuts than he called for in the 10-year budget-balancing plan he offered in June.

"If they say, 'Well, we think we can do $160 billion off the [Congressional Budget Office baseline],' then I think there might be some negotiating,' Packwood said.

Senate Finance is critical to Republicans' plans to pass a budget-balancing bill this year, since Finance is responsible for producing $530 billion of the $894 billion in seven-year spending cuts required to make the plan work. *(Weekly Report, p. 1900)*

---

middle of the struggle between old-guard Republicans and the new breed. The threats of activist junior members finally prevailed. "Newt and Dick Armey, you all created us," freshman lockbox backer Mark Foley, R-Fla., reminded his elders.

● **Moderates' concerns.** Seeking to stave off the rebellion among the party's outnumbered but critical moderates, leaders produced money for low-income programs and cleared the way for votes challenging key legislative provisions. Lewis added back more than $600 million to the VA-HUD bill that had been cut from housing and assistance programs for the elderly, disabled, people with AIDS and the homeless. "Restoring these funds goes to the heart of compassion and fairness," said Rep. Rick A. Lazio, R-N.Y.

In the move that led to the at-least temporary death of the EPA riders, leaders also agreed to clear the way for floor amendments to strike a wide variety of provisions that moderates

found particularly obnoxious, from the VA-HUD bill environmental provisions to abortion-related provisions in the Labor-HHS bill that would kill off the government's Nixon-era family planning program and allow states to deny Medicaid funding for abortions in cases of rape or incest.

"We want to make sure our members have every opportunity to express themselves," said Majority Whip DeLay. Livingston said it was a matter of simple arithmetic, since an exodus by moderates could doom controversial bills.

House leaders were confronting rebellions in the hurried final days before the August recess, largely because they left the two biggest and most controversial domestic spending bills — VA-HUD and Labor-HHS — until the very end.

Barring more problems with these two measures, or with the Defense spending bill, which was also set to come to the House floor the week of

July 31, appropriators were on track to finish everything but the District of Columbia bill before the recess. The entire process is about a month behind the usual pace.

Leaders are now starting to size up the endgame, which is complicated by the numerous veto threats President Clinton has issued against key spending bills. Livingston downplayed the notion that the process will collapse in a veto war, insisting that Clinton's threats are based on the House bills and implying that once the Senate weighs in, the measures will move closer to what Clinton wants.

Livingston predicted that Clinton ultimately would veto just one or two bills (most likely VA-HUD and Labor-HHS).

In the end, though, he predicted all 13 of the 1996 spending measures will be signed into law — though he said that would probably take until Christmas. "This will be a lengthy year," he said. ■

APPROPRIATIONS PROCESS

Members' Pet Projects Survive Despite Tight Fiscal Limits

Some freshmen frustrated by appropriators' traditions, but veterans say Congress should designate spending

When House Republicans served in the minority, Scott L. Klug, R-Wis., railed against funding projects nurtured by Democrats, saying that Washington should stop spending money on parochial projects.

Now that the Republicans are in charge, Klug said GOP appropriators are protecting the sort of pet projects that conservatives opposed for years. This year, Klug has been part of a losing battle to cut projects such as the $10.4 million included in the military construction bill for a physical fitness center at the Bremerton Puget Sound Naval Shipyard in Washington.

"It's frustrating for those of us who consider ourselves ideological purists," said Klug.

As House consideration of appropriations bills swings into full gear in July, one thing is becoming clear: While House appropriators are trimming the size of their spending bills and changing some of their habits, they are still ready, willing and able to finance projects that benefit individual members or districts.

In the Energy and Water Development bill (HR 1905 — H Rept 104-149), slated for floor action July 11, the appropriators pointedly rejected a Clinton administration proposal to limit financing to water projects that have national significance. Local flood control projects, enumerated in page after page of report language, are still highly prized by members.

In drawing up the bill, John T.

SCOTT J. FERRELL

Appropriations Committee members, including Harold Rogers, R-Ky., left, and Michael P. Forbes, R-N.Y., center, vote at June 27 markup.

Myers, R-Ind., chairman of the Appropriations subcommittee handling the bill, led the charge for the status quo, arguing that water projects generate economic benefits and serve a national interest.

This pattern of funding is being followed in other bills, although sometimes to a lesser degree. Frank R. Wolf of Virginia, the chairman of the Appropriations Transportation Subcommittee, boasted that his bill did not include any new money for highway "demonstration" projects, which are often derided as prime examples of pork barrel spending. But the bill does contain hundreds of millions of dollars for demonstration projects authorized in the 1991 surface transportation law (PL 102-240), and some members used other sections of the bill to get funding for favored causes. Enid Greene Waldholtz, R-Utah, won $5 million for a highway project on Inter-

state 15 in Salt Lake Valley, Utah, by using mass transit funds.

Appropriators jealously guard funding for such projects because even when they do not benefit their districts, they help them accrue power as colleagues beg to have their projects funded. They also say that taking care of such needs is exactly what a member of Congress is supposed to do.

"There's no question in my mind that the old bulls are retaining programs that conservatives have been trying to get rid of for 15 years," said Stephen Moore, director of fiscal policy studies at the Cato Institute, a libertarian think tank. "The real problem the Republicans have right now is that the big spenders are still in a position where they can spend."

The Defense

The Republican appropriators have mounted a vigorous defense of their actions. In a June 28 statement, Appropriations Chairman Robert L. Livingston, R-La., bristled at any suggestion that his committee was not doing its part to balance the budget.

He released a three-page list of program eliminations and major cuts in the bills already marked up by his committee, such as eliminating the Tennessee Valley Authority Environmental Research Center at Muscle Shoals, Ala., yielding $34.7 million in savings, and eliminating funding for all courthouse projects, for a savings of $286 million.

"We're more than halfway through the appropriations process, and we're keeping our promise to streamline the federal government and cut spending," he said.

Some groups that have vigorously protested congressional spending habits in the past, including the Council for Citizens Against Government Waste, have praised Livingston. While still taking issue with a number of projects, such as the space station, Thomas A. Schatz, the group's president, said the appropriators "deserve a lot of credit" for meeting their budget targets.

The leadership has not tried to dictate the content of appropriations bills so long as they stay within their limits. For his part, House Speaker Newt Gingrich, R-Ga., has been reluctant to attack particular projects as wasteful. Gingrich, a veteran of the Transportation Committee, describes himself as a "pro-infrastructure Republican."

In the past, House Majority Leader Dick Armey, R-Texas, has been willing to attack other members' projects, but as leader he must go where the votes are. And many Republicans say that while the federal government should not engage in social engineering, it does indeed have a role to play in building roads, bridges and other public works included in the appropriations bills.

"I think it's better for the federal government to make judgments that are regional in nature and industrywide in nature," said George Nethercutt, R-Wash., a freshman on the Appropriations Committee. "I don't think we can assume that because a special project is funded, that project is not meritorious."

A major test will come July 11 when the House is slated to take up the Energy and Water Development bill. Challenges are expected to such projects as the Advanced Light Water Reactor ($40 million in proposed fiscal 1996 spending) and the Gas Turbine Modular Helium Reactor, an experimental reactor fueled by weapons-grade plutonium.

But no major challenge is expected to the hundreds of water projects included in the bill. The legislation includes funding for about 20 construction starts, half of which were not requested by the Clinton administration. These include three unrequested projects in Myers' home state of Indiana that would get $6 million to start.

Opening Battles

So far, members who want to cut site-specific spending — headed by many of the Republican freshmen —

House Appropriations Calendar

The House Appropriations Committee has revised its timetable for action on its 13 bills. Dates for floor consideration are tentative, since action on this and other legislation may take longer than anticipated.

The committee plans to meet July 11 to set revised discretionary spending limits for each bill — so-called 602(b) allocations — in accord with the final budget resolution (H Con Res 67).

	Subcommittee	Committee	Floor
Agriculture	completed	completed	July 13
Commerce, Justice, State	completed	July 18	July 21
Defense	July 11-13	July 20	July 27
District of Columbia		Not scheduled	
Energy, Water	completed	completed	July 11
Foreign Operations	completed	completed	July 10
Interior	completed	completed	July 12
Labor, HHS, Education	July 11	July 20	July 26
Legislative Branch	completed	completed	completed
Military Construction	completed	completed	completed
Transportation	completed	completed	July 18
Treasury, Postal	completed	July 11	July 19
VA, HUD	July 10	July 18	July 25

have not commanded the votes to win consistently in committee or on the floor. They seem resigned to picking off projects that appear especially vulnerable.

Several lawmakers sought to challenge spending in the $11.2 billion military construction appropriations bill, passed by the House on June 21. But in the end only two amendments prevailed, one cutting $14 million the Army sought for land to build a museum and the other targeting $7 million in new housing for Air Force officers. (*Military construction, Weekly Report, p. 1857*)

"The bills are coming too fast for us to hit all of these things," said Mark W. Neumann, R-Wis., one of the few Republican appropriators who has openly challenged spending priorities. "We're trying to pick a few of the obnoxious things."

Part of the reason appropriators are succeeding is that they have shored up political support by working closely with authorizers, who help build coalitions.

The GOP leadership also is vested in moving the bills through the process and avoiding major conflict so long as the bills meet budget targets. Scott Hodge, the senior federal budget analyst at the Heritage Foundation, said that the message the leadership is

sending to the membership is: "We all know there is pork in there, but the goal is far more important than the specifics."

Nethercutt said that the challenges to future appropriations bills would be "match fires, not brush fires and not forest fires."

New Priorities

To protect funding for cherished projects, the appropriators have had to reorder priorities.

While the energy and water bill left few accounts untouched, Myers shielded the Army Corps of Engineers and the Bureau of Reclamation, the two major agencies that build water projects, from the kind of sizable reductions found in other parts of the bill.

The overall account for energy research and development dropped by $718 million, or 22 percent, from current year spending. But for the corps, the bill would provide $3.2 billion, or 6 percent less than fiscal 1995 spending, and the bureau would receive 3 percent less than current year spending.

Moore of the Cato Institute said, "The pork is still there, but it's now Republican pork, which could be damaging when people realize it's pork of a different color."

In the transportation bill, Democrats are howling over cuts in mass transit funding and money for Amtrak. The biggest cuts in the bill would be $618 million in transit, a 13 percent reduction; $305 million in Amtrak, a 30 percent reduction; and $199 million in the Federal Aviation Administration, a 3 percent cut.

By contrast, the federal-aid highway program would increase $884 million, or 5 percent, and grants for airport projects would go up $150 million, or 10 percent.

Many of these spending decisions are widely supported in the Republican Party.

"Infrastructure spending enables the private sector to create jobs and that has helped millions of Americans to become taxpayers," said Roger Wicker, R-Miss. "And it's a heck of a lot better than the government writing someone a check."

Klug said that the culture of the Appropriations Committee cannot be changed in a single session of Congress. But, he said, if all the Appropriations Committee does is substitute GOP priorities in spending for Democratic priorities, true change will not have occurred. Hodge acknowledged that appropriators are starting projects that will incur future costs, potentially undermining savings that will be needed to fulfill the goals of the budget resolution. But he said that pressure to balance the budget would increase in future years, forcing appropriators to change their ways.

"There is going to be some disappointment because the rhetoric of change is going to be dampened by the reality of how much is actually being cut out of government," said Hodge.

"We're not going to be able to get rid of all the pork at once."

Looking to speed the process of floor consideration, House leaders may push for more restricted rules that could limit amendments. That could anger the freshmen.

Fred Upton, R-Mich., predicted that efforts to change the process would be focused on legislation (HR 1162) that would ensure that any savings from a cut in an appropriations bill in committee or on the floor would be designated for deficit reduction, rather than being available for spending later in the process.

"The fervor at which we're balancing the budget is increasing rather than diminishing over time," predicted freshman Zach Wamp, R-Tenn. "The momentum is actually gaining, not losing." ∎

Lack of New Proposals Reflects New Dynamic on the Hill

Defining what he will accept, Clinton begins to cut his own swath between GOP, liberal Democrats

RICHARD ELLIS

The most stark symbol of change during Clinton's Jan. 24 address was the sight of Newt Gingrich, center, on the dais.

Acknowledging that "I have made my mistakes," a chastened President Clinton appealed for bipartisanship in his State of the Union address Jan. 24 and challenged the Republican-controlled Congress to work with him toward a "leaner, not meaner," government.

In its paucity of specific legislative proposals, the speech provided clear evidence that Clinton no longer controls the congressional agenda and knows it. Instead, Clinton adopted a posture more common to recent Republican presidents: He sought to set limits on Congress, not only on how far it may go in redirecting his policies but on how dismissive the new regime on Capitol Hill may be of his accomplishments.

In a speech notable as much for its length as for its wide-ranging content, Clinton walked a fine rhetorical line between defending his own record and acknowledging that he had gotten the message from voters' rebuke of his party in the 1994 elections. He vowed several times not to accept repeals of recent laws, such as the ban on imports of certain assault weapons. Yet he sounded positively Republican in his call to "cut yesterday's government to help solve tomorrow's problems."

Unlike his threat last year to veto anything short of a comprehensive health care bill, Clinton's warnings this time were delivered in terms that were largely non-threatening and thematic. In a sharp reversal, Clinton endorsed the idea of incremental health care legislation centered on insurance reforms. Even Clinton's once-confident vow to "invest in people" through more government spending on certain programs was replaced with

CQ Weekly Report January 28, 1995

a tepid appeal not to go too far in cutting spending.

"When we cut, let's remember that government still has important responsibilities," he said.

The new ideas that Clinton did propose — such as a campaign against teen pregnancy — were presented largely as decentralized, privately led efforts, reflecting how unfashionable it has become to propose new government programs.

Even so, in the official GOP response, New Jersey Gov. Christine Todd Whitman suggested that Clinton's level of commitment to the message of the 1994 election is uncertain. "If he has changed his big-government ideas, we say, 'Great — join us,'" she said.

But the normally combative House Speaker, Republican Newt Gingrich of Georgia, was not so dismissive of Clinton's ideas. "Every single policy proposal will be looked at; a number we support," Gingrich said. As if to emphasize the point, he pledged action by midyear on the kind of incremental heath care reform that Clinton had suggested.

Even as he was soliciting the cooperation of the GOP, Clinton began defin-

ing what he would and would not accept in the House Republicans' "Contract With America" and the rest of the party's GOP agenda. He declared he would not accept a tax cut that is not fully paid for. And he laid down a boundary on welfare reform, where divisions among Republicans are already beginning to appear.

"We should require work and mutual responsibility, but we shouldn't cut people off just because they're poor, they're young or even because they're unmarried," he said. That remark brought a smattering of applause from the GOP side.

In the Role of Whistleblower

No longer in the majority, Clinton and the Democrats now have an opportunity to hold the Republicans responsible for the battered ethical image of Congress, just as the Republicans held the Democrats in recent years. Clinton asked Congress to pass legislation to outlaw gifts to lawmakers from lobbyists, and he went one step further. "I challenge you to just stop taking them — now, without waiting for legislation to pass," he said.

But the political effectiveness of the challenge was quickly blunted by Senate Majority Leader Bob Dole, R-Kan., who pointed out that Clinton was collecting money from lobbyists for his legal defense fund. The trustees of the defense fund declared Jan. 25 that his fund would no longer take contributions from registered lobbyists.

One problem for Clinton is the skepticism of many congressional Democrats, his natural allies. After two years of an unfocused administration, some Democrats wonder whether Clinton can supply the necessary leadership. "The problem with this administration in the past has not been with speeches," said Rep. Bob Wise, D-W.Va. "The follow-through has been the problem. So far, we've seen a White House that is drifting."

Democrats concede that they are likely to be on the defensive through the first 100 days of the legislative session, as the Republicans move to bring floor votes on contract proposals. Republicans are divided about the specifics of the contract, but Democrats, too, are badly split and are having difficultly reaching consensus on alternatives to Republican proposals, such as welfare reform and tax cuts.

Even in areas where the administration has begun to develop alternatives, a lack of coordination between the White House and Democratic leaders in Congress has been apparent. In his speech, Clinton renewed his call for a middle-class tax cut that would provide a $500 per child tax credit for most families.

But that came after House Minority Leader Richard A. Gephardt, D-Mo., recently called for examining the current income tax, with its system of targeted credits and deductions, possibly to institute a flatter tax structure with fewer and lower rates. Some Democrats privately are distraught at Gephardt's comments because they appear closer to a plan by House Majority Leader Dick Armey, R-Texas, for a tax code with a single rate than they do to the middle-class cuts that the administration emphasizes.

Gephardt denied that there was distance between him and the White House on tax cuts. "We totally agree that when we come to the issue of tax cuts this year . . . it should go to middle-income families," he said. Consideration of the flat tax is a "long-term" issue, he said, that the two parties would debate. "Mr. Armey has a proposal out there, and I think it is a bad one."

Nonetheless, some Democrats contend that the party must offer a consistent, coherent alternative to the Republican agenda. "Clinton has to do it working with the Democratic leadership. There's too much one-upmanship," said Pat Williams, D-Mont.

Gephardt intends to use the newly created Democratic Steering Committee to build consensus among senior Democrats about how to respond to the Republicans, and that effort is be-

ginning, lawmakers said. In addition, the administration is stepping up its efforts to coordinate Democratic strategy. Treasury Secretary Robert E. Rubin met with Democrats on the House Ways and Means Committee the week of Jan. 23 to discuss the administration's views on tax cuts, although one participant said the meeting was "strictly informational."

Hailing Centrist Themes

Moderates hailed the generally centrist themes that Clinton sounded, say-

RICHARD ELLIS

Clinton makes his way out of the chamber after his speech.

ing that a move to the center is crucial if Clinton intends to reclaim the support of the voters who elected him. "I thought he tried to get back to the things that got him elected — expanding opportunity and not bureaucracy. I liked the fact that it wasn't a whole new laundry list of new programs," said Sen. John B. Breaux, D-La.

But to some Democrats, Clinton's emphasis on less government, personal responsibility and private charity grated. "I don't want my president sounding like a Republican. I want him sounding like a Democrat," said Rep. Charles B. Rangel, D-N.Y.

Several senior Democrats on the House Appropriations Committee, including David R. Obey of Wisconsin, John P. Murtha of Pennsylvania and Louis Stokes of Ohio, were among the only members who did not stand and applaud when Clinton called for a line-item veto to "save taxpayers money."

The presence of a strong liberal faction in the House Democratic ranks presents Clinton with a difficult challenge as he looks to restore the solid backing of his party in Congress. As he lays out his priorities and moves deci-

sively to the center, Clinton cannot ignore liberals without completely balkanizing his party. But unless he does take a more centrist stance on some issues, the few conservative Democrats left in the caucus will continue to gravitate toward the Republican side.

Conservative Democrats "present Clinton with a true Gordian knot," said Rep. Williams, a moderate. "When he moves to satisfy them, he appears to be pandering to Republicans."

On the other hand, liberals stood and cheered when Clinton defended the need for a federal role in childhood immunization, school lunch programs, early childhood education and assistance for pregnant women. But Clinton did not commit to expansion of such programs. Congressional aides have suggested that the nutrition programs will be studied for cuts this year.

Nor did Clinton offer anything other than rhetorical support for raising the minimum wage, declining to say in the speech how high an increase he supported. White House officials said the administration favored increasing the $4.25 minimum wage to $5 and added that the administration may or may not send a formal proposal to Congress in an attempt to find an acceptable increase.

That decision may reflect a judgment that a fight with Republicans, who oppose an increase in the minimum wage, would hardly represent a bold departure for an administration that has called for rethinking old approaches and putting aside partisanship.

Thus a fight over the minimum wage seems unlikely to develop, even though many Democrats would not mind one. "I think it's a great inconsistency to say we're going to get them off welfare, but we're not going to pay them a wage they can live on," said Rep. Barney Frank, D-Mass.

Perhaps the most apparent symbol of Clinton's changed circumstances was the presence of Speaker Gingrich behind him on the dais. Even some of Gingrich's common allusions, such as those to Alexis de Tocqueville, the Information Age and the pursuit of happiness, made it into Clinton's speech. His challenge now is to turn Gingrich's ideas to his advantage. ∎

Clinton Holds His Veto Power Over Heads of Republicans

Blocking bills may be his only way to influence GOP legislation, but the strategy is risky

Heading into a summer of heavy legislative work, President Clinton has made the veto threat his weapon of choice for trying to influence the Republican Congress.

In recent weeks, Clinton and other administration officials have threatened vetoes against a slew of major bills, including a welfare overhaul measure, a spending cut and disaster aid package, a House rewrite of the clean water law, and a bill that would slash and reorganize foreign aid programs.

In almost every case, Clinton wants to reshape the GOP agenda. He wants welfare reform, but not if it hurts children or slights work incentives. He wants spending cuts, but not in certain education programs. He wants regulatory reform, but not if it loosens environmental controls.

"I don't want to have a pile of vetoes," Clinton said at a Montana town meeting June 1. "So here I am — all dressed up and ready to cooperate.... I want to cooperate [with Congress], but it takes two to tango."

A veto strategy presents risks and opportunities for any president.

Using his power to block legislation provides an unavoidable reminder of the president's relevance in the legislative process. It forces Congress to consider his views more carefully when drafting bills.

On the other side, the veto or even the threat of one can make the president appear obstructionist, allowing him to be blamed for legislative gridlock. It can also prove an ineffective check of legislative ambitions if Congress overrides the veto.

For veto threats to magnify Clinton's influence over the legislative process, the president will first have to prove that he is prepared to use the veto and to make it stick by commanding enough votes not to be over-

Clinton traveled to Montana on May 31 to press his case with voters.

ridden by Congress.

Clinton has yet to reject any legislation during his presidency — a statistic that reflects his first two years with a Democratic Congress, but also his fondness for ameliorating differences with his opponents, not sharpening them.

The latest threats are serious, White House officials insist, and they say Clinton will prove it soon by vetoing a spending cut and disaster aid bill (HR 1158) that, they assert, would cut too much out of education and social programs. The override threat is acute with this bill because it contains disaster relief funds for Oklahoma and California.

"The veto has always been real to us," said White House lobbyist Patrick Griffin. "The only difference now is it's becoming more evident that it will manifest itself in the process."

Clinton faces only a moderate risk that his vetoes will be reversed, since the Republican majorities in the House and Senate are slim and large numbers of Democrats did not cross

over to support the Republican legislation now facing veto threats.

Clinton does not want to be perceived as obstructing the GOP agenda, but rather as exerting a moderating influence.

The challenge will be making that case in the face of inevitable GOP claims that he is blocking the changes voters called for in last year's election.

The biggest difficulty for Clinton may be picking which bills to seek to block. He is under pressure from factions in the Democratic Party to blunt the Republican agenda, but Clinton will have to be selective, observers say.

"If he vetoes everything, he looks like he's trying to satisfy his core constituency. If he signs everything, he looks weak," said Yale University political scientist David R. Mayhew.

Another complication is that many Republicans blanch at the idea of watering down their agenda to get Clinton's signature.

More ideologically driven members favor confrontation with Clinton, rather than the accommodation preached by Democrats and a few GOP colleagues.

A case in point is the welfare bill. To the extent they have concerned themselves with Clinton, Republicans in the House and Senate have said that they cannot imagine Clinton vetoing a bill to overhaul the widely unpopular federal welfare system. Such a step would be disastrous politically, they say.

"If he wants to make the case against reforming welfare, we'll take it to the American people in November of 1996," said Ed Gillespie, spokesman for House Majority Leader Dick Armey, R-Texas.

The House passed its welfare bill (HR 4) on March 24, and, like the version Senate Finance approved May 26, it would end the federal guarantee of Aid to Families with Dependent Children, the main cash welfare program, to all eligible applicants.

The administration has avoide dpublic statements outlining exactly what would provoke a veto, an administration official said, because they do not want to give Republicans "a road map" for producing a welfare bill that Clinton would be forced to veto. Clinton promised to overhaul the welfare system during his campaign and, above all, he wants a bill he can sign. (*Weekly Report, p. 1503*)

Lines in the Sand

Most presidents facing a Congress controlled by the other party must rely heavily on the veto to affect legislation and to communicate their priorities. President Harry S Truman, the last Democratic president in office during a GOP Congress, issued 250 vetoes during his two terms — a record Clinton is unlikely to match. (*Box, this page*)

Yet Clinton will face a stream of legislation this summer designed intentionally to overturn his policies and to highlight the differences between the White House and Congress. This dynamic is playing out in an environment increasingly dominated by presidential politics as Clinton and the field of GOP contenders maneuver in preparation for the 1996 race.

Clinton's caution about delineating differences between his priorities and those of congressional Republicans frustrates some Democratic Party allies. Vetoes alone may not help Clinton's image or restore his influence on Capitol Hill, they argue, unless voters understand — and support — the president's motives for blocking the GOP agenda.

"You've got to be making the case consistently with some broad principles," said Will Marshall, president of the Progressive Policy Institute, a group of centrist Democrats. "One day there's a veto threat from the White House, and the next day they are saying something else. There's no strategy for drawing crucial lines with the Republicans."

Yet administration allies contend that the White House is smart to remain vague about what welfare provisions would be acceptable and instead to concentrate on issues where polls suggest the Republicans are vulner-

Veto Scorecard

Presidents	Vetoes	Regular/Pocket		Overrides
Harry S Truman	250	180	70	12
Dwight D. Eisenhower	181	73	108	2
John F. Kennedy	21	12	9	0
Lyndon B. Johnson	30	16	14	0
Richard M. Nixon	43	26	17	7
Gerald R. Ford	66	48	18	12
Jimmy Carter	31	13	18	2
Ronald Reagan	78	39	39	9
George Bush	46	31	15	1
Bill Clinton	0	0	0	0

MARILYN GATES-DAVIS

able, such as environmental protection and education funding.

"It's important from the president's point of view to show that he stands for something," says Democratic pollster Mark Mellman, who is advising Senate Democrats. "People want action on the domestic front, especially on welfare, but they don't want it at the expense of cutting education or rolling back environmental standards."

All or Nothing

House Speaker Newt Gingrich, R-Ga., said in a June 2 speech that he expects a midsummer stare-down between Congress and the White House, with Clinton attempting to veto every major GOP initiative sent to him. Congressional Democrats have the numbers to block any effort to override a veto, although some members could stray on widely popular bills. Still, Gingrich has vowed to package vetoed bills into a must-pass omnibus measure, daring Clinton to veto it late this year.

"I don't believe we're going to have any choice but to wrap a lot of the year into [an omnibus bill]," said John A. Boehner of Ohio, chairman of the House GOP Conference, "because the president from a political standpoint is going to have to veto most of the Congress' initiatives."

White House officials say they would prefer to avoid an all-or-nothing showdown. "We certainly hope they don't pursue a train wreck strategy," said Griffin. "There's got to be a way this stuff can be resolved on a case-by-case basis."

Not all of the political heat will

automatically fall on Clinton if congressional Republicans dig in their heels. Republicans could be blamed by voters for inaction if they fail to send Clinton bills he can sign.

Already there are signs in the Senate that both parties are trying to avoid veto showdowns. The administration has focused on winning concessions allowing it to support some GOP bills. In a veto threat May 30, Clinton denounced the House-passed rewrite of the clean water act, saying the measure would allow "companies to get around the standards that have been designed to protect us all."

Senate Environment and Public Works Committee Chairman John H. Chafee, R-R.I., a longtime proponent of strong environmental protections, favors fine-tuning the existing law, not a sweeping rewrite like the House bill.

The more difficult dilemma for Clinton may be in handling the appropriations bills sent to him this year. For the first time in years, these 13 annual spending bills that fund most government programs and agencies will contain many deep cuts in areas Democrats have long protected. Some of the deepest cuts Republicans are proposing come from non-defense appropriations.

Democrats are already warning that dire consequences will accompany spending cuts the Republicans want to make in domestic appropriations. Publicly, the White House is saying it will wait for the specifics before passing judgment on cuts made by Congress.

Clinton has said he will be reluctant to accept cuts in programs he deems investments in future U.S. productivity. The House is slated to begin the appropriations process the week of June 5. Gingrich is assuming Clinton has almost no choice but to accept deep cuts eventually unless he wants to shut down the government, although the voters may not appreciate brinkmanship by either side. Still, said Yale's Mayhew, "On appropriations bills, the Congress has got a lot of leverage. The president has got to finally sign something."

Knowing this, Clinton is wielding veto threats now, hoping that what he ends up signing will reflect his priorities more than those of Republicans. ■

SUPREME COURT

It's Back to Drawing Board On Minority Districts

North Carolina, Texas cases may offer clearer guidelines for states

The tortuous lines drawn to create new minority-dominant voting districts have been the butt of numerous jokes likening them to squashed bugs, ink blots, even a sacred Mayan bird.

But many lawyers say the Supreme Court's guidance on when states can and cannot draw such congressional districts has become equally convoluted, creating a legal muddle for the states that is no laughing matter.

"I think that the court has acted terribly irresponsibly," said Samuel Issacharoff, a voting rights expert at the University of Texas law school. "They haven't offered any safe harbor. There is nothing you can do in redistricting now that can keep you from getting sued."

For better or worse, the high court is about to try again.

The Supreme Court opened its new term Oct. 2 with race-conscious redistricting once again on its agenda. The court will review cases from Texas, where a lower court struck down three minority districts, and North Carolina, where two controversial new districts have been upheld.

The decisions will affect not only those cases, but also political and legal developments in other states seeking to reconcile the mandates of the Voting Rights Act with constitutional prohibitions against taking race into account.

The rulings should flesh out the law regarding when and how states can consider race in redistricting.

CQ Weekly Report October 7, 1995

Texas Majority-Minority Districts

18

30

Dallas Area

29

Houston Area

The Supreme Court is expected to rule this year on whether these three odd-shaped districts bear what a lower court called "the odious imprint of racial apartheid."

Clark Kent

But the justices have been so sharply divided on the issue that they may once again stop short of a strong, clear decision capable of dispersing the legal fog.

In Flux

The current wave of voting rights litigation stems from the 1990 census, which reapportioned the 435 congressional seats among the states, setting off a flurry of redistricting.

States recast district lines under the provisions of the 1965 Voting Rights Act, which requires them to safeguard the influence of minority voters. Numerous states, on their own initiative or under pressure from the Justice Department, created districts in which minorities made up a majority of the voting age population, known as majority-minority districts.

As mapmakers pulled districts this way and that to pick up minority voters, established boundary lines were often tugged out of shape. Computer

technology, which provided intricate breakdowns of neighborhood demographics, also encouraged more detailed manipulation of district lines.

In the end, many of the new majority-minority districts came in fairly messy packages.

The Supreme Court raised a warning flag in 1993, ruling in *Shaw v. Reno* that race conscious redistricting can sometimes constitute unfair discrimination against white voters. That decision did not strike down the North Carolina districts in question. But it cast doubt on "bizarrely shaped" districts drawn to concentrate minority voting strength, and said they must be closely scrutinized.

The court went further last term, when, in *Miller v. Johnson*, it struck down Georgia's congressional district map. Writing for the majority in the 5-4 opinion, Justice Anthony M. Kennedy said oddly shaped districts were just one tip-off that race may have played too heavy a role in the districting process. Kennedy said that a constitutional violation may exist in any case in which race was the "predominant" factor in determining district lines — irregular or not.

But even the *Miller* decision did not close the door on race conscious districting.

The high court did not spell out how to determine when race is the "predominant" factor rather than one of several concerns. And even districts where race was a "predominant" concern would be permissible if states could present a compelling justification for them.

Moreover, the court agreed to hear the pending Texas and North Carolina redistricting cases, rather than summarily affirming or remanding the lower courts' decisions. That move suggests the justices are still developing the legal framework for deciding racial redistricting cases.

"They're sending mixed signals," said Daniel E. Troy, a lawyer for the voters challenging the Texas districts.

Justice Ruth Bader Ginsburg, writing the main dissent in *Miller*, cautioned that "the court has not yet spoken a final word."

Texas Tangle

The Texas case — a combination of three lower court cases, *Bush v. Vera, Lawson v. Vera* and *U.S. v. Vera* — will give the justices a chance to cover some new ground, including the complicated intersection of minority voting rights and what has traditionally been the dominant factor in redistricting — protecting incumbents.

After the 1990 census, Texas gained three congressional seats. State legislators subsequently created a congressional district map with three new or reconfigured majority-minority districts — the majority black 30th in Dallas and two in Houston, the majority black 18th and the predominantly Hispanic 29th.

Two African-Americans, Eddie Bernice Johnson and Sheila Jackson-Lee, represent the 30th and 18th districts respectively. A white state senator, Gene Green, won the other new Houston district.

The districts are oddly shaped, though that is a relative term in the world of redistricting.

In Dallas, Johnson's district sprouts tentacles from its city core that snake north and westward. And Houston's 29th has been compared to a Mayan bird with outstretched wings.

Six Republican voters challenged the congressional map, and a federal three-judge panel struck down the 18th, 29th and 30th districts as bearing "the odious imprint of racial apartheid."

But Texas Democrats insist the districts reflect coherent, urban neighborhoods — in contrast to the sprawling majority black rural districts that have come under fire in Georgia, Louisiana and North Carolina.

Nor was race necessarily responsible for some of the messy shapes.

Lawyers for the NAACP Legal Defense and Educational Fund and the Mexican American Legal Defense and

Other Cases To Watch

The Supreme Court will address several other issues of concern to Congress. Some key cases are summarized below (dates for oral arguments shown in parentheses):

● **Gay rights.** *(Romer v. Evans)* Does an amendment to Colorado's Constitution barring laws to protect homosexuals and bisexuals violate the 14th Amendment's guarantees of equal protection? The Colorado Supreme Court has said the amendment, approved by popular vote, is unconstitutional because it denies gays access to the political process. The state defends the measure as a legitimate public policy. *(Oct.10)*

● **Punitive damages.** *(BMW of North America v. Gore)* A well-publicized case of an Alabama BMW owner who collected $2 million in punitive damages after learning his supposedly brand new car — and others sold as new — had in fact previously been somewhat damaged and then refinished. The Supreme Court will consider whether the award was excessive and whether a state jury can impose punitive damages for conduct that takes place outside that state's borders and may be legal outside that state. *(Oct. 11)*

● **Voting rights.** *(Morse v. Republican Party of Virginia)* Does the Voting Rights Act, which protects minority voting rights, cover the nominating activities of a political party? At issue is the GOP's decision to charge a $45 fee for its 1992 senatorial nominating convention. Several law students challenged the fee as an unlawful "poll tax" and said the party at a minimum was required to "preclear" the fee with the Justice Department under the terms of the Voting Rights Act. The Virginia GOP has said the voting rights law does not apply to private party activities, such as a nominating convention. A three-judge federal court agreed and rejected the suit. *(Oral arguments were held Oct. 2)*

● **Census undercount.** *(Wisconsin v. New York City; Oklahoma v. New York City; Department of Commerce v. New York City)* How much latitude does the Commerce Department have in determining the nation's official head count? The core issue is whether the Commerce Department acted illegally when it refused to adjust the 1990 census to account for a likely underrepresentation of minorities. The Supreme Court will take up the more technical question of how much legal deference the administration should be given in making such determinations.

● **Telecommunications.** *(United States v. C&P Telephone; National Cable Television Association v. Bell Atlantic Corp.)* Is the 1984 Cable Communications Act an unconstitutional violation of free speech rights, as the lower courts have ruled? The Clinton administration is defending the law, which generally prohibits telephone companies from providing cable services within their own service territories.

● **Indian gaming.** *(Seminole Tribe of Florida v. Florida.)* Can the federal government, through the Indian Gaming Regulatory Act, force states to negotiate with Indian tribes over gambling on their reservations? The law allows tribes to sue states in federal court if the state fails to enter into good faith negotiations. Florida says that provision violates the 11th Amendment's guarantee of sovereign immunity. A federal appeals court agreed. *(Oct. 11)*

Educational Fund, who are fighting to uphold the districts, say the Texas Legislature could have created more compact, smoothly contoured minority districts, but was under pressure to accommodate white, primarily Democratic, incumbents in neighboring districts. It was the demands of these incumbents, they argue, that led to some of the irregular district lines. And courts in the past have given states consider-

able leeway to configure districts to protect incumbents' re-election prospects.

"The result of the ruling below is that the race conscious construction of an irregularly shaped district is permissible to help white incumbents, but if that construction of the majority white district causes a neighboring minority opportunity district to have an irregular shape, the minority district is unconstitutional," they argued in a brief to the Supreme Court.

Troy says that argument misses the point. While white incumbents undoubtedly did influence the final district lines, Troy said, "those accommodations always took a back seat to the primary goal of preserving these as racially safe seats."

Texas Attorney General Dan Morales, backed by the Clinton Justice Department, is defending the map and the underlying decision to create three majority-minority districts. Under the Voting Rights Act, states are generally obliged to draw a minority-dominant district if minority voters are sufficiently numerous and compact to make up the core of a district, and there is evidence that white voters will not vote for minority candidates.

But Troy believes Texas legislators and the Justice Department have misread the Voting Rights Act, which, he said, does not require states to draw minority districts where they cannot be fashioned in a reasonably compact and orderly way.

Troy is most critical of the Houston districts, where he says legislators intentionally split the black and Hispanic voters to create "safe" districts for each group.

"This is not what America is about, nor is it what the Voting Rights Act was ever meant to accomplish," he said.

Deja Vu

The North Carolina case, *Pope v. Hunt* and *Shaw v. Hunt*, is a continuation of the dispute that led to the well-known *Shaw v. Reno* decision in June 1993.

In 1992, North Carolina created two districts, the 1st and 12th, with a majority of black voters. Several white voters sued, alleging reverse discrimination, and the case reached the Supreme Court.

The justices ruled that race conscious redistricting may violate the constitutional rights of white voters and ordered the lower courts to examine the new districts under the toughest legal standard — strict scrutiny.

To pass the legal test of strict scrutiny in this context, the state government must show that it has a compelling reason to take race into account, and that it took the most "narrowly tailored" path possible to meet its goals.

That has traditionally been a very tough standard to meet, and critics of race conscious redistricting hoped the Supreme Court ruling would doom the new districts.

But the lower court in August 1994 upheld the North Carolina districts under the new legal test.

Now the Supreme Court will weigh in and presumably amplify what is required to survive strict scrutiny.

As a practical matter, "strict scrutiny" may mean whatever Justice Sandra Day O'Connor thinks it does. O'Connor provided a pivotal fifth vote for the *Miller* ruling. But she appeared

---

The Supreme Court's recent opinions are threatening to majority-minority districts, but analysts doubt the justices are ready to abandon such districts entirely.

---

to soften the potential force of that decision with a separate concurrence which specified that "strict scrutiny" should not be an impossible hurdle for the states.

Murky Outlook

The thrust of the Supreme Court's recent opinions is clearly threatening to minority groups, the Clinton Justice Department and others who have defended the new majority-minority districts as a means of empowering minority voters.

However, even those most disturbed by the thrust of the court's redistricting rulings doubt that the justices are ready to abandon such districts entirely.

Instead, the justices may continue to chisel out new limits in a sequence of cases, each of which presents slightly different circumstances.

For instance, a federal panel is currently reviewing a challenge to Louisiana's congressional map and is widely expected to strike it down as illegal racial gerrymandering.

Nevertheless, advocates of the Louisiana districts believe that there are key differences between their case and the Georgia case. The districts are somewhat more conventionally shaped, for example. Also, the Louisiana legislature acted without the same Justice Department pressure that the justices criticized as heavy-handed in *Miller*.

Therefore, if the Louisiana districts are struck down, it is possible the Supreme Court could take the case on appeal and restore them.

The high court's action on a Tennessee voting rights case may offer another piece of the final picture.

Tennessee drew state legislative districts that include majority-minority districts and several where minority voters constitute a significant portion of the vote, but not an outright majority.

Some minority voters protested, saying they were entitled to another district in which blacks would hold majority voting strength. But a federal court panel upheld the Tennessee "influence" districts as a legitimate way to empower minority voters under the Voting Rights Act, and the Supreme Court summarily affirmed that ruling Oct. 2.

Meanwhile, all the legal uncertainty has made the already contentious process of redistricting that much harder to resolve.

Brenda Wright, a voting rights expert at the Lawyer's Committee for Civil Rights Under Law, said the confusion and lawsuits are affecting not only congressional and state district mapmaking, but even redistricting by local authorities.

Georgia is a case study of the current confusion.

After the high court in June struck down Georgia's 11th congressional district, Democratic Gov. Zell Miller called a special session of the legislature to try again.

But lawmakers adjourned empty-handed after several weeks of bickering. Republicans, white Democrats and black Democrats divided into factions and could not find common ground.

Laughlin McDonald, director of the Southern regional office of the American Civil Liberties Union, said the vagueness of the Supreme Court's ruling is at least partly responsible for the impasse. "The legislature was convinced that there were no standards, that no matter what they did they'd get sued."

Now it will be up to a panel of three federal judges to approve a new district map for the state's congressional elections.

McDonald, whose organization had defended the plan struck down by the Supreme Court, hopes the political brawling in Georgia and elsewhere will help convince the courts to steer clear of the districting process.

"Legislatures should do it unless they really are violating somebody's constitutional rights," he said.

Issacharoff says the racial gerrymandering suits have put a spotlight on what was always an unseemly process.

"It's not like in the absence of race this is a purely sanitized process in which the angels come down to anoint the lines," he said. "This is nasty, backroom, cigar-chomping politics." ■

POLITICS AND PUBLIC POLICY

The term *public policy making* refers to action taken by the government to address issues on the public agenda; it also refers to the method by which a decision to act on policy is reached. The work of government—Congress, the presidency, the judiciary, and the bureaucracy—is to make and implement the policy decisions. The following articles explore major policy issues before the federal government through the fall of 1995.

The 104th Congress set a pace that had pundits comparing it to the Congresses that passed the New Deal and Great Society legislation of 1933 and 1965, respectively. The House voted on every plank in the Contract With America within the first 100 days, as the Republican leadership had promised, passing nine of ten. But much of that legislation stalled in the Senate, and the House then turned to more contentious issues—issues that the Republicans themselves did not always agree on.

In the latter half of 1995 the Republicans dove headlong into almost every hornet's nest in American domestic politics. At once they tried to reform Medicaid and Medicare, reducing the rate of growth of the programs; to reform welfare, turning it over to the states; and to overhaul farm programs that had endured largely unchanged since the 1930s. And they tried to achieve all of these profound programmatic changes while slashing spending and reducing taxes.

The weight of legislation, combined with inter- and intraparty squabbles, caused the legislative timetable to slip considerably in both the House and the Senate. By early November none of the major reform bills had passed Congress, and to speed up the process a wide array of legislation was combined in a massive budget reconciliation bill that would cut Medicare by $270 billion, Medicaid by $182 billion, and entitlements (including welfare) by $175 billion. The president was threatening to veto the bill.

The final three articles in this section of the *Guide* address topics that are certain to dominate discussion through 1996 and possibly beyond. Among them are prayer in public schools, anti-immigration sentiments in the key electoral vote states of California, Texas, and Florida, and the efficacy and fairness of affirmative action programs.

HEALTH CARE REFORM

Opponents Solidify Stands On Health Care Proposals

Battle lines becoming clearer as work continues on Medicare and Medicaid

Beyond the partisan trumpetings over the Republican plan to balance the budget, a shadowy picture is emerging of where the health care battle lines will be drawn — and perhaps where a final deal might lie, if there is one.

Republicans, Democrats and the White House began to solidify their positions during the week of Sept. 25 on their spending and taxing priorities. Party solidarity was still evident but slipping on a number of politically sensitive issues — which ultimately could lead to a compromise that pleases neither GOP conservatives nor liberal Democrats.

The Senate Finance Committee reflected some of those fissures as it forged ahead on GOP plans to squeeze more than $450 billion out of Medicare and Medicaid, as well as $40 billion out of the earned income tax credit (EITC) for the working poor. Democrats and moderate Republicans won small concessions and put up warning signs for a rocky road ahead. But Senate Majority Leader Bob Dole, R-Kan., said Sept. 29 that he expected the panel to approve the bill largely intact before adjourning.

On the House side, the Ways and Means and Commerce committees, tangled in internal and external problems with budget estimates and content, put off scheduled markups for their health care plans until the week of Oct. 9. *(Ways and Means, p. 89)*

Complicating the situation is the White House's public stance that President Clinton will veto any budget-reconciliation bill that cuts health programs on the scale supported by Republicans, especially when they are coupled with tax cuts for most Ameri-

SCOTT J. FERRELL

Senate Finance Committee marks up GOP plan Sept. 28.

cans and tax increases for the working poor. Privately, administration officials say they are discussing how far they can move toward the GOP without losing the support of the majority of Democrats.

Republicans have their own differences, principally over how much to cut Medicaid, a joint federal-state health care program for the poor and disabled, how big a tax cut to endorse and how much to increase taxes on the working poor. The Senate Republicans' appetite for both the spending reductions and the tax cuts appeared considerably less voracious than that of the House.

They also are dealing with a key agitator within their own camp: John

H. Chafee of Rhode Island. Chafee, who said he opposes the tax cuts and the plan to end Medicaid as an entitlement, has been siding with Democrats regularly in the Finance Committee on attempts to restore some of the protections for the poor. Although he is unlikely to scuttle Finance's entire bill, he has not hesitated to put his GOP colleagues on the spot.

And that could foreshadow difficulties when the budget reconciliation bill, which will be the vehicle for the deficit reductions proposals of Finance and other committees, gets to the floor.

Chafee has support among other Senate moderates who would like to maintain some of the federal coverage requirements in the program; conservatives want to hand out block grants and let states decide whom to cover while reducing the amount of the federal contribution to the program.

There also are divisions among Republicans and between the two chambers over formulas that would dole out federal Medicaid funds among the states.

Democrats are divided on Medicaid as well, with conservatives willing to cap the federal contribution but guaranteeing eligbility and coverage, while more liberal members are resisting any major changes. The Democratic Leadership Council, chaired by Sen. Joseph I. Lieberman, D-Conn., which represents the conservative wing of the party, endorsed a capped entitlement approach Sept. 27.

But perhaps more divisive for the Democrats is whether to make cuts in Medicare, the government health insurance for the elderly, that go beyond what is needed to make the hospital insurance trust fund solvent. They, along with the White House, have signaled they would be willing to work with Republicans on a smaller Medi-

Squaring Off Over Health Care

As Republicans forged ahead with their plans to cut federal health care spending, Democrats attempted to slow down the GOP juggernaut.

The Democratic goal was to gain time to raise questions about the impact of Republican proposals and to rally their own troops behind an alternative. The main targets of the Democrats' ire were the Republican proposal to reduce spending in Medicare — the government's health insurance for the elderly —

SCOTT J. FERRELL

Democrats hold "alternative" Medicare hearing outdoors Sept. 29. From left, Patricia Schroder of Colorado, Nita Lowey of New York, Nancy Pelosi of California, Ronald Coleman of Texas and Gene Green of Texas.

by $270 billion over seven years, and to cut Medicaid — the government's health program for the poor and disabled — by $182 billion over seven years.

In the Senate, Democrats were working on an alternative Medicare overhaul proposal at the same time they were trying to slow the action on Medicare and Medicaid in the Senate Finance Committee. In the House, Democrats remained fractured over what approach to take to revamp the Medicare system, or whether it needed to be overhauled at all. House Democrats devoted most of their energy to holding outdoor hearings with witnesses opposed to the GOP plan.

Senate Stall

"Our view has been all along that . . . we're making some very big decisions here," said Senate Democratic leader Tom Daschle, D-S.D. "And having hearings and having the opportunity to think through this a little bit, prior to the time we vote, just makes a lot of sense."

Daschle noted that the Democratic staff had only just begun to analyze the recently released Medicare plan and that crucial sections such as its proposed back-up spending controls known as the Budget Expenditure Limit Tool were poorly understood. This provision would automatically reduce payments to providers if the savings targets were not met. Daschle charged that it was just one of the "surprises" and "hatchets" in the proposal.

In the meantime, the Senate Democratic leadership was working on an alternative Medicare proposal that will be released Oct. 2. It would save $89 billion in Medicare over seven years. According to estimates by the Health Insurance Trust Fund's actuaries, savings of $89 billion could keep Medicare solvent through 2006, although a sudden rise in inflation rates or an increase in hospital admissions could leave it insolvent sooner.

The White House would like to go further and is now working on a plan that would make somewhat deeper reductions — at least $125 billion — in Medicare to help balance the budget. This is similar to the proposal the administration made in June. It is still unclear whether the cuts would be made over 10 years, nine years, eight years or even less. It also is unclear how many Democrats could stay on board if the administration unveiled such a scenario. Discussions are ongoing.

Democrats who support getting some savings from Medicare to reduce the budget deficit tend to be conservative. More liberal members such as Sen. Paul Wellstone, D-Minn., are reluctant to make any reductions in Medicare spending beyond what is needed to keep the system solvent.

The conservative Democrats released their plan for overhauling Medicare Sept. 22 though they did not introduce legislation. Sen. Joseph I. Lieberman, D-Conn., called the plan a "long-term" solution.

The proposal, written by the Progressive Policy Institute, an arm of the Democratic Leadership Council, includes aspects of both the Republican and Democratic proposals. It would privatize Medicare entirely and allow the elderly to choose among an array of health plans. The government would pay a set amount that would reflect the average price of competing plans. If the elderly chose an inexpensive plan they could get a cash rebate; if they chose a more expensive plan they would have to pay a premium for the difference between the price and the government contribution.

House Hearings

Meanwhile in the House, members held outdoor hearings with critics of the Republican plan including hospital executives, academic analysts and consumer groups. Among those testifying was Judith Feder, a former Clinton administration official who is now a professor of Health Policy at Georgetown University. Feder underscored that at least $100 billion of the Republican Medicare savings had nothing to do with making the trust fund solvent. "To pull $270 billion out of the Medicare program over seven years and claim that savings are the result of choice is to pursue retrenchment in the guise of reform," she said.

Simultaneously, Rep. Jim McDermott, D-Wash., introduced a health insurance bill (HR 2422) that is designed to save about $90 billion over seven years by reducing payments to hospitals and doctors. It also would set up a commission to study how best to overhaul Medicare to meet the flood of new beneficiaries after 2010 when the baby boom generation begins to retire. Last year, McDermott championed a single-payer health plan, under which all Americans would be guaranteed health insurance benefits through a taxpayer-financed system.

Senate Finance Plan Nicks Beneficiaries . . .

The plan marked up the week of Sept. 25 by the Senate Finance Committee includes these changes to Medicare:

Impact on Beneficiaries

● **Eligibility age.** Eligibility for Medicare would be raised gradually from the current age of 65 to 67 by 2027, in line with plans for Social Security.

● **Beneficiary payments.** The premium for the optional Medicare insurance for doctor bills (Part B) would be held to 31.5 percent of the cost of the program, with the rest paid for by general tax revenues. For fiscal 1995, the monthly premium was $46.10, which was scheduled to drop to $42.80 in fiscal 1996, enough to pay for 25 percent of the program. The committee proposal estimated the premium would rise to $54 in 1996, $58 in 1997, $63 in 1998, $69 in 1999, $77 in 2000, $84 in 2001 and $92 in 2002.

Another change in the premiums would require wealthier beneficiaries to pay the entire cost of Part B coverage. The Finance plan would begin to phase out the "subsidy" for individuals making $75,000 annually and for couples making $100,000. The government contribution would end at the $100,000 mark for individuals and $150,000 for couples.

Beneficiaries in the Part B program would have to pay the first $150 of expenses themselves in 1996, rather than the current $100; the deductible would rise by $10 annually through 2002.

From these changes, the committee expects about $71.2 billion in savings by 2002, with nearly $52 billion coming from maintaining the Part B premium rate.

HMOs, Medical Savings Accounts

While retaining their ability to remain in the traditional fee-for-service Medicare program, beneficiaries also will have a number of other health insurance options from which to choose. Among the choices are health maintenance organizations (HMOs), in which patients use a specific network of providers who have accepted a set fee for providing care; plans that would allow beneficiaries to go outside their network and use other physicians at a somewhat higher cost; health insurance policies offered by organizations or unions; medical savings accounts combined with a high-deductible catastrophic policy; or any other type of plan that meets requirements outlined by the plan. Expected seven-year savings: $48 billion.

● **Medical savings accounts.** The government would deposit funds in an individual's medical savings account. The amount would be the difference between the Medicare payment amount (what Medicare pays for a health maintenance organization, adjusted by region) and the cost of the beneficiary's medical coverage (HMO or a "catastrophic costs" insurance plan). Money from the account used for health expenses would not be taxed as income, but interest earned would be. Users would be permitted to roll over funds from year to year without other limits.

At the end of the year, beneficiaries could take up to 75 percent of the amount in the account as a cash rebate, but withdrawal would be subject to taxes and a 10 percent penalty.

Medicare Choice Requirements

In what the committee calls "Medicare Choice," a range of approaches of health care coverage would be offered to beneficiaries. To qualify with the federal government to offer plans, insurers would have to meet a number of federal requirements, including:

● **Eligibility and benefits.** The plans would have to cover anyone who is eligible for Medicare Part A and enrolled in Medicare Part B (except those with end-stage renal disease, which the secretary of Health and Human Services (HHS) is required to study to determine whether it should be included). They would also, at a minimum, have to cover the same items and services as traditional Medicare. The average total cost for a participant could not exceed the average out-of-pocket costs for the traditional program.

The plans would have to take anyone who wished to enroll and allow them to remain as long as they wished, provided they paid their bills.

● **Enrollment.** Beneficiaries could change plans only during an annual period, except during the first 90 days in a new program. Enrollees would be automatically re-enrolled in their current plans if they did not make a different choice.

● **Information.** HHS would be required to provide clear explanations of all plan options, including information on prices, services, co-payments, deductibles and other restrictions, and mail them to beneficiaries at least 30 days before the annual open enrollment period.

● **Consumer protections:** The choice plans would have to outline their strategies for quality assurance and receive annual accreditation from the secretary or from an agency recognized by HHS.

They must demonstrate they they have the capacity to adequately serve the number of beneficiaries they expect to enroll. Finally, they are expected to make all services accessible to their enrollees. The state plans must outline the procedure they would use if beneficiaries are unhappy with their coverage or decisions by their health plan. The choice plans are also supposed to provide limited coverage for any Medicare beneficiary who has a pre-existing condition and chooses to go to another plan.

● **Managed care payments.** Under current law, Medicare pays HMOs and similar managed care providers 95 percent of the average cost of treating a fee-for-service beneficiary in the area. The differences in payments can vary widely between states and even between counties in the same state.

The Finance proposal calls for a three-year overhaul of the payment method beginning in fiscal 1996. The new system would base costs on the per capita growth in the gross domestic product, one of several inflation indexes, and would create new payment areas, ending the current

...But Hits Medical Providers Hardest

county-by-county basis and terminating the link between HMO payments and fee-for-service payments.

For fiscal 1996, Medicare payments would be recalculated to adjust to the amount of money in the program. The rates would be calculated by adding 75 percent of the county rate to 25 percent of the national rate, which would be adjusted to account for differences in local prices.

For fiscal 1997, new payment areas would become effective. The new payment areas would consist of the metropolitan statistical areas within a state. If there are combined metropolitan areas, such as Baltimore-Washington, they would be considered separately. All areas outside of the metropolitan statistical areas would be considered as one for payment purposes.

The new formula would remove half of the Medicare payments for medical education and hospitals that serve a high percentage of poor patients. Providers could file a separate claim for those funds for Medicare recipients they had treated.

For fiscal 1998, the remaining hospital payments and medical education money would be removed. Beginning in 2000, the HHS secretary could make annual adjustments in the payment so long as they do not cause total Medicare spending to increase.

Reduced Payments to Providers

Doctors, hospitals and other providers of health services would bear the brunt of the savings.

• **Hospital reductions.** By using a variety of reductions in price indexes and readjusting the other scales by which payments to hospitals are determined, the committee would alter inpatient and outpatient hospital payments, would reduce the amount of money spent on capital costs of hospitals and nursing homes, and would recalculate other payment formulas. Expected seven-year savings: $73.6 billion.

Other provider changes include:

• **"Disproportionate share hospitals."** Medicare currently gives hospitals that serve a large number of low-income patients an extra payment. The committee proposal would reduce the payments by 5 percent a year from fiscal 1996-2000, freezing them for 2001-02. The committee proposal also would reduce adjustments for inflation. Expected seven-year savings: $4.5 billion.

• **Medical education.** The committee proposal would not change direct medical education payments, in which Medicare pays teaching hospitals for direct costs of residency training programs. But the proposal reduces the payment for indirect medical education, which includes costs from extra demands placed on staff and tests associated with teaching. Expected seven-year savings: $9.9 billion.

• **Nursing homes.** Medicare currently pays nursing homes on a per day basis for reasonable costs, subjected to per day costs limits. The payment is updated annually for inflation. The limits are applied only to the per day routine service costs (such things as nursing, room and board, administrative), which are updated annually for inflation. Non-routine costs are paid according to reasonable costs. For fiscal 1996, the proposal would extend a

R. MICHAEL JENKINS

Doctors, hospitals and medical training programs face cuts under Republican plans to hold down Medicare costs.

freeze on the inflation updates that was enacted in 1993. For fiscal 1997 and beyond, the plan would recalculate how other payments are made and subject them to limits as well. Expected seven-year savings: $10.4 billion.

• **Home health services.** Agencies that provide home health care are currently reimbursed on a "reasonable cost" basis. The committee proposal would institute a new payment formula that would attempt to restrict what has been one of the fastest growing parts of the Medicare system and would provide agencies with a financial incentive (50 percent of the savings) to keep costs below regional averages. Expected seven-year savings: $17.8 billion.

• **Physician services.** Currently, doctors are reimbursed on the basis of a fee schedule that is adjusted to reflect the "relative value" of their work, plus costs of running a practice, which is multiplied by a dollar amount for services such as surgery or primary care. The committee proposal would replace the current fee structure with a single payment factor to try to correct "distortions" and introduce a new formula. Expected seven-year savings: $22.6 billion.

• **Laboratory services.** The committee proposal would reduce the amount Medicare pays for lab tests and would eliminate all inflation adjustments through 2002. Expected seven-year savings: $6 billion.

• **Durable medical equipment.** The committee proposals would reduce the Medicare monthly payment for home oxygen equipment by 40 percent and eliminate automatic payment increases (except for the oxygen equipment) through 2002. Expected seven-year savings: $6.2 billion.

• **Ambulance services.** The proposal would eliminate any payment increases for ambulance services through 2002. Expected seven-year savings: $800 million.

care cut — say $90 billion, compared with the $270 billion envisioned in the GOP budget — if tax cuts are put off.

However, the White House and some conservative Democrats are willing to go further and reduce Medicare spending by as much as $125 billion to $130 billion, earmarking some of the money for deficit reduction, according to administration officials. So far, however, the administration says such reductions would have to be made over a longer time frame than the seven years required in the Republicans' balanced-budget plan.

Medicare Savings

The Senate Finance plan for Medicare, which the committee began marking up without having formal legislative language in hand, would allow seniors to stay in the traditional fee-for-service Medicare program.

But Republicans are counting on savings from new alternatives that seniors could select, such as managed care, private policies or medical savings accounts. These would be funded with a set federal amount, not an open-ended one. The plan would reduce payments to providers, raise the costs of premiums and the deductible for optional Part B insurance, make wealthier seniors pay more for their premiums, and would very gradually raise the eligibility age to 67. *(Highlights, p. 86)*

When it began meeting Sept. 26, Republican after Republican spoke of the need to shore up the Medicare hospital insurance fund (Part A),

SCOTT J. FERRELL

At Sept. 28 markup, Dole, left, and Roth put GOP fortunes in hands of Finance Committee.

which its board of trustees said would be insolvent by 2002 without changes in current law.

Majority Leader Bob Dole, R-Kan., acknowledged that the committee had "tough decisions to make," but that they were necessary to respond to the trust fund crisis. "We have to fix it in a way that does not adversely affect senior citizens," he said. "The larger challenge is to deal with the deficit and balance the budget by 2002."

Democrat Max Baucus of Montana agreed that Medicare needed a shot in the arm but disagreed with the Re-

publicans' plans.

"We need only about $90 billion to put it on solid footing," he said. "There never has been more than 14 years of solvency in the program. Nine times in 30 years, the trustees have warned of bankruptcy. Instead of fixing the basement, you're about to blow up the house."

In the first vote on the Republican plan in either chamber, the committee voted, 9-11, along party lines Sept. 27 to reject a substitute amendment from Democrats Daniel Patrick Moynihan of New York, and John D. Rockefeller IV of West Virginia, that would have saved about $106 billion over five years, more than the $89 billion that is necessary to extend the program's solvency through 2002.

Their plan differed from Republican plans in three areas: It would have allowed the Part B premium to drop to the point where it pays 25 percent of the program's costs instead of the 31.5 percent in the GOP plan; it would not have raised the premiums for wealthier beneficiaries as Republicans would; and it would have created a bipartisan commission to deal with long-term problems. It also would have sunk GOP plans for $245 billion in tax cuts.

William V. Roth Jr., R-Del., countered that the Democratic plan did not go far enough. "By 2002, Medicare won't be able to pay its bills, and $89 billion only delays the inevitable."

Other Amendments

Party unity faded on other amendments.

Republican Charles E. Grassley of Iowa proposed an amendment that would have altered the "sequester" function included in the measure to penalize states or individual areas that failed to stay within targeted spending goals. The sequester is what Senate Republicans call a "budget expenditure limit tool" that would automatically reduce payments to providers if the savings targets are not met.

Grassley argued that an across-the-board cut would provide high-cost areas, particularly those in large states, with no incentive to keep costs down, an argument that Democrats and Republicans from less-populous states joined.

Six Republicans voted for the amendment along with four Democrats. But it lost, 10-10.

Alan K. Simpson, R-Wyo., offered an amendment that would require all Medicare beneficiaries to pay $15 each time they receive a doctor's services,

EITC Changes Survive

Despite repeated assaults by Democrats, the Senate Finance Committee moved ahead on provisions that would drastically reduce the number of low-income working Americans who qualify for the earned income tax credit and would reduce the amount of the credit for many others.

The earned income tax credit (EITC), which currently helps reduce the tax burden for about 20 million taxpayers, costs the federal government about $25 billion a year. To qualify, a worker can make no more than $28,553, and the credit starts diminishing at $11,630. The maximum credit is $3,564 a year.

The Senate plan would exclude illegal aliens, low-income workers without children and low-income workers with children earning more than $27,731 a year. It also would count income from sources such as Social Security benefits, distributions from pensions and annuities, and child support. Taxpayers could not count losses from rents or royalties, or capital or net operating losses in a small business.

On a 9-11 party-line vote, the committee rejected three amendments that sought to eliminate or mitigate the EITC provisions. The Senate plan would save $42.4 billion over seven years; the House's version, about $23 billion.

Ways and Means' Medicare Proposal

House Republicans released long-awaited details of their proposal to reduce federal spending on Medicare on Sept. 29. And the preliminary review by nonpartisan congressional estimators backed GOP claims that the plan would save $270 billion over seven years.

According to the review by the Congressional Budget Office (CBO), health care providers such as hospitals and doctors would contribute about $151.5 billion of the total over seven years. Beneficiaries would contribute an additional $53.6 billion in payments. The balance would come from a variety of sources.

Markup of the Medicare bill (HR 2425) will begin in the House Commerce Committee on Oct. 2, but amendments will not start until Oct. 10, after the Columbus Day recess. The Ways and Means Committee will begin marking up its portions of the bill Oct. 9.

House Republican leaders said they were proud of their bill and for that reason were eager to let the public review it for a week before the markup. "We believe this is what we were elected to do," said Rep. Bill Archer, R-Texas, chairman of the Ways and Means Committee. "This bill saves Medicare for current retirees and protects it for those who are now in the prime of their lives."

The week also leaves time for Republican rank-and-file members to review the bill and sound out constituents. A number of lawmakers say they expect to make changes in the legislation, either in committee or before it reaches the floor.

According to the CBO analysis, the GOP proposal would achieve more than half its savings through traditional reductions in payments to hospitals and doctors as well as to health providers who offer care to the elderly in their homes. Significant savings also will come from restricting payments to managed care health plans. The GOP plan anticipates that an increasing number of elderly will subscribe to such plans.

However, because the CBO is far less optimistic than lawmakers about the number of people who will migrate to managed care plans, the total savings in this category fall about $32 billion short of the $270 billion total savings. To make up the difference, the proposal contains a strict "fail-safe" mechanism that would force deeper reductions in provider payments if the savings from Medicare fell short of annual targets.

Here are some of the key provisions and savings in the plan:

● **Care choices.** Each year Medicare beneficiaries could choose to: stay in a traditional Medicare program; enroll in a managed care organization or in new groups known as provider-sponsored networks that will be set up by doctors and hospitals; or begin a medical savings

SCOTT J. FERRELL

Chairman Archer: "We believe this is what we were elected to do."

account. According to CBO, about 25 percent of the Medicare population is expected to migrate into managed care plans by 2002.

● **Cost containment.** The Medicare program would become a "capped entitlement," meaning that while everyone who qualified for it would receive benefits, the money available to pay doctors and hospitals would be capped.

Individual doctors and hospitals and other health providers would be reimbursed at lower rates. The rate of overall spending would be incrementally reduced from 10 percent a year to about 6 percent. Savings: $151.5 billion over seven years.

Managed care providers would receive a set amount annually for each Medicare patient they care for. The annual rate of growth in the payment would vary from year to year. But it would be considerably lower than the growth rate for traditional Medicare. Savings: $30.8 billion over seven years.

● **Budget fail-safe.** To ensure that traditional Medicare meets its budget targets each year, the secretary of Health and Human Services would determine whether spending constraints in the law were sufficient to ensure that budget targets would be met; if they were not, the secretary would have authority to reduce reimbursement rates for hospitals, doctors and others.

If the budget targets were missed, the secretary could reduce future payments to the sectors of the industry that were responsible. Savings: $32.1 billion.

● **Premium increases.** The elderly would continue to pay premiums based on 31.5 percent of the cost of the doctor portion of Medicare, which would bring the cost of the monthly premium to between $90 and $93 in 2002. Under current law, the percentage is expected to decline to 25 percent. Wealthy beneficiaries — single people earning more than $100,000 a year and couples earning more than $150,000 a year — would pay all the premiums for the doctor portion of Medicare. The elderly who elected to enter a managed care plan could be charged unlimited additional copayments for services. Savings: $53.6 billion.

● **Medical education.** The proposal would set up a new $50 billion trust fund to finance the costs of teaching hospitals. The trust fund would eventually replace the current money available to teaching hospitals through Medicare. Savings: about $8.2 billion over seven years.

● **Medical malpractice.** The proposal limits noneconomic damages (pain and suffering) to $250,000 and limits on punitive damages to $250,000 or three times the amount of the economic loss to the patient, whichever was greater. No savings.

GOP Answers Lobby Effort

A coalition of labor unions and advocacy groups has launched a $2 million grass-roots media campaign in an effort to defeat efforts by congressional Republicans to overhaul Medicare. Now, the GOP leadership is fighting back.

The TV, radio and print campaign by the coalition, known as Save America's Families, seeks to apply political pressure on 34 targeted Republicans, including moderates, freshmen, House and Senate members. The advertisements feature an all-

SCOTT J. FERRELL

The National Council of Senior Citizens, part of the Save the Family coalition, protests the GOP Medicare plan Sept. 29, using a Trojan horse as a symbol of the proposal.

American couple fretting over the financial burden of caring for their elderly relatives if the Republicans cut the nation's Medicare program.

The advertisements are the handiwork of Vic Fingerhut, whose Washington polling and media firm does work for unions, liberal organizations and Democrats. For Fingerhut, such campaigns are not new; he ran similar ads in New York state earlier this year to fight reductions in the state's health care spending proposed by Gov. George E. Pataki, a Republican.

The campaign is part of a larger grass-roots lobbying effort aimed at getting voters to write or call Democratic and GOP lawmakers in 80 House districts to help derail the Medicare plan. "We will concentrate our efforts in areas where we think we can make a difference," said Cathy Hurwit, legislative director for Citizen Action, a consumer and environmental group that is part of the Save America's Families coalition.

Irate House Republicans have pointed to the campaign as evidence that tough new restrictions are needed to curb the lobbying activities of nonprofit and "advocacy" groups that receive federal grants.

"It illustrates our point for us," said Ernest Jim Istook Jr., R-Okla., the chief sponsor of a measure to rein in the lobbying activities of such groups.

Just 10 days after the advertisements started to run, Speaker Newt Gingrich, R-Ga., on Sept. 20 summoned Istook and his two cosponsors, David M. McIntosh, R-Ind., and Robert L. Ehrlich Jr., R-Md., to his office and told them to hold firm on their demands to attach the House lobbying provision to the Treasury-Postal Service appropriations bill (HR 2020), which would prohibit such organizations that receive federal grants from spending more than 5 percent of their budgets on lobbying.

The House language is far more sweeping than the Senate's version, which would limit the lobbying activities of only one class of nonprofit organizations that receive federal grants. The Senate language would bar federal grants from going only to 501(c)(4) corporations that lobby; it is in its version of the Treasury Postal Service spending bill. The two sides' inability to reach a compromise on the issue has delayed approval of a final appropriations bill. *(Weekly Report, p. 2882)*

Coalition representatives contend that Gingrich is trying to silence their opposition. "It's clearly an attempt to intimidate individuals and groups," said Charles Loveless, director of legislation for the American Federation of State, County and Municipal Employees, which is part of the coalition. Gingrich dismisses the criticism, saying groups dependent on taxpayer funds should be providing services, not lobbying against public policy. "The point is: It is wrong and it needs to be fixed," said Tony Blankley, Gingrich's spokesman.

which he said would not be applied to an annual deductible or covered under supplemental insurance policies.

He described the measure as a "fair and equitable way to effect change in people's behavior."

Rockefeller retorted that he was "fascinated" to see illness described as behavior, and Bill Bradley, D-N.J., noted that beneficiaries already have copayments under Part B.

Even after he agreed to drop the per-visit fee to $5, Simpson was defeated, 9-11, with three other Republicans (Orrin G. Hatch of Utah, Larry Pressler of South Dakota, and Don Nickles of Oklahoma) and five Democrats (Moynihan, Baucus, John B.

Breaux of Louisiana, Kent Conrad of North Dakota, and Carol Moseley-Braun of Illinois) voting with him.

"No way, my mother would string me up," said Alfonse M. D'Amato, R-N.Y.

In other action, the committee:

● Rejected, 8-12, a Rockefeller amendment designed to limit so-called balance billing by private managed-care plans that take on Medicare patients. His amendment specified that the alternative Medicare plans could require patients to pay some share of their medical bills, but no more than the average amount they would have had to pay in a traditional Medicare fee-for-service plan. Baucus joined the 11 Republicans

in voting against the amendment.

● Rejected, 9-11, along party lines, a Conrad amendment that used nonbinding language to declare that any "fiscal dividend" savings should go toward deficit reduction or toward mitigating the reduction in social programs.

● Rejected, 9-11, on party lines, a Breaux sense of the Senate amendment that any economic dividend should be used first to alleviate taxes for the working poor and to restore the EITC reduction in the bill.

● Rejected, 10-10, a Moynihan amendment that would establish a trust fund for teaching hospitals, a key home state concern. D'Amato voted with the Democrats. ■

Managed Care May Save Money, But Hard To Say How Much

In 1994's health care debate, some Republicans treated managed care as an enemy, equating it with rationing and government efforts to limit citizens' choices of doctors.

What a difference a year makes. In 1995's debate over how to constrain spending on entitlement programs, Republican leaders tout managed care as a way for Medicare, and Medicaid as well, to save money and also offer enrollees more health care choices.

A key question, however, remains: How much can managed care save as part of the Republicans' plan to squeeze $270 billion out of Medicare and $182 billion out of Medicaid over the next seven years?

House Republican leaders are counting on increased use of managed care — in which a specified network of providers agrees to offer services for a set fee — for a windfall. But the Congressional Budget Office, which must "score" budget proposals to compute anticipated savings, and many health care analysts caution that the Republicans may be disappointed. The reason is that no one knows whether the older, generally less healthy senior citizens will opt for such plans as health maintenance organizations (HMOs) or whether they will stay put in the current program, which lets them select their own doctors and pays their fees on a service-by-service basis.

Rep. James C. Greenwood, R-Pa., a member of the House task force that is writing the Medicare changes, has suggested that managed care could account for half of the $270 billion target, but he has offered no specifics. However, a preliminary CBO estimate of the Republican plans suggested that the figure is closer to $30 billion than $135 billion over seven years.

Despite that discouraging news,

CQ Weekly Report September 23, 1995

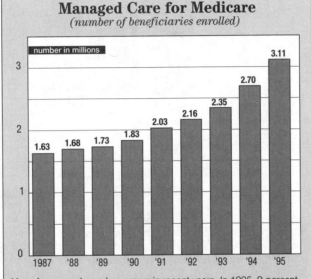

Managed Care for Medicare
(number of beneficiaries enrolled)

number in millions

1987	1.63
'88	1.68
'89	1.73
'90	1.83
'91	2.03
'92	2.16
'93	2.35
'94	2.70
'95	3.11

Use of managed care has grown in recent years. In 1995, 9 percent of Medicare beneficiaries were enrolled in some type of managed-care health plan.

SOURCE: Health Care Financing Administration

proponents are optimistic about the potential for savings if significant numbers of beneficiaries choose managed care. And the burgeoning managed care industry is eager for the opportunity to prove that it can offer subscribers better coverage than traditional fee-for-service providers.

Savings are not the only benefit that managed care proponents envision. They say many senior citizens would welcome the chance to have one place to turn for all their health care needs. They believe managed care can reduce paperwork and reduce out-of-pocket costs for beneficiaries. And they expect that additional competition in the medical marketplace will force other providers to lower costs and work more efficiently.

But skeptics doubt whether seniors, who often have a long-term relationship with their physicians, will embrace managed care's limits on doctors and services.

"For most people, the quality of care is symbolized by choosing your own doctor, even though there is no scientific evidence that that is the case," said David B. Kendall, a health

policy analyst at the Progressive Policy Institute, an offshoot of the Democratic Leadership Council.

Henry J. Aaron of the Brookings Institution, a centrist think tank, notes that "Medicare already pays at deep discounts for services for the elderly" and says it will be impossible to achieve big savings without charging seniors more.

Critics also have concerns beyond the realm of savings. They worry that beneficiaries who choose to remain in traditional fee-for-service plans will have to pay more to do so, despite House Republicans' early vows to the contrary. And they fear that the changes will further limit doctor choices or hospital services for the poor or for rural residents.

Not a New Concept

Managed care is not a new concept for either Medicare or Medicaid. Currently, about 9 percent of Medicare's 37 million beneficiaries are enrolled in some form of managed care plan. And Medicaid has boosted its managed care enrollment from 9.5 percent of eligible beneficiaries in 1991 to more than 23 percent in 1994. *(Chart, this page)*

Nearly 51 percent of Medicare beneficiaries currently in managed care live in California, Nevada, Hawaii and Arizona, with California having the largest share. Participation has been growing rapidly in Florida, Georgia, the Carolinas, Tennessee, Kentucky, Mississippi and Alabama, which now enroll nearly 17 percent of the Medicare managed care population.

With interest and participation in managed care on the rise, analysts suggest that Congress could bolster savings by changing the way it pays Medicare managed care providers.

Medicare currently pays managed care groups 95 percent of the average per beneficiary cost of traditional fee-for-service coverage in an area. The method has been widely criticized as overpaying for healthier beneficiaries, who may have cost the program far less if it had paid only for their specific costs.

"I think the law as currently structured is not likely to generate savings, because of the way it overcompensates," said Karen Davis, president of the Commonwealth Fund, an independent philanthropy that studies health and social issues. "Studies have indicated that every Medicare beneficiary in managed care costs about 6 percent more than one in traditional fee-for-service plans."

Revising the formula would be one way to increase savings, although suggestions to pay providers less may cause some of them to refuse to accept Medicare recipients. Medicare already pays doctors only about 68 percent of what private insurers pay.

Another way would be to allow competitive bidding among managed care plans, a concept that the Health Care Financing Administration has supported.

One way to pressure people to use managed care would be to raise the costs of staying in the traditional fee-for-service program, whether through higher co-payments or higher deductibles for services.

However, the House plan rejects that concept, protecting members from Democratic charges that seniors would be "coerced" into joining HMOs.

A key benefit of managed care, from the federal Treasury standpoint, would be that having a fixed annual payment to a provider would allow the government to better control costs than in the current open-ended program, where expenditures rise to whatever level of services people use. But if large numbers of Medicare recipients choose to remain in the traditional program, an option under the House plan, questions arise about whether any money would be saved.

Concerns about "cream skimming" also have been batted about, a concept that angers the managed care industry.

If insurance companies and other providers somehow select only the healthiest beneficiaries, the critics say,

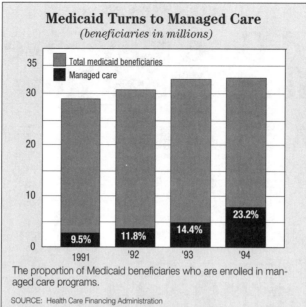

Medicaid Turns to Managed Care
(beneficiaries in millions)

- Total medicaid beneficiaries
- Managed care

	1991	'92	'93	'94
Managed care	9.5%	11.8%	14.4%	23.2%

The proportion of Medicaid beneficiaries who are enrolled in managed care programs.

SOURCE: Health Care Financing Administration

costs of insurance will rise for those remaining in fee-for-service plans. Managed care providers say there is no evidence that such practices exist, and the Republican plan requires that managed-care plans take all Medicare

---

"Our biggest concern is that Congress won't keep the standards high enough, and we'll have some real bad experiences with some fly-by-night plans."

—Carmen Ness,
Pacificare Health Systems

---

beneficiaries who apply if they want to participate. Still, it may be that older and sicker seniors would stay out of managed care plans.

Among other concerns about managed care that may be addressed by the Medicare legislation is the expense of long-term care, how to deal with the small percentage of beneficiaries who account for as much as 50 percent of the costs and how to handle the fact that the costliest part of health care is usually the last few months of life.

"It is reasonable for Medicare to pay the same amount regardless of the nature of the delivery system, so long as — and this is an important qualifer — the payment is adequate without imposing excessive costs for the bene-

ficiaries," Aaron said.

Quality of Care

Finally, health care experts believe Congress also will need to address such issues as the quality of care and its oversight functions if more beneficiaries embrace managed care options.

Maintaining government oversight and attempting to ensure quality are key elements to providing care for beneficiaries, said Diane Rowland, executive director of the Kaiser Commission on the Future of Medicaid.

"We still don't know much about how to monitor quality of care in managed care," she said, noting that managed care keeps costs down by trimming services and minimizing tests. "In many ways, a change to a different system requires greater state oversight and monitoring than in some of the earlier systems where people could vote with their feet. And it comes at the very time we're talking about reducing government involvement."

Carmen Ness, vice president of government relations for Pacificare Health Systems, the nation's largest provider of Medicare managed care with about a half-million beneficiaries in California, Washington, Oregon, Oklahoma and Texas, said his organization supports government scrutiny.

"Our biggest concern is that Congress won't keep the standards high enough, and we'll have some real bad experiences with some fly-by-night plans," he said.

Defenders of the GOP plan say that ultimately, there is little choice about whether the nation must turn to managed care and a host of other options if it wants to stay solvent.

"The White House is saying that it's bad to reform Medicare in the way that the Republicans are proposing, but if you don't reform it largely in the way that the Republicans are proposing, it will be catastrophic for the rest of us," said Robert Moffit, deputy director of domestic policy studies at the conservative Heritage Foundation and a Reagan administration official. "If Gingrich and company do not deliver on their promise to reduce Medicare, the consequences for working American families will dwarf the tax increases they've already endured under this administration." ∎

WELFARE REFORM

Putting Recipients to Work Will Be the Toughest Job

The Republican welfare bills making their way through Congress have three main goals: limit federal spending, hand welfare programs to the states and put welfare recipients to work.

The first two goals can be accomplished by legislative fiat. But putting people to work is more complicated.

Congress can write laws requiring work. It can limit the amount of time that welfare recipients can receive benefits. It can even order states to place a certain percentage of their welfare caseload in jobs. Republicans have put those provisions, and much more, in the welfare overhaul measures (HR 4) approved by the Senate Finance Committee (S Rept 104-96) and passed by the House. *(Weekly Report, pp. 1842, 1747)*

But none of those requirements offer any assurances that more welfare recipients will actually work. And getting them to work is arguably the only way to truly transform the welfare state and meet the public's hopes for reform.

Republicans hope to change the welfare equation by giving states unprecedented control over the programs and relying on them to link welfare recipients to work.

The states have undeniably become the focus of welfare-to-work efforts in the past decade. State experiments have included subsidizing jobs, conditioning benefits on willingness to perform community service, and forcing recipients to sign contracts requiring them to take more responsibility for their lives.

But since 1988, when putting people to work became a main goal of the welfare program, the states have had only modest success. Only about 9 percent of the roughly 5 million adults now receiving Aid to Families with Dependent Children (AFDC), the nation's main cash welfare program, are working.

CQ Weekly Report July 8, 1995

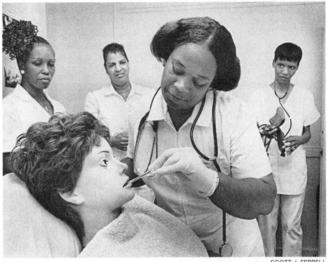

SCOTT J. FERRELL

Mary Rainey practices taking a patient's temperature during class at Vital Management Team Education Center. Her class participates in Project Independence, the Maryland JOBS program.

Improving on that record depends not only on motivating recipients, many welfare experts say, but also on committing sufficient resources to local welfare offices. It is there that, with the proper expertise and wherewithal, welfare recipients can be matched with the jobs, child care and career counseling that can get them into the work force and keep them there.

Most GOP lawmakers believe that getting the federal government out of the way will allow welfare programs to be customized to fit local needs. They also count on motivating welfare recipients by requiring them to work within two years of receiving benefits and denying any welfare checks after five years. In addition, they would set specific work goals for states.

"What we're looking for is an attitudinal change across the entire country," said Rep. E. Clay Shaw Jr., R-Fla., chairman of the House Ways and Means Human Resources Subcommittee and a leading proponent of the House welfare bill. The idea, he said, is to make welfare "not a way of life, but simply a short-term bridge over tough times."

But moving people from welfare to work depends on some elements that cannot be legislated. Time limits and work requirements may be enough to spur some welfare recipients to work, but their jobs might be temporary and the pay insufficient to move them out of poverty or off welfare. For others — especially those who lack skills, job experience and education — the task is more challenging.

Moreover, finding jobs would not be easy even under the best circumstances. "It's not like America needs 5 million single mothers looking for work at the low end of the labor market," said Judith M. Gueron, president of the Manpower Demonstration Research Corp., which evaluates social programs for the disadvantaged.

State efforts to help welfare recipients get jobs and keep them has initially required more money for such things as child care and administrative oversight. Reorienting welfare offices from places that mainly verify eligibility into placement centers for the hard-core unemployed will not be easy.

Even as GOP lawmakers relish the notion of cutting the federal welfare bureaucracy to reduce costs, their hopes of moving welfare recipients into the work force depend partly on spending those funds to reorient local offices.

Lawrence M. Mead, a visiting professor at the Woodrow Wilson School at Princeton University, summed up successful welfare-to-work programs in Wisconsin, pointing out that "reforming welfare may save money on balance, but it requires more bureaucracy rather than less."

And these qualified welfare managers are hard to come by, added Robert Rector, a senior policy analyst at the Heritage Foundation and an influential conservative on this issue among GOP lawmakers.

"A lot of the success of these programs has to come from high-level or midlevel bureaucrats who are committed to making the programs work," Rector said. "We may have a shortage of those."

States Experimenting With Ways ...

All states run welfare-to-work programs as part of the Job Opportunities and Basic Skills (JOBS) program Congress enacted in the Family Support Act of 1988 (PL 100-485). Several states have tried experimental programs to lure welfare recipients into the work force and help them stay there. Here are a few that have had some success:

Iowa

Under Iowa's Family Investment Program, most adult welfare recipients are required to work either full- or part-time, search for a job, enter an education or training program or perform unpaid community service. Those who don't lose benefits.

The program allows welfare recipients who have jobs to earn more than would otherwise be permitted and still keep a large portion of their benefits.

Each family in the program must sign an individually tailored Family Investment Agreement, which specifies the education, training and employment goals its members must meet to continue to receive benefits. For example, one parent may be required to study and take the high school equivalency exam. A high school graduate may be required to take a job training course. The Family Investment Agreement is a binding contract that also says the state will provide such supports as job training and child care.

State figures show that from January 1994 to February 1995, 25,694 families signed agreements and 881 families lost their benefits because they did not sign one. Most of those who do not comply with their agreement lose some benefits after three months and all benefits after six months.

The Iowa Department of Human Services reported that in March 1995, almost one-third of families in the Family Investment Program included someone who was employed — compared with less than one-sixth of families receiving traditional welfare checks in September 1993. That's partially because certain families with earned income now qualify for benefits.

Feedback from clients has been telling, said Douglas Howard, administrator of the Economic Assistance Division for the Department of Human Services. Many families reported that working on the investment agreement was the first time a caseworker had asked about their plans.

California

California's welfare-to-work program, Greater Avenues for Independence (GAIN), views welfare as a two-way street: The state provides job search and training services, subsidized child care and transportation costs for families in the program; certain welfare recipients must participate in GAIN activities — working, job search, education, training — or lose cash benefits.

GAIN, which differs from county to county, has been modestly but notably successful in Riverside and Sonoma counties.

In Riverside, near Los Angeles, GAIN officials emphasize one thing: getting a job.

In Sonoma, outside San Francisco, welfare recipients' monthly checks go directly to employers to subsidize wages for recipients who work.

Riverside. Riverside County encourages GAIN enrollees to get education and training but stresses employment. Program managers try to place clients as soon as they apply for welfare. They do everything they can to help clients get jobs, including reading the want ads. They put enrollees in any job available on the theory that work experience is more important than education or training. Staff workers also can reduce or withhold welfare benefits to clients who do not follow the rules.

Studies by the Manpower Demonstration Research Corp., a nonprofit research organization based in New York, show modest gains in moving Riverside welfare recipients into the work force.

For example, a 1994 study showed that close to one-quarter of participants earned at least $5,000 in their third year in GAIN, compared with less than one-fifth in a Riverside control group.

Sonoma. Sonoma County has implemented a GAIN program known as "grant diversion" that uses cash welfare benefits to subsidize wages for welfare recipients who receive on-the-job training through private employers. The welfare benefits are sent directly to employers for up to nine months.

The program aims to encourage welfare recipients to work and to encourage employers to hire them. It works best with older recipients who have previous work experience.

Sandy Sweitzer, supervisor of vocational counselors in Sonoma's GAIN office, said that of the 88 clients who finished on-the-job training through grant diversion since 1989, only nine are still receiving welfare checks.

Utah

Beyond a standard welfare-to-work program, Utah has a program that gives certain welfare applicants a one-time lump sum — on the theory that the family can

Troubled Program

The federal government's current thinking on welfare-to-work programs is embodied in the Family Support Act of 1988 (PL 100-485). It requires states to run a Job Opportunities and Basic Skills (JOBS) program, providing welfare recipients with work, remedial education and training. *(1988 Almanac, p. 349)*

The law is credited with advancing the idea that in exchange for receiving benefits, welfare recipients must take steps to improve their lives. In practice, though, JOBS has had limited success — partly because of the economy and partly because of flaws in the program.

Never envisioned as a quick fix, the legislation was hampered by the 1990 recession: First, the weak economy contributed to an explosion of welfare rolls. Then the drain on state revenues limited states' ability to pay for education, training and job placement. The welfare rolls also swelled from the continued rise of out-of-wed-

...To Help People Stay Off Welfare

stay off the welfare rolls if it gets emergency help. The one-time payment, equal to as much as three months of cash benefits, can be used to get the family through emergencies such as layoffs, overdue car notes and overdue rent or mortgage payments. This option is typically offered to a parent, usually a woman, who is either working or ready to work. During the three-month period, Utah also provides child care, Medicaid, food stamps and extra cash for needs such as work clothes and baby supplies.

The average payment is about $900. Of 280 families that have received the payments since January 1993, fewer than 40 (13 percent) have since requested regular payments under Aid to Families with Dependent Children (AFDC), according to Office of Family Support Program Specialist William Biggs.

Wisconsin

Wisconsin restructured its welfare program in 1987 to emphasize two things: putting welfare recipients to work and ensuring care for their children. The new approaches include these five programs:

Work First. Work First, implemented in 1994, encourages people to look for alternatives to applying for welfare benefits. Work First counsels would-be AFDC recipients on managing their finances and job-hunting. "The best thing that you can do for a family in terms of helping them get off of AFDC is to help them not need it in the first place," said J. Jean Rogers, administrator of the Division of Economic Support, Department of Health and Social Services.

Parental and Family Responsibility Demonstration Project. This program tries to keep young couples with children together by removing typical disincentives to marriage and working. It targets welfare mothers under 20 who are first-time parents and the fathers of their children.

The parents receive help with family planning, parenting skills and job searches. The project encourages marriage between the young parents by allowing certain couples — married or single — to receive welfare bene-

SONOMA COUNTY GAIN PROGRAM

Lisa Davenport works as a chart-room attendant at Kaiser Permanente after getting help from Sonoma County's Greater Avenues for Independence.

fits. The parents receive higher benefits if they stay together than if the mother applies alone. Couples are also given incentives to work. For example, they can earn more than is usually allowed without losing benefits.

The project also discourages the couple from having more children while on welfare by stipulating that benefits do not increase after the second child.

Work Not Welfare. An experiment in Pierce and Fond du Lac counties, Work Not Welfare requires welfare recipients to sign an agreement to work for their benefits, which are initially limited to two years. Within 30 days, recipients must take unsubsidized or partially subsidized jobs, community service positions or education and training.

Education and training can last no longer than 12 months, after which the recipient must work in a private-sector job for pay or for the government in exchange for benefits. After receiving two years of benefits, Work Not Welfare families are ineligible for three years.

Children First. The Children First program tries to enable fathers to pay child support by helping them get jobs. Under the program, a non-custodial parent — usually the father — can have his wages partially withheld when a child support order is established.

The program also provides job training and search services.

In 1993, 6,400 families got off welfare because fathers paid child support regularly, Wisconsin officials said.

Learnfare. Wisconsin developed this program to encourage welfare recipients to graduate from high school, thereby increasing their employability.

Learnfare reduces welfare benefits for teenage mothers and welfare children ages 13 to 19 who do not attend school regularly. The state provides support services such as child care and transportation subsidies.

In the one-year period from 1992 to 1993, 97 percent of Learnfare teens complied with school attendance requirements, and others lost benefits.

lock births which, particularly among teenagers, is often associated with long-term stays on welfare.

Some analysts have also faulted the JOBS programs themselves. A General Accounting Office (GAO) report released in May said most JOBS programs failed to move welfare recipients to work. Local administrators cited insufficient staff and resources, as well as recipients' discouragement about taking low-paying jobs. They also said they wanted more flexibility to subsidize jobs and give recipients more on-the-job experience.

The report also concluded that many JOBS programs "emphasize preparing participants for employment without also making strong efforts to help them get jobs."

Some states have conducted welfare experiments by obtaining waivers from federal laws, an approach that started under President Ronald Reagan and then accelerated. These waivers have, for example, given certain states more leeway to impose time limits on benefits and to transform AFDC or food stamp benefits into wage subsidies.

"Despite very cumbersome federal laws and waiver processes, the states have been leaders in the last decade in changing public welfare from a 50-year-old program in income maintenance toward one that has a new goal of self-sufficiency and reducing dependence," said A. Sidney Johnson III, executive director of the American Public Welfare Association, which represents state social service departments and local welfare agencies.

The nation's most widely heralded JOBS program is in Riverside County, Calif. Single-parent participants in the program there earned an average of $3,562 a year, or 40 percent more per person than those not in the program, according to a 1994 study by Manpower. Because of these earnings, the state reduced annual AFDC payments to participants by an average of $584, paying them 17 percent less than those not in JOBS.

Among the keys to Riverside's success, Gueron said, were getting welfare recipients into jobs quickly, relying heavily on job searches, strictly enforcing participation rules and maintaining close links to area businesses.

A subsequent study released July 7 by Manpower found that participants in JOBS programs in Riverside, Atlanta and Grand Rapids, Mich., which strongly emphasized immediate employment, needed 22 percent less in AFDC benefits and 14 percent less in food stamps than those not in JOBS programs. Participants also were 24 percent more likely to be employed and had 26 percent higher earnings than others.

Even so, Gueron has cautioned lawmakers that large numbers of welfare recipients across the country are unlikely to move quickly into the work force. Many welfare recipients will be unable to earn enough to get off welfare, she said, and those who do work can easily lose their jobs. Others, perhaps one-quarter of welfare recipients, lack the skills, experience or stability to maintain unsubsidized jobs.

Can States Get the Job Done?

Under the GOP welfare bills, states would be given broad flexibility to use federal money to help find jobs for welfare recipients. But how they would use these funds is unclear.

Federal welfare money now essentially goes to states in two pots. One provides welfare checks, mainly

UTAH DEPARTMENT OF HUMAN SERVICES

Former welfare recipient Lori Sather now works as a graduate program assistant at the University of Utah.

through AFDC. The federal share of AFDC benefits and administrative costs was $14.1 billion in fiscal 1994; states paid $11.9 billion.

Another fund provides matching funds to states to run job training and placement programs through JOBS. That amounted to $786 million in federal funds and $514 million in state money in fiscal 1994.

The House and Senate GOP welfare bills would consolidate these funds, so that states would receive one block grant from which to provide checks and pay for work programs. The House version of HR 4 would consolidate AFDC and three related programs into a block grant worth $15.4 billion annually for five years. The Senate version would consolidate AFDC and six related programs into a $16.8 billion block grant.

But under those circumstances, states might give work programs short shrift. It would be cheaper, at least in the short run, to hand checks to welfare recipients than to provide what they might need to help them get jobs: placement assistance, child care, wage subsidies, and remedial education or training. The Finance Committee bill, but not the House bill, would require states to provide child care to welfare recipients who have children younger than 6 and who need it to work.

Money is a critical element in helping welfare recipients find work, said Mark S. Greenberg, a senior staff attorney at the Center for Law and Social Policy, a liberal public research group. States already can require nearly 80 percent of welfare recipients to take part in a JOBS program,

Greenberg said, but only about 13 percent participate.

"The principal barrier to expanding JOBS participation has not been federal rules," he said. "It has been the cost of increasing the number of participants."

How then can states be expected to react to a welfare system with restraints on federal funding and time limits on benefits? Or as Gueron put it, "Under fiscal pressure and with a short time horizon, will states make the upfront investments that we know can produce the longer term savings?"

No, according to the nonpartisan Congressional Budget Office (CBO). It concluded that 44 states would be unable to place half their welfare caseload into work or training programs by fiscal 2001, as required by the Senate Finance Committee bill.

John W. Tapogna, a CBO analyst, told the Finance Committee on May 26 that most states would simply accept a reduction of up to 5 percent of their welfare block grant rather than meet the work requirement.

Other observers say there are limits to the effectiveness of even well-funded work programs, and they say only a tough approach will get people off welfare.

Rector of the Heritage Foundation played down the importance of job preparation programs such as JOBS, saying that states respond best to requirements that they find work for a certain percentage of welfare recipients. Beyond that, he said, the only sure way to reduce welfare is to minimize the number of out-of-wedlock births that lead families into poverty.

Gary Burtless, a senior fellow at the Brookings Institution, noted the limited success of the approaches used in Riverside. Even if they were duplicated across the country, he said, "I would not anticipate lots and lots of people moving off the rolls." That, Burtless said, would be accomplished by time limits on benefits.

How Best to Find Jobs

Republicans are counting on the time limits and work requirements to motivate welfare recipients, creating a stronger expectation that they find jobs. That leaves open the question of the proper route for welfare recipients — gaining experience by accepting the first job offer or gaining skills through training and education.

To some extent, welfare recipients

can be motivated by higher expectations. Johnson said that in Oregon, for example, case workers are instructed to ask from the outset, "How can I help you get a job?" rather than trying primarily to verify eligibility for benefits. "It sounds like not a big difference," Johnson said. "But it sets up quite different expectations."

Elsewhere, welfare recipients are being challenged to take practical steps to improve themselves even if they might be unable to hold a full-time job.

In inner-city Chicago, a welfare-to-work program known as Project Match assumes that all welfare recipients can help themselves. Working mainly with residents of the Cabrini-Green public housing development, Project Match helps recipients with even the barest job skills become more self-sufficient. It encourages them to become better parents and to do volunteer work if they are unprepared for full-time jobs, and it gives wide discretion to caseworkers.

"We feel people should be doing something," said Toby Herr, director of Project Match. "What they should do should be flexible." Caseworkers assist welfare recipients even after they obtain jobs, because many recipients quit their jobs or are fired after the first setback at home or at work.

Project Match stresses practical experience as a stepping stone toward working, rather than emphasizing education. "If they saw there was a link between education and income," Herr said, "they would have stayed in school in the first place."

That sentiment seems to fit with the growing sense that education and training are less important than gaining on-the-job experience as quickly as possible. "If people have failed conspicuously to prosper in school between the ages of 6 and 18," Burtless said, "the notion that when they're 25 they're suddenly going to be receptive and able to absorb a good education is far-fetched."

But Greenberg said that point can be overstated. He maintained that education and training can improve the earnings of welfare recipients, particularly for those who already have some work experience.

He cited evidence from the Manpower study of California's JOBS program. Riverside County, which emphasized work, increased the employment

Fixing a Schedule

Senate Republican leaders have talked about sending the welfare overhaul bill (HR 4) to the floor the week of July 17, but that is contingent upon resolving fierce intraparty disputes over the measure's funding formula, work requirements and lack of provisions aimed at decreasing out-of-wedlock births.

Those arguments, which erupted soon after the Finance Committee finished work on its bill May 26, already forced one postponement of floor action, which was initially set for June 14.

If the Senate does not pass a free-standing bill before the August recess, the bill's major components may be rolled into the omnibus budget reconciliation bill in September. Doing so would still require Republicans to agree among themselves on key points.

rate of welfare recipients — but not necessarily their pay. By contrast, a JOBS program in Alameda County that relied more on vocational training and post-secondary education had more success than Riverside in increasing earnings.

"It is important to continue to focus on approaches that can raise the earnings and reduce the poverty of families," Greenberg said. "The idea of 'work first' may be entirely appropriate for a parent with little or no work history. But many of the parents who enter the welfare system have substantial prior work experience but in low-wage jobs with little mobility."

Are Recipients Employable?

Ultimately, the question becomes: How many welfare recipients are likely to become permanently employed? Can the labor market even absorb a large number of them?

"Yes," said Mead, the Princeton welfare analyst, "provided it's not done overnight." He said the labor market could stretch to accommodate new employees, though many jobs would be low paying. But he acknowledged that analysts "really don't know how many of the mothers are employable because we haven't tried to make them work until recently, and only in certain localities."

Mead said he is unsure whether welfare recipients are likely to earn enough to get off welfare, something that is nominally easier to do in states with low welfare benefits such as Mississippi (where a mother and two children can get up to $120 monthly) than in states with high benefits such as California (where they can get up to $607).

Shaw expressed confidence that jobs were available to most of those who want one. "I'm always hearing from people who can't fill $5- and $6-an-hour jobs," he said. "The reason is people who know how to really game the system can get a lot more from welfare."

Burtless has said that most labor economists believe that employers could find work for 2 million to 3 million AFDC recipients, especially if they were willing to accept low-wage jobs with few fringe benefits.

Overall, Burtless said that about a quarter or more of the welfare mothers who would be pushed into the work force when their benefits ran out would succeed in maintaining a job, earning at least as much as they now receive on welfare.

But about half the mothers pushed off welfare would be worse off than they are now, earning less than they now get on welfare.

And another one-quarter of recipients are "going to be in such severe difficulty that they will have to give up their children or, in trying to keep their families together, they will spend time as homeless people."

It is the thought of this last group — of welfare mothers and their children sent into the streets to fend for themselves — that energizes liberal critics of the GOP approach. They say that states would find it cheaper to withhold job assistance and simply drop welfare recipients from the rolls when they hit the time limit rather than help them get jobs.

Rector maintains that public pressure will keep that from happening to any large degree. "The ability of states to kick highly dependent people off the rolls is highly limited," he said, because widespread media coverage of hapless welfare recipients would stop officials from neglecting them.

But clearly not all welfare recipients will find jobs, something that Shaw acknowledged would be particularly true in poverty-stricken areas.

"In some areas this is going to be a problem," Shaw said. "We're going to have to monitor the situation very closely, particularly where you've got large pockets of unemployment and poverty in the inner cities."

And in words rarely used this year by key Republicans as they talk about welfare, Shaw said that dealing with the situation in these neighborhoods would be "a federal responsibility." ■

AGRICULTURE

In Farm Debate, GOP Risks Cultivating Enemies

Budget cutters must decide whether to take on one of their most important constituencies

Now comes the time for budget-slashing Republicans to decide whether to wield the knife at programs that benefit one of their core constituencies: farmers.

Soon, Agriculture subcommittees will begin marking up the farm bill, a sprawling piece of legislation that governs policy on farm subsidies, soil conservation and nutrition programs. The legislation is so byzantine that lawmakers tackle it only about twice a decade, typically reauthorizing the controversial programs for five years.

It already is threatening to shatter GOP unity this year and complicate the legislative agenda until the late fall.

Central issues to be debated include rewarding farmers who grow designated crops, protecting agricultural wetlands, and spending billions to promote food exports. The bill could have far-reaching effects on consumer prices, America's trade deficit and the jobs of the one in six American workers employed in the agriculture sector.

The policy debate will focus on technical economic issues, but the biggest question appears to be political. Will the ascendant Republicans, who voted for cuts in such Democratic-backed programs as welfare and environmental regulations, be willing to take on one of their most important constituencies?

The debate puts congressional Republicans in a delicate position, as they try to demonstrate their commitment to fiscal austerity without driving rural voters into the Democratic fold.

"The Republicans have been talking about cutting pork and so forth, and there's not a bigger waste of taxpayer dollars and transference of wealth than the periodic farm bills," said Edward L. Hudgins, director of regulatory studies at the conservative Cato Institute and one of the most outspoken critics of farm programs.

PATT CHISHOLM

CQ Weekly Report June 24, 1995

Defying conservative analysts who back them on other issues, some of the most stalwart Republicans argue that farm programs stimulate the economy and guarantee Americans an abundant supply of inexpensive food.

"The great challenge is to move toward a balanced budget and at the same time preserve those programs that are really important," said Sen. Thad Cochran, R-Miss., chairman of the agriculture subcommittee of the Senate Appropriations Committee. "Our commodity-support programs work well for America and need to be continued."

Lawmakers don't have the luxury of doing nothing. The provisions of the 1990 farm bill will expire this year and would be superseded by underlying farm laws of the 1930s and 1940s if Congress doesn't take action. That could result in chaos for the agriculture economy, potentially requiring the government to virtually double its support prices for certain commodities, while forcing some farmers to drastically cut production.

This year's debate cuts across party lines, with rural lawmakers of both parties forming traditional alliances to try to protect crop subsidies that date back to the 1930s. But the deficit-cutting tide now sweeping through the Capitol is threatening to put an end to the programs, which have cost an estimated $55 billion in the last five years.

The farm programs are in the cross-hairs of groups that span the political spectrum, including free-market conservatives, consumer advocates and environmentalists. Even a smattering of farmers are demanding major changes, saying that government policies are squeezing family farms and harming American exports.

If those policies were abruptly swept away, however, veteran agriculture lobbyists warn that rural America would be devastated. Farmers could be knocked out of business by their subsidized counterparts overseas, they say, ratcheting up food prices and threatening agriculture jobs across the nation.

Presidential politics also are intruding into the legislative picture, with President Clinton and two prominent challengers — Senate Majority Leader Bob Dole, R-Kan., and Senate Agriculture Committee Chairman Richard G. Lugar, R-Ind. — all staking out prominent and sometimes conflicting positions in the debate.

For those keeping score, much of the action may take place outside the farm bill reauthorization process. That is because both the budget-reconciliation and the appropriations bills are likely to get ensnared in the debate over farm subsidies, since farm spending is a key budget issue.

Amid the swirling currents of politics and budget cuts, farm bill markups that were scheduled for the week of June 26 now have been postponed until July.

Whatever the scenario, lawmakers are bracing for a repeat of 1985, when the farm bill was not signed into law until Dec. 23.

"It's really going to be a wild process through the rest of the year," said Charles Benbrook, an agricultural consultant who is monitoring the debate.

The Major Programs

The federal government began intervening in the farm economy during the Depression, when commodity prices were in a disastrous slump and farm income averaged about half that of non-farm families. Starting with the Agriculture Adjustment Act of 1933, one of the first major pieces of New Deal legislation, Washington began to try to prop up prices by cutting supplies of basic commodities.

At the time, Agriculture Secretary Henry A. Wallace wrote that government payments to farmers who plowed under crops and slaughtered surplus livestock were "but a temporary method for dealing with an emergency."

But getting out of the farm business proved more difficult than getting into it. The government remains as deeply involved as ever in curtailing supplies of commodities to control the market, and the scope of farm legislation has expanded beyond basic commodities to include nutrition and conservation programs. Nearly 60 years after that first New Deal legislation, the approximately 750-page 1990 farm bill encompassed 25 titles, governing use of the nation's 435 million acres of cropland.

The total agriculture budget this year is $63 billion, of which $8 to $10 billion goes for farm subsidies and related programs depending on market conditions.

The major components of the nation's farm policy include:

● **Payments to farmers.** To guarantee farmers a return on their crops, the government sets a "target price" for wheat, cotton, rice and feed grains such as corn. In general, when market prices are depressed, the government pays farmers the difference between the price they received for their crop and the target price. This is known as a deficiency payment.

● **Price supports.** The government props up the income of the producers of certain crops, such as peanuts, tobacco and sugar, by giving them non-recourse loans and establishing marketing quotas or allotments that limit supply. If the producers cannot pay back the loans, they hold on to the money and forfeit the crop to the government instead.

● **Supply control.** The government gives incentives to farmers who set aside a portion of their land, thereby cutting supply and raising the price of commodities. The land may either be diverted for a different crop than it is normally used for, or idled altogether.

● **Exports.** The government, to boost demand for American crops, helps food companies market their products overseas and subsidizes the sale of certain commodities. It also assists countries that are short on cash to obtain credit to buy American agricultural products

● **Conservation.** To curb soil erosion and water contamination, the government pays farmers to idle environmentally sensitive land and restricts production in wetland areas. The government also provides funding to farmers who build projects on their land to prevent the loss of soil and water.

The goal of these policies is to shield farmers from the vagaries of weather and the marketplace, thereby keeping them in business and assuring the country of a stable food supply. Nonetheless, analysts debate whether the programs are continuing to do much good.

On the positive side, the programs have helped make

Total Farm Assets and Liabilities

USDA

The government began boosting crop prices during the Depression, when farmers were being driven off their land by dust storms and disastrously low prices. Even though government intervention was seen as a "temporary method for dealing with an emergency," the government continues to intervene in the agricultural economy.

Farmers have enjoyed considerable stability over the last 10 years. Thanks to growing markets, total farm assets have climbed to about $930 billion, while debt has dropped to about $150 billion.

SOURCE: USDA

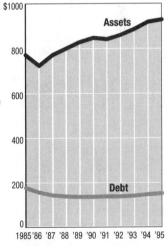

MARILYN GATES-DAVIS

commodities so accessible that Americans pay only about 10 percent of their disposable income for food. That is virtually the lowest rate of any nation in the world, although part of the reason is the high level of American income, rather than the low cost of food, according to the Congressional Research Service.

Even with programs to protect the environment and restrain production, the United States will export an estimated $49 billion of agricultural products this year, generating a $20 billion trade surplus. In addition, the government spreads

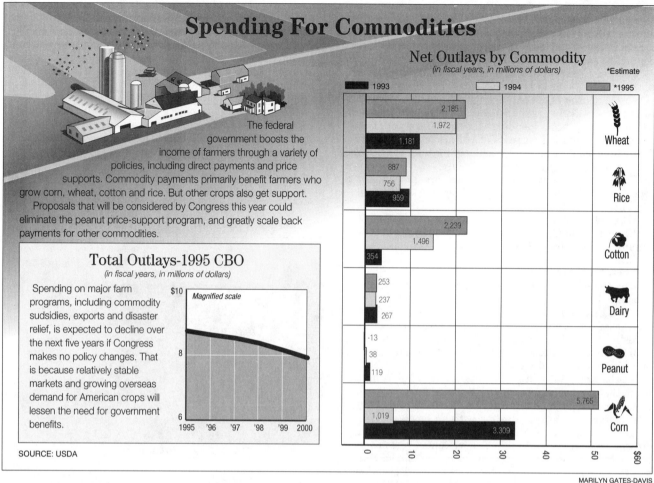

Spending For Commodities

The federal government boosts the income of farmers through a variety of policies, including direct payments and price supports. Commodity payments primarily benefit farmers who grow corn, wheat, cotton and rice. But other crops also get support. Proposals that will be considered by Congress this year could eliminate the peanut price-support program, and greatly scale back payments for other commodities.

Net Outlays by Commodity
(in fiscal years, in millions of dollars)

■ 1993   □ 1994   ▨ *1995   *Estimate

Wheat: 2,185 / 1,972 / 1,181
Rice: 887 / 756 / 959
Cotton: 2,239 / 1,496 / 354
Dairy: 253 / 237 / 267
Peanut: -13 / 38 / 119
Corn: 5,765 / 1,019 / 3,309

Total Outlays-1995 CBO
(in fiscal years, in millions of dollars)

Spending on major farm programs, including commodity sudsidies, exports and disaster relief, is expected to decline over the next five years if Congress makes no policy changes. That is because relatively stable markets and growing overseas demand for American crops will lessen the need for government benefits.

Magnified scale — $10 / 8 / 6 — 1995 '96 '97 '98 '99 2000

SOURCE: USDA

MARILYN GATES-DAVIS

goodwill by donating food to famine-ravaged countries.

Growers, aided by government-sponsored research and more consolidated farm operations, are becoming increasingly efficient. Each farmer and rancher produces enough food and fiber to feed 129 other people, compared to just 19 in 1940, according to statistics compiled by Rep. George Nethercutt, R-Wash.

And the farm economy, which suffered wild swings and massive bankruptcies in the early and mid-1980s, is now back on solid footing. Total farm debt, for example, declined by about 17 percent between 1985 and 1994, while total farm equity reached $772 billion, an increase of about 30 percent.

Armed with such statistics, backers strongly praise the farm programs. Agriculture Secretary Dan Glickman characterized them as "the extraordinary success story of American agriculture"; Nethercutt credited them with extending the average American life span by a third.

But there is also a down side that has attracted the attention of powerful business groups and government auditors. And at least two farmers in Congress, Lugar and Rep. Cal Dooley, D-Calif., say the programs are seriously flawed.

Critics say that, far from helping family farmers, the programs have squeezed them to the point where farmers constitute less than 2 percent of the population today, compared with a fourth in the 1930s.

That is because the subsidies primarily benefit large landowners, some of whom exploit loopholes to earn hundreds of thousands of dollars in government payments every

year, according to groups such as the Progressive Foundation, a public policy center affiliated with moderate Democrats. This has the effect of distorting land values, enriching farmers who already have an average net worth of $300,000 or more and undermining the family farmers who were the original beneficiaries of the Depression-era programs.

Furthermore, the programs are driving up the price of commodities such as peanuts and sugar by hundreds of millions of dollars a year, according to General Accounting Office estimates.

This means that taxpayers, already footing the bill for federal farm programs, are getting hit a second time at the supermarket checkout line.

Analysts with the U.S. Chamber of Commerce also warn that the programs are undercutting American exports by requiring farmers to set aside land and plant the rest with crops supported by government programs, rather than those that are in demand overseas.

Even though consumer advocates and urban liberals are heaping scorn on the farm programs, perhaps the harshest rhetoric of all is coming from free-market conservatives.

House Majority Leader Dick Armey, R-Texas, denounced the "staggering waste and inefficiency" of the programs, likening them to failed Soviet attempts to control supply and demand. And in his 1991 book, "Parliament of Whores," conservative humorist P. J. O'Rourke tartly recommended, "Drag the omnibus farm bill behind the barn, and kill it with an ax."

The Political Calculus

At first glance, the political landscape this year would appear to be hostile for the farm programs.

For one thing, farm-area representatives are outnumbered in the 435-member House. There are only 76 to 110 rural congressional districts, based on differing estimates by the Agriculture Department and the Congressional Rural Caucus.

Moreover, the GOP leadership is insisting on unprecedented spending cuts in agriculture and other programs in a bid to balance the budget by 2002. Conservative Republicans have been cool to farm programs since President Reagan tried unsuccessfully to scale them back in 1981, although he later changed course and proposed expanded policies.

But farmers have been beating the political odds for at least a decade, and it appears to be too early to count them out this year. That's because Republicans may not be able to afford swinging a hatchet at farm programs.

"Agriculture is important to us as a party," said Saxby Chambliss, R-Ga., a freshman who has lobbied House Speaker Newt Gingrich, R-Ga., and other House leaders to protect farm programs.

The GOP has a narrow majority in both the House and Senate, and rural Republicans openly worry that they may have trouble holding on to their seats if the farm programs are gutted. They are only too aware that their party lost its majority in the Senate in 1986 partly because proposed cuts in the 1985 farm bill spurred an anti-Republican backlash in rural states.

Indeed, senior members of both parties appear to be maneuvering for the farm vote. President Clinton has advocated a farm bill that would "do no harm," and Gingrich also has indicated a concern over the farm vote.

"The goal is to make sure that as we get to the ideal policy, we don't do damage to the agriculture sector in the process," said a Gingrich spokesman, Tony Blankley. "If your policies were to do damage to the agriculture sector, you would deserve to be punished at the polls."

In the Senate, Dole is one of the biggest defenders of farm programs. He has discussed rolling them into the budget reconciliation bill, which could shield them from hostile floor amendments, but Lugar and House Agriculture Committee Chairman Pat Roberts, R-Kan., are anticipating a separate farm bill.

Party politics aside, a study this month by the nonpartisan watchdog group Center for Responsive Politics demonstrated the financial clout of the farm lobby. Agriculture political action committees (PACS) made $15.5 million in campaign contributions in the 1993-94 election cycle, which ranked third among business PACs, the study concluded.

Displaying their muscle, rural lawmakers in both chambers have won an impressive string of early skirmishes in recent months.

First, Roberts won concessions from the House Budget Committee, persuading committee Chairman John R. Kasich, R-Ohio, in May to recommend no more than $9 billion in farm cuts over the next five years. That was significantly lower than a preliminary figure of at least $11 billion.

Then, Roberts won a written guarantee that the House would re-examine the farm cuts in two years if rural land values declined. "We know that farmers and ranchers have been among the strongest supporters of the kind of federal fiscal responsibility we are undertaking," stated a May 17 letter Gingrich and Kasich sent to Roberts.

The Senate Budget Committee adopted a non-binding amendment by Charles E. Grassley, R-Iowa, that would limit farm cuts to about $5.5 billion over the next five years. *(Weekly Report, p. 1316)*

Senate staffers said they could meet such cuts without making major changes to farm programs.

The budget resolutions, however, call for steeper cuts in 2001 and 2002 to achieve a balanced budget.

Without any change in policy, the Congressional Budget Office has estimated that farm programs would cost about $41 billion over the next five years. Part of the reason that farm spending would be less than in the past five years is that the agriculture economy is stable, reducing the need for the deficiency payments that make up for low market prices.

The success of rural legislators is not surprising, given that they are under heavy pressure by some of their con-

REUTERS

During his visit to Montana in early June, President Clinton talks to a farmer after touring a wheat field near Billings.

stituents to fight for federal dollars.

"A lot of it is the consequence of ideology bumping up against political reality," said former Rep. Timothy J. Penny (1983-1995), a Minnesota Democrat who has called for a revision of farm programs. "Legislators who largely believe the federal government is big, fat and out of control now are coming to the defense of farm programs because that's the one goverment program that affects their constituency."

A Long-Term Battle

But farm advocates are not yet out of the woods. Even if they can meet the budget guidelines, they still face a ferocious floor fight over the programs.

This year's assault on farm subsidies, curiously enough, was begun by the chairman of the Senate Agriculture, Nutrition and Forestry Committee. Lugar, himself a corn and soybean farmer, set the stage in February for a fiery battle over farm spending by proposing to eliminate an export subsidy program and reduce target prices. His plan would save nearly $15 billion over five years. *(Weekly Report, p. 522)*

It was immediately denounced by members of his own committee. Sen. Kent Conrad, D-N.D., said the plan would lead to "mass bankruptcy" among North Dakota wheat farmers.

Lugar, however, is refusing to back down. He said his proposals would create a more market-oriented farm policy, and he may take them to the Senate floor if they are rejected by his committee.

In the House, a bipartisan coalition led by Charles E. Schumer, D-N.Y., and Dick Zimmer, R-N.J., is going Lugar one better by calling for a complete phaseout of deficiency payments over five years. The proposal would save $29 billion by 2002, they say.

In addition, the two congressmen want to end the sugar and peanuts price support programs and the Market Promotion Program, which helps advertising efforts by companies seeking to expand their overseas sales of U.S. food products. Zimmer conceded that his proposal may be too radical a step for Congress to take this year, but he said it may stir up support for Lugar's comparatively moderate plan. "Our pro-

The vastly differing views of Roberts, left, and Lugar could delay passage of the farm bill for months.

posal to phase out the programs completely is one end of the spectrum of the debate," he said. "By introducing our proposal, we are, I hope, changing the tone of the debate to help Lugar."

Other lawmakers, such as Richard J. Durbin, D-Ill., have said they may propose doing away with the tobacco price-support program, which is controversial even though it is not up for reauthorization. Other proposals are being floated by California's Dooley, a grower of cotton and other crops, who wants to cut subsidies and expand America's export markets.

Rural lawmakers are clearly nervous over the coming floor fights, which are likely to erupt in the late summer or early fall. Roberts said he may remove two titles from the farm bill, which govern research and credit issues, in part because there doesn't seem to be enough time to push through a complete farm bill.

One major problem for farm bill supporters is the unraveling of the longtime alliance between urban liberals who supported nutrition programs and rural conservatives who supported farm subsidies. Unlike past years, when the groups worked together to enact controversial programs, they are now at odds because of Republican efforts to cut welfare and food stamps.

Sen. Patrick J. Leahy of Vermont, the ranking Democrat on the Senate Agriculture Committee, said he will propose doing away with farm subsidies to large farmers unless Republicans restore some funding to nutrition programs. Both farm and nutrition programs compete for the same pot of money in the Agriculture Department's budget.

"If I have to choose between very wealthy farm interests and needy children, I am going to pick children every time," Leahy wrote in a June 6 letter to Lugar.

Leahy predicted that amendments to cut benefits to large farmers would win approval on the Senate floor.

A Market-Driven Program

In order to steer a farm bill through Congress this year,

members of the Agriculture committees believe that they have to create a more market-oriented farm policy that would encourage farmers to plant for growing export markets.

One proposal under discussion is a "total acreage base" that would give farmers the flexibility to plant a variety of crops and still receive deficiency payments. Under current law, by contrast, farmers who have used their land historically to plant a certain subsidized crop generally have to keep planting that same crop.

The proposal is backed by Clinton as well as a number of rural legislators in the Midwest and West. But the powerful cotton lobby opposes it because of concerns that more farmers will plant cotton, depressing the market.

Another proposal would do away with "acreage reduction programs" that reward farmers for idling land. Although this is a top priority of agribusinesses that export commodities, it may not win congressional approval, due to a preliminary CBO estimate that it would cost the government $8.7 billion over five years in higher deficiency payments. CBO revised its estimate down to $6.6 billion after Roberts and other agriculture leaders complained that the earlier figure misjudged market conditions.

To protect the embattled peanuts program, both Clinton and rural lawmakers are looking at ways to make the program self-supporting, possibly by charging assessments on peanut growers.

The committees also will discuss various environmental proposals, such as paring back the 36.4 million acre Conservation Reserve Program, which pays farmers to take environmentally sensitive land out of production. In addition, lawmakers also have said they will consider changes to wetlands regulations, possibly narrowing the definition of a wetland to allow farmers to plow on more of their land. *(Weekly Report, p. 1631)*

Indeed, Roberts said one of his top priorities is to ease environmental and other regulatory restrictions on farmers. He believes this will help make farms more profitable, compensating growers for subsidy cuts.

"If the farm bill is going to be more market-oriented on the dollar side, it will also have to be more market-oriented on the regulatory side," he said.

The committee will also have to make deep cuts in spending as outlined in the budget resolution.

One possibility would be to reduce target prices, although farm groups generally want target prices maintained.

Another, more politically popular way to achieve savings may be to increase the amount of acres that are not covered by government subsidies. *(Weekly Report, p. 1316)*

If the committees can craft a bill that cuts spending and helps farmers compete in the global marketplace, farm lobbyists are hopeful that it could withstand a floor assault.

"If it's a palatable budget number to the rest of Congress, I don't think they care what the programs per se look like," said Chandler Keys, senior director of congressional relations for the National Cattlemen's Association. "I don't see a lot of people running around saying we need to radically alter the way the corn program works." ∎

Prayer Amendment Unlikely Despite Push From Right

Press of business and lack of deep GOP support make constitutional change a long shot

When 10-year-old Joshua Burton brought a Bible to his Orange County, Fla., elementary school last March, a teacher told him he had violated the Constitution's provisions on the separation of church and state.

The school's principal told the fourth-grader that he could bring his Bible to school if he read it silently and did not discuss it with anyone. But two days later, he was expelled after two other students complained that he had been reading his Bible before school.

"All I could think of doing was just to sit at my desk and cry," Joshua said during a June 23 House Judiciary subcommittee hearing in Tampa, Fla.

Citing a long list of similar incidents around the country, a growing chorus of conservatives is calling for a constitutional amendment to allow free religious expression at schools, the display of religious symbols and student-initiated group prayer during sports contests, graduation ceremonies and other events.

With Republicans controlling Congress, proponents of school prayer believe they have their best chance ever of returning organized religious expression to public places. Prominent GOP House members such as Majority Leader Dick Armey of Texas and Judiciary Committee Chairman Henry J. Hyde of Illinois have expressed support for the cause.

But despite the momentum provided by the GOP electoral sweep in November, an effort to promote school prayer through a constitutional amendment is still a long shot.

Working against it is a calendar crowded with other measures that are

ST. PETERSBURG TIMES

At a hearing in Tampa on June 23, Joshua Burton told lawmakers he was expelled for bringing a Bible to school.

higher congressional priorities. And, for all the high-profile advocates, support for a constitutional amendment to restore school prayer does not run very deep among members.

Democrats are nearly unanimous in opposition to an amendment, contending that it is unnecessary at best and could discourage the expression of minority religions. President Clinton also is opposed.

And many Republicans are ambivalent, questioning either the need for an amendment or the potential risks in alienating moderates in their party.

"Congress reacts to complaints that are brought to us by our constituents around the country," Rep. F. James Sensenbrenner Jr., R-Wis., said during the hearing in Tampa. But "I sure would like to have the solution

fall short of a constitutional amendment," he added.

Legislative Outlook

Several drafts of a proposed amendment encouraging school prayer are circulating on Capitol Hill. The most prominent are two almost identical drafts proposed by the Traditional Values Coalition, a grass-roots church lobbying organization based in Anaheim, Calif., and by Focus on the Family, a media ministry based in Colorado Springs, Colo. Both would state that religious expression in schools or other public places could not be abridged by states or the federal government.

The drafts also state that the free exercise of religion under an amended Constitution would not constitute establishment of an official religion.

Adopting a constitutional amendment requires a two-thirds vote of the House and Senate and approval by three-quarters, or 38, of the states.

Michael W. McConnell, a University of Chicago law professor who helped draft the Focus on the Family proposal, said in an interview that an amendment is needed because religion has been incrementally squeezed out of public life as the government's influence has increased over time. Ultimately, he said, "that area of life that had been pluralistic, all of a sudden it becomes secularized."

GOP conservative Rep. Ernest Jim Istook Jr. of Oklahoma plans to propose a measure similar to the amendment he introduced just before the 1994 elections. That bill stated that nothing in the Constitution could be construed to prohibit individual or group prayer in schools and other public institutions. The amendment also said that no person would be re-

CQ Weekly Report July 8, 1995

Major Decisions on School Prayer

A Supreme Court ruling in 1963 that banned mandatory, government-sponsored school prayer marked the end of an era in which Bible readings, devotional exercises and prayer were common in public school classrooms across the nation.

In that case, *School District of Abington Township v. Schempp*, the court cited a violation of the Constitution's Establishment Clause, finding that such exercises infringed on the religious rights of some students, and in some instances, could tend to advance certain religions over others.

Cases challenging prayer in the schools and at graduation ceremonies have been brought repeatedly in subsequent years. But the outcomes have varied, leading to some confusion about what the law allows.

As recently as June 26, for example, the Supreme Court dismissed a federal appeals court ruling that had held in *Joint District No. 241 v. Harris* that student-led prayer at a public school graduation is unconstitutional. The court, however, did not address the question of whether students should be allowed to pray at such events.

Listed below are several of the Supreme Court's major decisions regarding prayer in public schools.

● *Engel v. Vitale* (1962): By a 6-1 vote, the Supreme Court reversed a lower court's ruling and found that the New York State Board of Regents had violated the Establishment Clause by recommending that school districts adopt a specific non-denominational prayer to be recited by public school students at the beginning of each school day. Writing for the majority, Justice Hugo Black found that such government sponsorship might have a coercive effect on students to conform, even if they or their families were opposed to such a prayer.

● *School District of Abington Township v. Schempp* (1963): One year after *Engel,* the court, by an 8-1 vote, banned government-sponsored Bible reading and recitation of the Lord's Prayer, both of which were routinely practiced in the public schools in Pennsylvania and Baltimore. The court found that both violated the Establishment Clause and were therefore unconstitutional. A constitutional amendment to overturn the decision was introduced in the House shortly thereafter, but died in committee.

● *Lemon v. Kurtzman* (1971): The court ruled, 8-0, that government funding of secular education programs in private or parochial schools led to unavoidable entanglement of religious and secular purposes, thereby violating the Establishment Clause.

● *Wallace v. Jaffree* (1985): The court struck down, 6-3, a 1981 Alabama law that required up to one minute of silence for the purposes of meditating or engaging in voluntary prayer. The court ruled that the Alabama law violated the Establishment Clause because its clear intent was to restore prescribed prayer to the public schools.

● *Lee v. Weisman* (1992): The court voted 5-4 to prohibit official prayer at high school graduation ceremonies, ruling that under such circumstances, students who objected to such prayers might nonetheless feel induced to conform.

● *Joint School District No. 241 v. Harris* (1995): The court vacated as moot a lower court's ruling that student-initiated prayers at graduation ceremonies are unconstitutional but offered no explanations or guidelines.

quired to participate in prayer and that neither the states nor the federal government would compose any prayers said in public schools. *(1994 Weekly Report, p. 3353)*

"We are talking about permitting religious expression, not compelling it," Istook said at a June 8 hearing in Washington of the House Judiciary Subcommittee on the Constitution. "Why can students not do voluntarily what adults can do?"

Subcommittee Chairman Charles T. Canady, R-Fla., said he is not leaning toward any of the drafts in particular at this point. "We are in the process of trying to get a full understanding of the problem," he said in an interview. "I think we need to listen to everybody on this issue."

In addition to the hearings in Washington and Tampa — and one held June 10 in Harrisonburg, Va. — the subcommittee is planning sessions in New York City, Los Angeles and Oklahoma City.

Opponents as well as supporters are testifying, occasionally producing lively exchanges that underscore the difficulties facing the proposals. In Tampa, for example, Canady had to appeal for order several times from a crowd that was largely opposed to amending the Constitution. The crowd at the Harrisonburg hearing was largely supportive of an amendment.

At the Washington hearing, com-

mittee Democrats, including Melvin Watt of North Carolina, contended that expressions of minority and majority religions are already protected under current law. "What you are saying is that you want to amend the federal Constitution to give that control to the majority," he said. "If everything that was in the Constitution was done by a simple majority, then I guess you would have a Constitution that was based on protecting the rights of the majority."

Canady conceded that the path to a constitutional amendment would be arduous and said other options may have to be considered. These include attaching, to unrelated legislation, language that would promote school prayer but fall short of a constitutional amendment. Such statutory language, if upheld by the Court, could remain in effect until enactment of a more specific constitutional amendment.

"We have to recognize that we might fail," Canady said. "I don't know if a statutory approach could successfully address the problem. But that is something that should not be rejected out of hand."

One likely avenue for such an approach would be the fiscal 1996 appropriations bill that is scheduled to be marked up by the Appropriations Labor, HHS, and Education Subcommittee on July 11. "There will be some legislating on the bill," Chairman John Edward Porter, R-Ill., predicted in an interview. But he also suggested that a school prayer provision may ultimately get lost among more pressing fiscal concerns.

"I think there's going to be so much going on," Porter said, "people won't be able to focus on things like this."

In the Senate, where hearings are not yet under way on school prayer, a constitutional amendment would be a harder sell than in the House.

There, "religious equality" language would probably face a filibuster from nearly all Democrats and several Republicans, including Mark O. Hatfield of Oregon, Arlen Specter of Pennsylvania, James M. Jeffords of Vermont and Orrin G. Hatch of Utah.

"A Place at the Table"

Much of the driving force behind the effort to amend the Constitution comes from Christian conservatives, who played an influential role in the 1994 elections.

A "religious equality" amendment was the first item in the "Contract With the American Family," which Ralph Reed, executive director of the Christian Coalition, unveiled on Capitol Hill on May 17. The document, patterned after the House GOP's "Contract With America," drew praise from Republican Party leaders. House Speaker Newt Gingrich of Georgia and Majority Whip Tom DeLay of Texas also spoke at the news conference. *(Weekly Report, p. 1448)*

Later, in a June 11 appearance on ABC-TV's "This Week With David Brinkley," Gingrich said, "We have to bring God and the concept of a creator

back more into the public square than it has been in recent years."

But Gingrich says he is not convinced a constitutional amendment is required, and he is exploring the feasibility of a statute that could withstand a court challenge.

Senate Majority Leader Bob Dole of Kansas, a candidate for the GOP presidential nomination in 1996, has also praised the concept. But it remains unclear whether Dole would prefer an amendment or a statutory approach.

RICHARD ELLIS

A "religious equality" amendment was the first item in the "Contract With the American Family" that Ralph Reed, executive director of the Christian Coalition, unveiled May 17.

Reed's announcement also served to rally opponents, however. The newly formed Coalition to Preserve Religious Liberty, which consists of numerous mainstream religious organizations and interest groups such as the American Civil Liberties Union and liberal People for the American Way, held their own news conference the same day to underscore their opposition.

The Rev. J. Brent Walker, general counsel for the Baptist Joint Committee on Public Affairs in Washington and chairman of the coalition, conceded that religious expression is sometimes stifled in school settings through unwitting ignorance or neglect. But Walker said the answer should not be amending the Bill of Rights for the first time in more than 200 years.

"We need to educate our educators, teach our teachers and inform our students" about what is permissible under current law, Walker said. "I don't think a constitutional amendment is going to make the line any brighter."

Jesse Choper, a professor of law at

the University of California at Berkeley, said prayer in schools "wouldn't be the end of the world," but would have a coercive effect on some students, especially young children who are members of religious minorities. "Sometimes majorities succumb to the passions of the moment," Choper said, but "majorities don't need constitutional rights to protect them. They have the political process to protect them."

Feasibility Doubted

Others have questioned the practicality of a school prayer amendment. Jorge Osterling, director of community services for the Arlington County, Va., public schools, said an amendment could complicate the already difficult job of educating in diverse areas such as Arlington, where students come from more than 50 countries and represent nearly 20 religions.

"The fact is, we cannot facilitate any public place to pray, because if we do it for one, we have to do it for everybody," Osterling said in an interview. "We cannot paralyze the school by turning it into a temple."

Still, for dedicated advocates of school prayer nothing short of an amendment will do. "We need to have something definitive," said Beverly LaHaye, president of the conservative Concerned Women for America in Washington. "The underlying conflict is basically hostility toward religion."

In Tampa, Joshua Burton and his family are not waiting for a constitutional amendment. With the help of an Orlando law firm specializing in religious liberty cases, the family has sued the school in federal district court.

Joshua's father, Mark Burton, who also testified at the Tampa hearing, said that parents need help raising their children in a socially fraying society that seems increasingly hostile toward religion.

"It seems to me," he said, "that in this age where children are taught by the state school system that they must be tolerant of racial differences, tolerant of homosexuality, tolerant of political differences and tolerant of cultural and language diversity, that this same system should be tolerant when it comes to religious freedom." ■

IMMIGRATION POLICY

Immigration: Bridging Gap Between Ideas and Action

Tightened borders are gaining support; experts debate costs, benefits of newest arrivals

If the 104th Congress does not enact major new laws on immigration, it will not be for lack of suggestions: Various members want to boost border patrols and deportations; impose border fees, worker identification cards and new immigration ceilings; stem public benefits for non-citizens; and end citizenship for the children of illegal aliens.

Lawmakers are exploring these new restrictions amid concerns that the costs of new arrivals outweigh the advantages they provide.

Illegal immigrants are the primary target. "People are fed up," said Sen. Alan K. Simpson, R-Wyo., chairman of the Judiciary Committee's immigration panel and an advocate of new restrictions. "They see people violating our law come here and be treated hospitably."

There is also a new skepticism toward legal immigration, which has surged in recent years. Already, House lawmakers have voted to restrict public benefits for lawful immigrants who have not become citizens — triggering an emotional debate about the rights of recent arrivals vs. the native-born.

"It's simply targeting people because of their political vulnerability," said Lincoln Diaz-Balart of Florida, a Cuban-born Republican who split with his party leadership on the issue.

At a minimum, lawmakers and the Clinton administration are prepared to invest more in policing the nation's borders and deporting illegal entrants. They may do more, such as creating a

CQ Weekly Report April 15, 1995

RICHARD ELLIS

Immigrants take the citizenship oath at a ceremony April 11 in Washington. Total immigration increased from 853,000 in 1989 to 1.3 million in 1993.

national computer registry to identify work status or narrowing the channels for legal immigration.

But the policy landscape is not as straightforward as the desire for action.

Increased border patrols, for example, cost money — at a time when Republicans are trying to curb government spending. National registries raise civil liberties issues among liberals — and also alarm conservatives hostile to the idea of increased government oversight in the workplace.

It is not clear that immigrants pose an economic threat: Some economists say that immigrants overtax public services while making it harder for the native-born to find jobs. But other studies indicate that immigrants are an economic windfall, or even a necessity, for the United States.

And economics cannot answer some of the social questions at the heart of immigration policy in a nation founded by immigrants: Who deserves to be in the United States? What are immigrants supposed to bring to the

country, and how much are they allowed to take?

Some of the strongest voices for restrictions have come from within the Republican Party, where some complain that immigrants are overburdening public services or creating a balkanized community by failing to learn English and otherwise assimilate.

Other Republicans, however, argue that newcomers inject critical vitality into the nation's economy. They are wary of proposals that send a restrictionist or anti-foreign message, which could be perceived as racist and could jeopardize the party's appeal among ethnic communities — such as Cuban-Americans — that share many Republican values.

"This is one of those issues that really threatens to tear the Republican Party in half," said Stephen Moore, an economist specializing in immigration at the libertarian CATO Institute.

For their part, Democrats must balance their traditional allegiances to minority and civil rights organizations against the public appetite for immigration restrictions that those groups may find offensive.

As California Goes

The impetus for national action on immigration begins with California. Anti-immigration sentiment often tracks hard economic times, as it did during the 1990 recession. Much of the nation has pulled out of that slump, but California is still reeling. It also hosts more legal and illegal immigrants than any other state.

The combination has been explosive. It prompted the now widely known Proposition 187, a successful 1994 state ballot initiative to deny most public services to illegal aliens. The Proposition 187 argument spilled into the national political debate, nurturing seeds of discontent already planted by publicized abuses in the asylum system and other aspects of the immigration system.

Rep. Howard L. Berman, D-Calif., said such problems have generated public agitation even in areas with few immigrants. "It's almost a national test of will of the effectiveness of government to enforce its laws," he said. Proposition 187 is on hold pending a court challenge, but the issue remains on the nation's front burner.

California and five other states also have tried to sue the federal government for billions of dollars in reimbursement for providing services to illegal aliens. Their claims focus attention on the costs of immigration in increased public services or displaced workers.

Academics generally agree that illegal immigrants take more in public services than they pay in taxes (although they typically pay some taxes and contribute indirect economic benefits that may make them an overall plus).

The fiscal picture for legal immigrants is more confusing. Donald Huddle, an economics professor at Rice University, estimates that legal immigrants directly cost taxpayers about $17 billion more in 1993 than they paid in taxes. But researchers at the Urban Institute, a nonpartisan public policy research and education organization, have calculated these immigrants as a net plus for taxpayers. And many economists say the contribution from immigrants is even more positive when broader economic factors are included — such as their strong record of starting and sustaining small businesses, or the health of industries that benefit from their labor.

Disputed cost estimates notwithstanding, analysts generally agree that the direct economic benefits from immigrants flow disproportionately to the federal government in the form of payroll taxes, while the major direct costs, such as education, are borne primarily by states and localities.

And states have little power to legislate their way out of these costs. The federal courts, and sometimes state constitutions, dictate that states cannot discriminate against non-citizens when providing welfare benefits. In some cases — public education, for example — they must provide services to illegal aliens as well.

That financial scenario helps account for some of the political pressure — particularly from governors and state legislatures — for Congress to do more to stem new arrivals.

But money is not the only concern among politicians and voters.

The current wave of immigration is not only large, but also culturally distinct from earlier influxes. In 1965,

REUTERS

Cubans paddle their rafts toward the U.S. coast in August 1994.

Congress adjusted immigration laws to place less emphasis on nationality — which had favored Europeans — and more on admitting relatives of U.S. citizens or legal residents. Over time, that policy has worked to bring in ever greater proportions of immigrants from Asia and Latin America.

Their arrival has been met with disquiet in some communities, where some native-born citizens complain that newcomers are not assimilating.

Daniel Stein, executive director of the Federation for American Immigration Reform (FAIR), said that culture shock may be particularly pronounced when it coincides with low birth rates or shifting demographics among the native-born. "Suddenly, what used to be their own neighborhood shopping strip, there's not a sign in English," said Stein, whose 70,000-member group supports restrictions on immigration.

The resulting disorientation helps feed public apprehension about more immigrants, who can become easy scapegoats for economic or cultural problems in the community.

Moore, of the Cato Institute, also connects anti-immigration sentiment with an inward-looking mood he perceives in certain foreign policy arguments, such as calls to defeat the North American Free Trade Agreement. "I think there is a real danger in this country in terms of a re-emerging economic nationalism," he said.

Political Heat

The desire for political action brewed throughout the 103rd Congress, popping up on spending bills and on spontaneous floor amendments. When Congress approved emergency earthquake aid to California, for example, lawmakers sought to stop most of the assistance from going to illegal aliens. *(1994 Weekly Report, p. 319)*

The Clinton administration proposed sizable budget increases for the Immigration and Naturalization Service (INS) and an overhaul of the rules for processing asylum claims. These efforts won credit even from some Republicans, who conceded that the INS had languished under GOP administrations.

But other GOP lawmakers said President Clinton did not go far enough.

Congress moved no major legislation on immigration, in part because Clinton and some Democratic congressional leaders were reluctant to take on the issue in such a politically charged climate.

Republicans are showing far less hesitancy.

Proposals Would Crack Down on Illegals...

Congress is likely to take up an array of immigration-related proposals as part of a comprehensive legislative package. Many measures are aimed at keeping — or throwing — illegal immigrants out of the country. Others would change the terms for legal immigrants to enter and live in the United States. Below are key proposals:

Illegal Immigration

● **Border security.** Many lawmakers support increased resources to secure the nation's borders. Most of the attention is on expanding staff and equipment for the Border Patrol along the U.S.-Mexico border. The Immigration and Naturalization Service (INS) currently employs about 4,500 Border Patrol agents; lawmakers want to boost that to as high as 10,000, although some are concerned about the cost and potential human rights abuses by the patrols.

The Clinton administration originally suggested a border crossing fee to help finance border security and processing for legal entrants but retreated amid howls of protest from some affected communities and their congressional representatives, who feared it would squelch commerce in the border region. Clinton is now suggesting a voluntary crossing fee plan, with enhanced border services going to those communities that "opt in." Some key congressional voices on immigration, such as Sens. Alan K. Simpson, R-Wyo., and Dianne Feinstein, D-Calif., support the idea.

Lawmakers also want to explore ways to improve compliance with visa regulations or tighten qualifications for receiving entry visas. Officials estimate that about half the illegal immigrant population entered the country legally but overstayed their visas. Ideas include giving the State Department more resources to screen visa applications or requiring applicants to post a financial bond to help ensure that they will return to their home country.

Some lawmakers may want to reconsider the current Visa Waiver Program (PL 103-416), which allows short-term tourists and business travelers to enter the United States without a visa if they are from countries that have a low rate of denials and violations on U.S. visas. However, this program is popular as a means to promote tourism and commerce.

● **Employer sanctions.** The 1986 Immigration Reform and Control Act (PL 99-603) for the first time made it illegal to hire undocumented aliens, with punishments including civil fines and, in egregious cases, jail time. But so far the federal government has devoted few resources to enforcing the provisions, and there is widespread

agreement that the law has had little effect in deterring illegal immigration. Policy-makers differ on what to do now. The Clinton administration and some lawmakers propose putting new resources into enforcing employer sanctions as well as general labor laws upholding minimum workplace standards. But others are hostile to increased government interference in the workplace or skeptical that the program can work. In the past, lawmakers such as Senate Judiciary Chairman Orrin G. Hatch, R-Utah, and Sen. Edward M. Kennedy, D-Mass., have called for scrapping employer sanctions, citing claims that the law has led to incidents of job discrimination against citizens who look "foreign."

● **Verification.** Closely related to the employer sanctions debate is the question of verification. Momentum is increasing behind proposals to create a national registry enabling employers to check the legal status of potential employees. The proposal — which would probably rely on Social Security numbers and could be accompanied by some sort of enhanced Social Security or work authorization card — has long been anathema to certain minority groups and civil libertarians, who fear it would be costly and inaccurate and lead to discrimination against those who appear foreign-born. However, members of both parties are interested in the idea as perhaps the only way to curtail employment of illegal aliens. The Clinton administration is proposing several pilot programs for a national registry, in keeping with recent recommendations by the bipartisan Commission on Immigration Reform.

Lawmakers have also proposed tougher penalties for those who use or manufacture fraudulent visas or other documents for immigrants.

● **Reimbursement.** Six states are suing the federal government to recover money spent on services to illegal aliens. While the legal actions are not expected to prevail, the federal government is moving to quell some of the irritation. Pending anti-crime legislation (HR 667 — H Rept 104-21) would guarantee a total of $650 million annually from fiscal 1996 through 2000 for the costs of incarcerating illegal aliens, building on money already approved in the 1994 crime law (PL 103-322). The Clinton administration's fiscal 1996 budget proposed $250 million to help affected states pay for certain medical and education expenses for immigrants.

Legal Immigration

● **Immigration ceilings.** While much political attention has been focused on illegal immigration, some lawmakers insist that the United States also must scale back

Immigration politics do not fall along party lines, but the recent calls to restrict immigration — legal and illegal — have been more potent within the Republican Party. Republicans are typically less dependent on support from Hispanics and other minority groups that are sensitive to potential discrimination, and sometimes perceive racist undercurrents in restrictionist proposals.

Moreover, the Republican takeover in Congress has delivered the House and Senate Judiciary committees on immigration policy into the hands of two lawmakers with a longstanding interest in tightening the nation's borders: Sen. Simpson and Rep. Lamar Smith, R-Texas.

Simpson already has introduced a major proposal on illegal immigration (S 269) and plans to offer a bill addressing legal immigration later this year.

...And Tighten Rules for Legal Immigrants

RUDY GUTIERREZ/EL PASO TIMES

In El Paso, Texas, border agents seal off the border, but it requires one agent stationed every 50 to 200 yards along the 26-mile stretch.

fits for many legal immigrants who have not become U.S. citizens. In some cases these aliens would be banned outright from receiving benefits; in others, their access would be restricted by stepping up requirements that their sponsors' financial resources be taken into account (a process known as "deeming") when determining the applicant's eligibility. The legislation also would clarify that illegal aliens cannot receive most federal benefits. (That is generally the case now.) Republicans are touting the proposal as a way to save money and draw a closer connection between benefits and full citizenship. But it has generated fierce opposition in several camps, including among governors who say states will be forced to pick up the cost when needy immigrants who have been receiving federal aid turn to state programs for increased help. Key Senate Republicans appear cool to the proposal. *(Weekly Report, p. 872)*

the number of newcomers it allows to enter each year through lawful channels. Regular legal immigration has climbed to more than 800,000 people annually, including refugees, relatives of U.S. citizens and those admitted because they have work skills in high demand. Simpson, chairman of the Senate immigration subcommittee, last session proposed dropping those levels to about 600,000; other lawmakers advocate steeper cuts or a temporary moratorium on immigration.

Besides questioning the overall numbers, lawmakers are likely to consider changing the priorities for who gains legal admission. Family reunification now accounts for more than half of all legal immigration. Several members have suggested that the United States should emphasize admitting people with needed work skills or language proficiency and cut back on the ability of citizens or legal permanent residents to bring in relatives. Family reunification currently can apply to siblings and adult children. Some lawmakers have suggested limiting the provision to members of the nuclear or immediate family.

Simpson also wants to repeal the 1966 Cuban Adjustment Act, which lets any Cuban who arrives on U.S. soil qualify for work papers and legal status after one year.

● **Benefits**. House Republicans have passed a bill (HR 4) to prohibit or restrict welfare and other federal bene-

There is broader support for the more general principle of requiring sponsors to help support new immigrants who need assistance. Sponsors currently sign an affidavit promising to provide their charges with financial support, but these pledges are not legally enforceable.

Related Concerns

● **Deportation.** Several lawmakers have proposed ways to send more immigrants home, faster. The primary focus is on steps to speed deportation of aliens — both legal and illegal — who commit serious crimes. But there are also proposals to expedite deportation for asylum seekers without valid claims, for would-be entrants who are apprehended at sea, and for newcomers who enter legally but quickly become dependent on public assistance. Current law allows for deportation of immigrants who become dependent on government benefits, but this "public charge" provision is rarely enforced.

● **Citizenship.** One of the most dramatic proposals is to deny automatic U.S. citizenship to the children of illegal aliens born in this country. California Gov. Pete Wilson has proposed a constitutional amendment to this effect. On Capitol Hill, members have proposed making that change by constitutional amendment or by statute.

Smith is holding hearings on the issue and is expected to craft his own comprehensive bill.

The administration plans to weigh in with a legislative package on illegal immigration, relying in part on recent recommendations from the bipartisan U.S. Commission on Immigration Re-

form, created by the 1990 Immigration Act (PL 101-649) and chaired by former Texas Democratic Rep. Barbara Jordan.

Bright Line

The starting point for the debate is cracking down on illegal immigrants.

Government officials estimate that about 4 million people are living in the United States illegally, many of them concentrated in a few states.

Tightening the border has become an automatic cause for most politicians — either as a prelude to cutbacks in legal immigration or as an

Defining the Terms

The term "immigrant" applies broadly to any person who comes to the United States, legally or otherwise, intending to stay. Immigrants are broken into categories depending on the terms under which they entered the country. They are known as "aliens" until they undergo the naturalization process and become citizens.

Legal immigrants age 18 or older are generally eligible to naturalize after they have lived in the United States for at least five years and can show proficiency in English and U.S. history.

Legal Immigrants

Most legal immigrants are admitted as lawful permanent residents, also called permanent resident aliens. Of this group, most are admitted for "family-related" reasons — i.e. they are close relatives of U.S. citizens or other lawful permanent residents. Another large group are "employment-related," admitted because they possess needed job skills.

The United States also admits immigrants for humanitarian reasons, if they are trying to escape persecution in their home country. These "refugees" and "asylees" often become "lawful permanent residents" after arriving in the United States.

● **Refugees**. Refugees are people who have fled their home countries because of fear of persecution based on race, religion, nationality, political views or social affiliation. Refugees are admitted to the United States while still outside the country after consideration by the State Department and the Immigration and Naturalization Service.

● **Asylees**. Asylees, like refugees, are fleeing persecution. However, asylum-seekers are those who arrive on American soil first and then apply for protection and permission to live in the United States.

Illegal or Undocumented Aliens

These are people living in the United States without governmental permission. Officials estimate that about half of them enter the country illegally, such as by sneaking across the U.S.-Mexico border. The other half enter the country legally, often on a student or tourist visa, and stay after the visa expires.

---

attempt to forestall them.

The result has been a virtual bidding war among policy-makers pledging to expand personnel and equipment along the southwest border. The Border Patrol now consists of about 4,700 agents. Lawmakers are talking seriously about doubling that.

Many policy-makers and analysts also say the government must look beyond the borders to what primarily draws immigrants across — jobs.

The administration wants to improve enforcement of the law that prohibits hiring undocumented workers, targeting industries known for relying on them.

Clinton officials and many Democrats also call for tougher enforcement of general labor laws, saying that illegal aliens are often attractive hires because they are afraid to challenge exploitative working conditions that legal citizens would not tolerate.

"You can drive up and down the state of California on Highway 89 . . . and the people working the crops are still not U.S. citizens," said Xavier Becerra, D-Calif., a member of the House Judiciary Committee's immigration panel.

"If we were to just follow some of our own labor standards, you'd see a change," Becerra said.

But some conservatives are skeptical about increased government intervention in the workplace. That extends to proposals to create a national registry to verify that a job applicant can work legally.

This puts conservative organizations in an odd political alliance with various minority and civil liberties groups, who have long decried such proposals as tantamount to a national identification card that would be wielded primarily against those who appear "foreign."

Cecilia Muñoz, an immigration policy specialist at the National Council of La Raza, a national Hispanic group, said those types of abuses are already occurring in the wake of Proposition 187. "There are people getting carded in grocery stores in California."

Still, the political tide seems to be going the other way.

Both the Clinton administration and the Jordan Commission have called for pilot programs to test verification methods. Many lawmakers in both parties say they do not understand what the fuss is about, because citizens are routinely asked to provide their Social Security numbers and other identification for tasks official and mundane.

"If we can protect a $2 charge at Kmart," said Rep. Elton Gallegly, R-Calif., "we should be able to protect American jobs." Gallegly chairs an immigration task force appointed by House Speaker Newt Gingrich, R-Ga.

Another key proposal is to cut illegal immigrants' access to government benefits. These aliens are not legally entitled to most federal aid, but some lawmakers say they tap into the system anyway.

Rooting out such abuses, however, will require costly or otherwise controversial improvements to government records that verify immigration status.

The acid test will be whether lawmakers, in tight budget times, put up the money required for any or all of these initiatives. As Susan Martin, executive director of the Jordan Commission, told the Senate Judiciary Committee: "No solution to the problem of illegal immigration is going to come cheap."

Closing the Front Door

Some lawmakers say that legal immigration has also gotten out of hand. It is at historic highs, with between 700,000 and 1 million people lawfully admitted each year from 1990 to 1993. During that time, the government also legalized more than 2 million people already living in the United States, under the terms of the 1986 Immigration Reform and Control Act (PL 99-603). *(Weekly Report, p. 1067)*

That is more new legal residents per year than the boom immigration years of the early 1900s, although they represent a smaller proportion of the native population.

"We don't need all these people," said Stein of FAIR, which advocates a temporary moratorium on immigration, then greatly reduced levels of admission with more emphasis on immigrants who provide needed job skills.

Sen. Simpson has called for more modest changes, but also wants to lower legal immigration ceilings and rethink who gets preference for admission.

On the House side, Smith also is inclined to curtail legal immigration, although he speaks of "trimming around the edges" rather than dramatic cutbacks.

Smith's caution may reflect the ambivalence within his party leadership about tackling legal immigration. Gingrich says he sees no need to cut immigration ceilings. Nor is Gallegly interested: "We've got enough work to do to address the illegal problem."

Others are quick to affirm their enthusiastic support for lawful immigration, saying it has brought the country economic and cultural vitality. "Legal immigration is a great plus for this country and it continues to be," said Sen. Paul Simon, D-Ill., a member of the Judiciary Committee's immigration panel.

INS Commissioner Doris Meissner said the administration is withholding judgment on proposed changes in legal immigration until the Jordan Commission releases its recommendations on that issue in June.

Considering Citizenship

Despite such skittishness about overhauling the rules for legal immigration, a new examination of citizenship seems inevitable.

Already, the welfare reform debate has revealed a willingness to adjust the contract between legal immigrants, their sponsors and the govern-

Simpson   **Smith**

Simpson and Smith have a longstanding interest in tightening the borders. "People are fed up," Simpson says of illegal immigration. Smith talks of "trimming around the edges" rather than dramatic cutbacks in legal immigration.

ment. The House welfare bill (HR 4) would greatly restrict legal aliens' access to certain federal programs, either by banning them outright or by requiring sponsors to assume greater financial accountability. Some Republican advocates of the change suggested these non-citizens were making excessive use of the benefits. *(Weekly Report, p. 872)*

Studies do indicate that elderly immigrants and refugees rely on some federal benefits at a higher rate than the native-born. Other immigrants traditionally have been somewhat less likely to make use of federal assistance programs, although that may be changing.

Gallegly is among those who think Congress should draw a connection between citizenship and public benefits. "If they don't want to pledge their allegiance to the United States," he said, "they shouldn't be eligible for food stamps."

But numerous Democratic lawmakers said the welfare plan is being promoted primarily as a way to free up funds — about $20 billion over four years — for other GOP priorities. They are indignant about denying benefits to legal immigrants who generally bear the burdens of full citizenship, such as paying taxes.

"If you are a legal immigrant in this country, you are working here, you are paying taxes, and bad times

come to you, you ought to be entitled to everything else that every American is," Jim McDermott, D-Wash., said during floor debate on the welfare proposal. The Jordan Commission likewise came down against denying benefits to legal immigrants.

Still, even some critics are uneasy about the many legal immigrants who do not seek to become citizens.

Rep. John Bryant, D-Texas, put the question this way at a February hearing: "Are you coming here because you love us or are you just coming here to make money?"

Smith says it is this question of allegiance that drives controversial movements such as efforts to make English the country's official language. While critics see the language movement as an intolerant swipe at the foreign-born, Smith says it is motivated by a desire to promote a unified culture.

Across the Capitol, Simpson agrees: "The magic of America, corny as hell as it sounds, is common flag, common language, public culture."

Yet Frank Sharry, executive director of the National Immigration Forum, an umbrella group for pro-immigration organizations, believes fears about non-assimilation are often ill-founded: "People don't give up everything they've known to come to the United States so they can reject it."

There are several reasons why many legal immigrants do not pursue citizenship, including emotional ties to their homeland, skittishness about interacting with government officials and difficulty passing the English or history tests for naturalization.

INS Commissioner Meissner said her agency is making a push to promote naturalization, an issue that often has been ignored. And as politicians step up talk of cutting benefits to non-citizens, record numbers of legal immigrants are applying for citizenship.

Meanwhile, some immigration advocates say lawmakers should not lose sight of what immigrants stand for — whether or not they are on the track to formal citizenship. When it comes to hard work, determination and other values extolled by politicians, said Becerra, "they do the things that we talk about at a higher clip than the citizen population." ∎

AFFIRMATIVE ACTION

Pressure Builds for Retreat On Affirmative Action

Even supporters wonder whether diversity programs have gone too far; critics seize the moment

Sen. Joseph I. Lieberman, D-Conn., disregarded affirmative action critics in 1991 and supported a job discrimination bill that they said would lead to hiring quotas for women and minorities. But he has grown increasingly sympathetic to arguments that affirmative action has gone too far. "It's been building in me," Lieberman says of his concern. "We have to find another means" to ensure equal opportunity.

Lieberman is one of a growing number of moderate lawmakers who are rethinking affirmative action and helping to throw its future into question. The political tremors are felt in California, where an anti-affirmative-action ballot initiative is roiling state politics and where Gov. Pete Wilson announced June 1 that he was curtailing controversial programs. The tremors reach to the White House, where President Clinton has ordered a review of federal programs that give special consideration to women and minorities. And in Congress, Republicans are leading an even more aggressive push to re-examine and perhaps roll back affirmative action laws.

Several policies are under fire, from race-conscious redistricting for political elections to minority scholarships. But it is affirmative action in the workplace — policies such as numerical goals and timetables to move women and minorities into certain jobs — that appears to be generating the most concern. There is particular

CQ Weekly Report June 3, 1995

RICHARD ELLIS

New employees undergo job training at the Manassas, Va., training center for AT&T, which operates under a 1973 consent decree requiring the company to promote more women and minorities.

agitation over government programs that give women and minorities special consideration for federal contracts and jobs, and lawmakers are expected to at least trim these programs.

The debate could heat up later this month. Charles T. Canady, R-Fla., who chairs a House Judiciary subcommittee with responsibility for civil rights, is poised to introduce legislation erasing virtually all federally sponsored affirmative action. The Supreme Court is due to rule on a case involving federal contracting by summer, and the Clinton administration nearly has completed its affirmative action review.

Affirmative action has withstood numerous past assaults, however, and the current criticism may not be sufficiently deep or focused to prompt an overhaul. Big business, for example, generally has grown to accept affirmative action.

"We feel diversity is critical," says Johanna Schneider, a spokeswoman for the Washington office of the Business

Roundtable, a group of large-company executives. "CEOs think it's the right thing to do and it only makes sense."

Moreover, some GOP leaders have yet to specify what changes they would like to see in employment and contracting policies that aim to promote women and minorities.

Still, members are at least talking seriously about doing away with officially sanctioned preferential treatment or replacing race and gender-conscious programs with those targeting poor people.

Opponents of affirmative action say either that it has worked so well that it is no longer needed or that it always has been an ill-conceived effort that promotes women and minorities at the expense of more qualified white men. They say that ongoing affirmative action will exacerbate racial and gender divisions in society and lead to a balkanized polity.

Advocates insist that affirmative action has worked and has yet to outlive its usefulness. Any substantial retreat, they argue, will invite a resurgence of discrimination.

Antipathy toward affirmative action is driven in part by economic unease, as well as by resentment that newly arrived immigrants may be eligible to participate in such programs.

Yet some activists on both sides say the biggest change is not economic or demographic, but political: It has become more acceptable to criticize affirmative action. Where most political leaders once supported affirmative action even in the face of considerable popular skepticism, many of these lead-

A 30-Year Experiment

It has been roughly three decades since the nation began experimenting with special programs known collectively as "affirmative action." The term embraces an array of initiatives, including special recruiting and hiring goals, designed to help racial minorities and women become full participants in the nation's economic life.

The effort came initially from the executive branch.

In 1961, President John F. Kennedy ordered federal contractors to make special efforts to ensure that workers were hired and treated without regard to race or ethnicity. President Lyndon B. Johnson expanded the directive significantly, requiring contractors who do business with the federal government to adopt affirmative action plans for all their operations — including goals and timetables for increased minority hires. He later enlarged federal affirmative action rules to include women.

But it was President Richard M. Nixon who ushered in a markedly more aggressive — and controversial — form of affirmative action. Nixon in 1969 initiated the "Philadelphia plan," which required minimum levels of minority participation on federal construction projects in Philadelphia and three other cities. The next year, similar standards were adopted for virtually all federal contractors.

The 1964 Civil Rights Act

Congress, meanwhile, had weighed in with the 1964 Civil Rights Act, which marked a huge advance for the principle of non-discrimination in employment. The law did not establish or explicity require affirmative action programs. In fact, sponsors assured critics that the law would not force employers to use hiring quotas or give preferential treatment to blacks or other groups.

But Title VII of the law did set out principles of employment non-discrimination and a mechanism to redress violations. Courts have since interpreted the law to allow or even require various types of affirmative action. And many private and state employers adopted voluntary affirmative action plans. *(Court rulings, p. 115)*

These policies continually drew some criticism, but they survived key court challenges and became standard operating procedure.

At the request of Senate Majority Leader Bob Dole, R-Kan., the Congressional Research Service compiled a list this year of more than 100 federal programs that could roughly be categorized as affirmative action — programs as precise as setting aside a fixed percentage of crime assistance grants for minority or female-owned institutions, and as general as urging recipients of federal agriculture or housing assistance to use minority-owned banks.

Backlash in the Reagan Era

The first major political assault on affirmative action came from the Reagan administration, which vocally opposed most affirmative action programs as examples

Presidents Johnson, left, and Nixon worked to increase minority participation in federal construction projects.

of reverse discrimination and unwarranted preferences. Reagan weakened enforcement of some programs and challenged others in court.

However, advocates and their congressional allies withstood his administration's attempts to undo many affirmative action requirements for federal contractors — a testament to the effort's ongoing support and, perhaps, reluctance to take on the debate's volatile racial politics.

"Nobody wanted to make an issue of it, because you're opening yourself to charges of racism or sexism," said Seymour Martin Lipset, a public policy professor at George Mason University who has written about affirmative action.

The Fatal Quota Label

As recently as 1991, Congress indirectly endorsed some of the principles of affirmative action when it passed civil rights legislation (PL 102-166) that made it easier for workers to sue for job discrimination. *(1991 Almanac, p. 251)*

Still, an earlier version of the bill was defeated amid bitter arguments over whether it was a "quota bill" that would force employers to hire by the numbers.

Fixed hiring quotas are unlawful in virtually all contexts and were not called for in the 1991 bill. But critics said some aspects of that legislation — for example, requiring employers who are sued for employment discrimination to show why workplace demographics did not roughly track that of the available labor pool — amount to de facto quotas as nervous employers seek to avoid discrimination lawsuits.

Former Sen. John C. Danforth, a Missouri Republican who struggled to pass a version of the bill, recalls the opponents' initial success. "It was very clear at that time that if something could be successfully labeled quota legislation, it wasn't going to go anywhere."

Danforth and other supporters eventually prevailed, but uneasiness about the nation's affirmative action policies has lingered and grown, feeding into the current critical mood.

ers are hostile or at least questioning.

"The difference is the perception in political circles," says Linda Chavez, president of the Center for Equal Opportunity, a conservative think tank, and an opponent of affirmative action. "A lot of politicians seem to have suddenly discovered that these programs are preference programs."

Alternately, some defenders of affirmative action say critics are distorting the facts — falsely equating affirmative action with quotas and overstating the incidence of reverse discrimination — to exploit public apprehension.

Rep. John Conyers Jr., D-Mich., a senior black lawmaker who supports the programs, puts it this way: "It's just people making the most of a sensitive issue that people can get some political mileage out of."

New Attitude

Some of the current tensions about affirmative action surfaced during congressional debate on the 1991 civil rights legislation (PL 102-166) that made it easier for workers to sue for job discrimination. An early version went down amid criticism that it was a "quota bill" that would force employers to hire women and minorities according to strict ratios. *(1991 Almanac, p. 251)*

The 1994 elections brought a clearer opportunity to challenge affirmative action, simultaneously signaling a more conservative electorate and putting some affirmative action skeptics in charge of key congressional posts. *(Weekly Report, p. 819)*

Presidential politics have helped prod opponents into high gear, as Clinton and the Republican contenders jostle for position on the issue. The controversial ballot proposal to undo affirmative action programs in California — a key electoral state in national politics — ensures that the issue will figure in the 1996 presidential race.

The Republican Party has long included strong critics of affirmative action, so it is not surprising that members' success in the 1994 elections would embolden them to attack. Even Senate Majority Leader Bob Dole, R-Kan., who has supported affirmative action, is now critical and may sponsor legislation to undo most federal efforts.

Many Democrats have been strong supporters of the policy, reflecting its importance to minority and women's groups, which are among the party's most steadfast allies.

Yet elements of the Democratic co-

"I think the current system cannot stand."

—Sen. Joseph I. Lieberman, D-Conn.

alition, such as working-class whites, have been uncomfortable with affirmative action for years. And now Clinton and other key Democrats seem to be struggling to find a proper stance on the issue.

Clinton has said he still supports affirmative action and is looking to improve rather than abandon it. Even that is considered a betrayal by some within the party, where liberal politicians are bracing to defend the embattled programs. Key Democrats, such as House Minority Leader Richard A. Gephardt of Missouri and Sen. Christopher J. Dodd of Connecticut, while publicly welcoming the review, have pledged ongoing support for affirmative action.

But Lieberman, who chairs the centrist Democratic Leadership Council, said he and some colleagues are increasingly hard put to reconcile the notion of group preferences with the ideal of individual opportunity.

"That inconsistency has become more and more evident over time and has become less and less tenable politically," he says. "I think the current system cannot stand."

Pressure Points

The term "affirmative action" embraces a range of initiatives, including special recruiting, goals and timetables for hiring or promoting minorities and women, as well as rules to allot a portion of government contracts for minority- or female-owned companies.

There is little dissent over recruiting and outreach programs for women and

minorities, which make up a large portion of affirmative action efforts. On the other end, policy-makers also unite against fixed hiring quotas, which are unlawful in virtually all contexts.

The friction comes over whether race or gender should factor into hiring and firing decisions. For example, is it sometimes appropriate to look beyond pure test scores and give an extra plus to a diversity candidate? What about set-asides in government grants or procurement rules?

Lawmakers' differing responses to such questions reveal large gaps in the way discrimination and affirmative action are perceived.

Studies indicate that affirmative action has helped to move women and minorities into traditionally segregated professions, although these studies differ on the impact of the gains. Yet Chavez and other critics insist that the policies have taken a far greater toll on individual fortunes and societal values than can be set off by any gains they may have provided.

They see affirmative action as a departure from principles of meritocracy and individual striving and as a policy that costs white men who may have had no part in any past or present discrimination.

Hiring quotas are illegal, but critics say managers are nonetheless "hiring by the numbers" to avoid discrimination lawsuits. And over time, such perceived or real abuses have accumulated. "I think more and more people are being impacted by affirmative action," says House Judiciary Committee Chairman Henry J. Hyde, R-Ill.

Critics also charge that many affirmative action programs benefit only a few, privileged minorities or women rather than helping the truly disadvantaged. Early in 1995, Republicans eagerly attacked a tax credit for companies that sell television and cable stations to minorities. The tax break figured in plans by Viacom, a media and entertainment giant, to sell its TV systems to a black-owned company and defer millions in taxes — a scenario many lawmakers decried as far removed from the guiding aspirations of the civil rights movement. *(Weekly Report, pp. 1016, 602)*

These criticisms appear to resonate with voters, white men in particular. Some women and minorities also have voiced ambivalence toward affirmative action, arguing either that it is unneeded or that it is harmful because personal achievements may be attributed to "preferences" rather

Courts Establish Boundaries

Many of the rules for affirmative action have been written not in Congress, but in the federal courts.

The courts have sanctioned, and even required, employers to take race or gender into account to promote equal opportunity. But they have sprinkled this legal path with strong caveats and marked some forays into the world of race and gender preferences as off-limits. A case pending before the Supreme Court could change some of those rules once again.

General axioms have emerged from more than two decades of complex and often closely decided affirmative action rulings by the U.S. Supreme Court and other federal courts. They can be summarized as follows:

● "Preferences maybe, quotas no." Employers can use race or gender as a "plus factor" in certain cases, but are almost always forbidden from employing strict, numerical quotas to fill jobs.

● Affirmative action programs should be temporary efforts to correct past wrongs — specific or general — rather than permanent features of the employment landscape. No one has defined temporary, however, prompting disputes over how much affirmative action is enough.

● Employers must take into account the burden any affirmative action program would place on workers or potential workers outside the plan.

Current Law

Private employers are governed by rulings on Title VII of the 1964 Civil Rights Act, which prohibits employment discrimination on the basis of race, gender or ethnicity. That language might appear to preclude taking race or gender into account in workplace decisions, and some affirmative action programs have been struck down as violations of Title VII. Overall, however, courts have ruled that affirmative action is consistent with Title VII goals and may even be required to remedy past violations.

Employers can undertake affirmative action programs voluntarily if they aim to erase entrenched racial or gender imbalances in job categories. For example, the Supreme Court in 1979 upheld a steel manufacturer's voluntary program to reserve half of the training slots for skilled craft jobs for African-Americans. At the time, virtually all such jobs were held by whites.

But these programs cannot unduly impinge on other workers or prospective workers: A company's recruiting program would probably pass muster but reserving all job openings in a given category for women or minorities probably would not. Also, a program must be a transitional scheme to break down longstanding barriers rather than a permanent preference or a guarantee of a certain level of minority or female representation.

If an employer is found guilty of discrimination under Title VII, the courts may order the company to adopt an affirmative action program. Here, however, the court would have to establish that discrimination had taken place, not simply that a pattern of segregation existed.

When the government does the hiring — directly or by contracting work — the legal ground rules for affirmative action are set by the Constitution as well as Title VII. Governments can adopt affirmative action policies through legislative or executive branch action. Ultimately, such programs must square with the Fourteenth Amendment guarantee of "equal protection" under the law to all people.

State or local affirmative action policies must meet "strict scrutiny" by the courts: They must serve a compelling public policy goal and take targeted action to achieve that goal. This has been translated into showing that such plans are making up for past discrimination in a particular field, not for societywide biases.

The Supreme Court has accorded the federal government a little more latitude than the states to undertake affirmative action in the name of broad social goals such as diversity. The high court in 1990 upheld a controversial Federal Communications Commission policy that gives minorities preference for broadcast licenses to promote diverse viewpoints on the airwaves — not specifically to remedy past discrimination.

On Trial

A case pending before the Supreme Court, *Adarand Constructors Inc. v. Pena*, could alter the rules for affirmative action — at least where the federal government is concerned.

At issue is a Transportation Department policy designed to steer some federal contracts to "socially and economically disadvantaged" businesspeople. The policy gives contractors a bonus if they hire a disadvantaged subcontractor. Minority-owned businesses automatically qualify for "disadvantaged" status (subject to an income cutoff), while others can petition for the designation. A white contractor says the policy is discriminatory. If the high court agrees, it could curtail federal affirmative action in the contracting arena. A ruling is expected in June.

A New Jersey case before a federal appeals court is generating even more political fireworks and could further refine the parameters of affirmative action. Two business education teachers — one black, one white — were hired on the same day by the Piscataway school board. When the board was forced to fire one eight years later, it dismissed the white teacher rather than her black colleague, who was at the time the only black teacher in the 10-member department. In the past, the decision would have been settled by a coin toss.

Sharon Taxman, the white teacher, filed a reverse discrimination suit with the support of the Bush administration Justice Department. But under President Clinton, the department switched sides and argued that the school district could take race into account in this instance.

than merit.

But some policy-makers are bitter about calls for a meritocracy in which race and gender would play no role. It is precisely because the qualifications of some women and minorities have been slighted, they say, that affirmative action is important. "How do we go back to this colorblind society when we didn't have it in the first place?" asked Rep. Donald M. Payne, D-N.J.

Advocates say affirmative action forces employers to scrutinize the explicit or hidden biases that can close opportunities for women and minorities. They say everyone benefits from this broadening: Employers get a more diverse work force, and white men may have more opportunities when employers go beyond the "old boy network" to hire based on objective factors.

To a great extent, the current fight revolves around whether that kind of hiring has become the norm and would exist without affirmative action.

American Telephone & Telegraph, for example, has been under a consent decree since 1973 to promote more women and minorities. Spokesman Burke Stinson says what began as an exercise in court-ordered compliance has now become a way of doing business. "The concept of including people, no matter their race, creed or color, is now pervasive," he says.

Rep. Harris W. Fawell, R-Ill., who has conducted hearings on affirmative action as chairman of the Economic and Educational Opportunities Subcommittee, says most employers today look for the most qualified worker, regardless of race or gender. He says that while his grandparents undoubtedly discriminated, "my children and my grandchildren don't. . . . They just can't be held accountable for those societal wrongs" of earlier generations.

But Conyers says many critics are too quick to see discrimination as a thing of the past. "It's easy to think things are better than they are."

Deval Patrick, head of the Justice Department's civil rights division, told members of a House panel that they would be "astonished and saddened" by the egregious cases that continue to land on his desk. In 1994, Patrick says, the Equal Employment Opportunity Commission received 91,000 complaints of job discrimination. And a recent study by the Glass Ceiling Commission indicated that white men still hold the vast majority of upper-level jobs.

Supporters do not embrace proposals to recast affirmative action to help those who are economically disadvantaged. Civil rights advocates say such efforts should be made in addition to affirmative action, not in place of it.

"Affirmative action was never meant to be an anti-poverty program," says Ralph G. Neas, a veteran civil rights lobbyist who is coordinating a pro-affirmative action campaign for the Leadership Conference on Civil Rights. "It enabled people who were discriminated against to have an equal opportunity."

"It's easy to think things are better than they are."

—Rep. John Conyers Jr., D-Mich.

Muddied Field

During the 1991 legislative debate, civil rights groups had positive momentum as they sought to overturn or restrict the effect of several Supreme Court decisions that were seen as unfairly burdening plaintiffs in job discrimination suits.

This round, they are on the defensive while affirmative action critics appear to have the upper hand. "Clearly the ground has shifted," says Chavez.

Just throwing a spotlight on affirmative action may help generate opposition to the programs.

Seymour Martin Lipset, a public policy professor at George Mason University, says that many politicians in the past avoided the issue for fear of opening themselves to charges of racism or sexism. Now that events like the California ballot initiative have placed affirmative action on the table, political sentiment favors at least some retrenchment. "The politicians now find it hard to resist," Lipset says.

But opponents' newfound momentum does not automatically translate into legislative success.

The simplest action would be to scale back or eliminate federal programs that give special consideration to women and minorities. These include hiring requirements or incentives for federal agencies, grant recipients and federal contractors.

These federal programs affect many jobs and serve as a signal to other employers on affirmative action issues. Many lawmakers and policy analysts consider it likely that Clinton, Congress or both will support some adjustments in this area.

Canady's bill would eliminate such programs and also would seek to restrict programs ordered by the federal courts in response to proven discrimination.

However, Congress cannot alter voluntary affirmative action programs in the private sector or by state and local governments unless lawmakers are prepared to rework the 1964 Civil Rights Act.

Hyde and others say that is a complicated proposition and one that Congress may not have the stomach for — especially absent a strong, organized lobbying effort.

That sort of campaign has yet to materialize. Religious conservatives are more focused on other social issues, such as school prayer and abortion. Nor is the business community clamoring for lawmakers to act.

Women, who arguably have benefited more than minorities from affirmative action, also represent a large political force to block or limit revisions. Many national women's groups have expressed vehement opposition to a rollback of affirmative action, although polls suggest women voters are more equivocal.

Such political uncertainty — and a packed legislative calendar — have raised hurdles for the issue in Congress. However, the issue is heating up in the race for the Republican presidential nomination — a race that includes Dole, Sen. Phil Gramm of Texas and Sen. Richard G. Lugar of Indiana — and could easily spill over into the Senate. Jesse Helms, R-N.C., has introduced bills to outlaw preferential treatment on the basis of race or gender. Canady's legislation should help focus attention on the matter in the House.

Clint Bolick, a conservative activist who has been working with lawmakers on the issue, predicts that legislation to end federally sponsored affirmative action will pass both chambers.

For their part, affirmative action supporters acknowledge that they have plenty of work ahead to bolster political and popular support for their cause, but remain optimistic their position will improve as the focus shifts from the abstract to the specific.

"I am confident that a bipartisan majority will defeat efforts to undo affirmative action," says Neas.

Chavez, from a different viewpoint, says Neas may be right. "I've spent too many years in this to think it's an easy battle," she says. "This is a long haul." ∎

APPENDIX

The Legislative Process in Brief

Note: Parliamentary terms used below are defined in the glossary.

Introduction of Bills

A House member (including the resident commissioner of Puerto Rico and non-voting delegates of the District of Columbia, Guam, the Virgin Islands and American Samoa) may introduce any one of several types of bills and resolutions by handing it to the clerk of the House or placing it in a box called the hopper. A senator first gains recognition of the presiding officer to announce the introduction of a bill. If objection is offered by any senator, the introduction of the bill is postponed until the following day.

As the next step in either the House or Senate, the bill is numbered, referred to the appropriate committee, labeled with the sponsor's name and sent to the Government Printing Office so that copies can be made for subsequent study and action. Senate bills may be jointly sponsored and carry several senators' names. Until 1978, the House limited the number of members who could cosponsor any one bill; the ceiling was eliminated at the beginning of the 96th Congress. A bill written in the executive branch and proposed as an administration measure usually is introduced by the chairman of the congressional committee that has jurisdiction.

Bills—Prefixed with HR in the House, S in the Senate, followed by a number. Used as the form for most legislation, whether general or special, public or private.

Joint Resolutions—Designated H J Res or S J Res. Subject to the same procedure as bills, with the exception of a joint resolution proposing an amendment to the Constitution. The latter must be approved by two-thirds of both houses and is thereupon sent directly to the administrator of general services for submission to the states for ratification instead of being presented to the president for his approval.

Concurrent Resolutions—Designated H Con Res or S Con Res. Used for matters affecting the operations of both houses. These resolutions do not become law.

Resolutions—Designated H Res or S Res. Used for a matter concerning the operation of either house alone and adopted only by the chamber in which it originates.

Committee Action

With few exceptions, bills are referred to the appropriate standing committees. The job of referral formally is the responsibility of the Speaker of the House and the presiding officer of the Senate, but this task usually is carried out on their behalf by the parliamentarians of the House and Senate. Precedent, statute and the jurisdictional mandates of the committees as set forth in the rules of the House and Senate determine which committees receive what kinds of bills. An exception is the referral of private bills, which are sent to whatever committee is designated by their sponsors. Bills are technically considered "read for the first time" when referred to House committees.

When a bill reaches a committee it is placed on the committee's calendar. At that time the bill comes under the sharpest congressional focus. Its chances for passage are quickly determined — and the great majority of bills falls by the legislative roadside. Failure of a committee to act on a bill is equivalent to killing it; the measure can be withdrawn from the committee's purview only by a discharge petition signed by a majority of the House membership on House bills, or by adoption of a special resolution in the Senate. Discharge attempts rarely succeed.

The first committee action taken on a bill usually is a request for comment on it by interested agencies of the government. The committee chairman may assign the bill to a subcommittee for study and hearings, or it may be considered by the full committee. Hearings may be public, closed (executive session) or both. A subcommittee, after considering a bill, reports to the full committee its recommendations for action and any proposed amendments.

The full committee then votes on its recommendation to the House or Senate. This procedure is called "ordering a bill reported." Occasionally a committee may order a bill reported unfavorably; most of the time a report, submitted by the chairman of the committee to the House or Senate, calls for favorable action on the measure since the committee can effectively "kill" a bill by simply failing to take any action.

After the bill is reported, the committee chairman instructs the staff to prepare a written report. The report describes the purposes and scope of the bill, explains the committee revisions, notes proposed changes in existing law and, usually, includes the views of the executive branch agencies consulted. Often committee members opposing a measure issue dissenting minority statements that are included in the report.

Usually, the committee "marks up" or proposes amendments to the bill. If they are substantial and the measure is complicated, the committee may order a "clean bill" introduced, which will embody the proposed amendments. The original bill then is put aside and the clean bill, with a new number, is reported to the floor.

The chamber must approve, alter or reject the committee amendments before the bill itself can be put to a vote.

How a Bill Becomes Law

This graphic shows the most typical way in which proposed legislation is enacted into law. There are more complicated, as well as simpler, routes, and most bills never become law. The process is illustrated with two hypothetical bills, House bill No. 1 (HR 1) and Senate bill No. 2 (S 2). Bills must be passed by both houses in identical form before they can be sent to the president. The path of HR 1 is traced by a solid line, that of S 2 by a broken line. In practice, most bills begin as similar proposals in both houses.

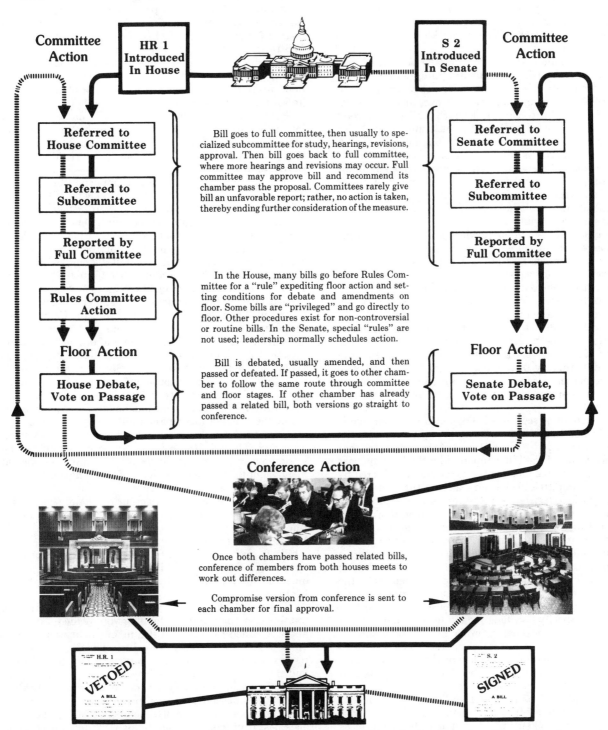

Committee Action

HR 1 Introduced In House

S 2 Introduced In Senate

Committee Action

Referred to House Committee

Referred to Subcommittee

Reported by Full Committee

Rules Committee Action

Floor Action

House Debate, Vote on Passage

Referred to Senate Committee

Referred to Subcommittee

Reported by Full Committee

Floor Action

Senate Debate, Vote on Passage

Bill goes to full committee, then usually to specialized subcommittee for study, hearings, revisions, approval. Then bill goes back to full committee, where more hearings and revisions may occur. Full committee may approve bill and recommend its chamber pass the proposal. Committees rarely give bill an unfavorable report; rather, no action is taken, thereby ending further consideration of the measure.

In the House, many bills go before Rules Committee for a "rule" expediting floor action and setting conditions for debate and amendments on floor. Some bills are "privileged" and go directly to floor. Other procedures exist for non-controversial or routine bills. In the Senate, special "rules" are not used; leadership normally schedules action.

Bill is debated, usually amended, and then passed or defeated. If passed, it goes to other chamber to follow the same route through committee and floor stages. If other chamber has already passed a related bill, both versions go straight to conference.

Conference Action

Once both chambers have passed related bills, conference of members from both houses meets to work out differences.

Compromise version from conference is sent to each chamber for final approval.

H.R. 1 VETOED A BILL

S. 2 SIGNED A BILL

Compromise bill approved by both houses is sent to the president, who may sign it into law, allow it to become law without his signature, or veto it and return it to Congress. Congress may override veto by two-thirds majority vote in both houses; bill then becomes law without president's signature.

Floor Action

After a bill is reported back to the house where it originated, it is placed on the calendar.

There are five legislative calendars in the House, issued in one cumulative calendar titled *Calendars of the United States House of Representatives and History of Legislation.* The House calendars are:

The Union Calendar to which are referred bills raising revenues, general appropriations bills and any measures directly or indirectly appropriating money or property. It is the Calendar of the Committee of the Whole House on the State of the Union.

The House Calendar to which are referred bills of public character not raising revenue or appropriating money.

The Corrections Calendar to which are referred bills to repeal rules and regulations deemed excessive or unnecessary when the Corrections Calendar is called the second and fourth Tuesday of each month. (Instituted in the 104th Congress to replace the seldom-used Consent Calendar.) A three-fifths majority is required for passage.

The Private Calendar to which are referred bills for relief in the nature of claims against the United States or private immigration bills that are passed without debate when the Private Calendar is called the first and third Tuesdays of each month.

The Discharge Calendar to which are referred motions to discharge committees when the necessary signatures are signed to a discharge petition.

There is only one legislative calendar in the Senate and one "executive calendar" for treaties and nominations submitted to the Senate. When the Senate Calendar is called, each senator is limited to five minutes' debate on each bill.

Debate. A bill is brought to debate by varying procedures. If a routine measure, it may await the call of the calendar. If it is urgent or important, it can be taken up in the Senate either by unanimous consent or by a majority vote. The majority leader, in consultation with the minority leader and others, schedules the bills that will be taken up for debate.

In the House, precedence is granted if a special rule is obtained from the Rules Committee. A request for a special rule usually is made by the chairman of the committee that favorably reported the bill, supported by the bill's sponsor and other committee members. The request, considered by the Rules Committee in the same fashion that other committees consider legislative measures, is in the form of a resolution providing for immediate consideration of the bill. The Rules Committee reports the resolution to the House where it is debated and voted on in the same fashion as regular bills. If the Rules Committee fails to report a rule requested by a committee, there are several ways to bring the bill to the House floor — under suspension of the rules, on Calendar Wednesday or by a discharge motion.

The resolutions providing special rules are important because they specify how long the bill may be debated and whether it may be amended from the floor. If floor amendments are banned, the bill is considered under a "closed rule," which permits only members of the committee that first reported the measure to the House to alter its language, subject to chamber acceptance.

When a bill is debated under an "open rule," amendments may be offered from the floor. Committee amendments always are taken up first but may be changed, as may all amendments up to the second degree; that is, an amendment to an amendment to an amendment is not in order.

Duration of debate in the House depends on whether the bill is under discussion by the House proper or before the House when it is sitting as the Committee of the Whole House on the State of the Union. In the former, the amount of time for debate either is determined by special rule or is allocated with an hour for each member if the measure is under consideration without a rule. In the Committee of the Whole the amount of time agreed on for general debate is equally divided between proponents and opponents. At the end of general discussion, the bill is read section by section for amendment. Debate on an amendment is limited to five minutes for each side; this is called the "five-minute rule." In practice, amendments regularly are debated more than ten minutes, with members gaining the floor by offering pro forma amendments or obtaining unanimous consent to speak longer than five minutes.

Senate debate usually is unlimited. It can be halted only by unanimous consent by "cloture," which requires a three-fifths majority of the entire Senate except for proposed changes in the Senate rules. The latter requires a two-thirds vote.

The House considers almost all important bills within a parliamentary framework known as the Committee of the Whole. It is not a committee as the word usually is understood; it is the full House meeting under another name for the purpose of speeding action on legislation. Technically, the House sits as the Committee of the Whole when it considers any tax measure or bill dealing with public appropriations. It also can resolve itself into the Committee of the Whole if a member moves to do so and the motion is carried. The Speaker appoints a member to serve as the chairman. The rules of the House permit the Committee of the Whole to meet when a quorum of 100 members is present on the floor and to amend and act on bills, within certain time limitations. When the Committee of the Whole has acted, it "rises," the Speaker returns as the presiding officer of the House and the member appointed chairman of the Committee of the Whole reports the action of the committee and its recommendations. The Committee of the Whole cannot pass a bill; instead it reports the measure to the full House with whatever changes it has approved. The full House then may pass or reject the bill — or, on occasion, recommit the bill to committee. Amendments adopted in the Committee of the Whole may be put to a second vote in the full House.

Votes. Voting on bills may occur repeatedly before they are finally approved or rejected. The House votes on the rule for the bill and on various amendments to the bill. Voting on amendments often is a more illuminating test of a bill's support than is the final tally. Sometimes members approve final passage of bills after vigorously supporting amendments that, if adopted, would have scuttled the legislation.

The Senate has three different methods of voting: an untabulated voice vote, a standing vote (called a division) and a recorded roll call to which members answer "yea" or "nay" when their names are called. The House also employs voice and standing votes, but since January 1973 yeas and nays have been recorded by an electronic voting device, eliminating the need for time-consuming roll calls.

Another method of voting, used in the House only, is the teller vote. Traditionally, members filed up the center aisle past counters; only vote totals were announced. Since 1971, one-fifth of a quorum can demand that the votes of individual members be recorded, thereby forcing them to take a public position on amendments to key bills. Elec-

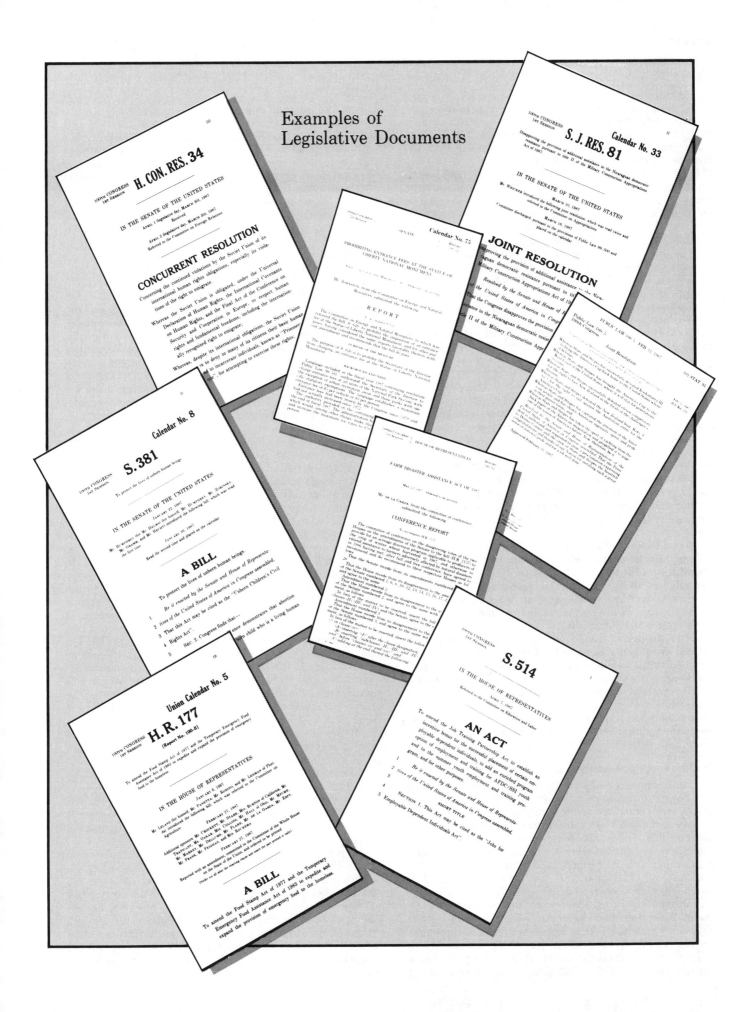

Examples of
Legislative Documents

tronic voting now is commonly used for this purpose.

After amendments to a bill have been voted upon, a vote may be taken on a motion to recommit the bill to committee. If carried, this vote removes the bill from the chamber's calendar and is usually a death blow to the bill. If the motion is unsuccessful, the bill then is "read for the third time." An actual reading usually is dispensed with. Until 1965, an opponent of a bill could delay this move by objecting and asking for a full reading of an engrossed (certified in final form) copy of the bill. After the "third reading," the vote on final passage is taken.

The final vote may be followed by a motion to reconsider, and this motion may be followed by a move to lay the motion on the table. Usually, those voting for the bill's passage vote for the tabling motion, thus safeguarding the final passage action. With that, the bill has been formally passed by the chamber. While a motion to reconsider a Senate vote is pending on a bill, the measure cannot be sent to the House.

Action in Second House

After a bill is passed it is sent to the other chamber. This body may then take one of several steps. It may pass the bill as is — accepting the other chamber's language. It may send the bill to committee for scrutiny or alteration, or reject the entire bill, advising the other house of its actions. Or it simply may ignore the bill submitted while it continues work on its own version of the proposed legislation. Frequently, one chamber may approve a version of a bill that is greatly at variance with the version already passed by the other house, and then substitute its contents for the language of the other, retaining only the latter's bill number.

A provision of the Legislative Reorganization Act of 1970 permits a separate House vote on any non-germane amendment added by the Senate to a House-passed bill and requires a majority vote to retain the amendment. Previously the House was forced to act on the bill as a whole; the only way to defeat the non-germane amendment was to reject the entire bill.

Often the second chamber makes only minor changes. If these are readily agreed to by the other house, the bill then is routed to the president. However, if the opposite chamber significantly alters the bill submitted to it, the measure usually is "sent to conference." The chamber that has possession of the "papers" (engrossed bill, engrossed amendments, messages of transmittal) requests a conference and the other chamber must agree to it. If the second house does not agree, the bill dies.

Conference, Final Action

Conference. A conference works out conflicting House and Senate versions of a legislative bill. The conferees usually are senior members appointed by the presiding officers of the two houses, from the committees that managed the bills. Under this arrangement the conferees of one house have the duty of trying to maintain their chamber's position in the face of amending actions by the conferees (also referred to as "managers") of the other house.

The number of conferees from each chamber may vary, the range usually being from three to nine members in each group, depending upon the length or complexity of the bill involved. There may be five representatives and three senators on the conference committee, or the reverse. But a majority vote controls the action of each group so that a large representation does not give one chamber a voting advantage over the other chamber's conferees.

Theoretically, conferees are not allowed to write new legislation in reconciling the two versions before them, but this curb sometimes is bypassed. Many bills have been put into acceptable compromise form only after new language was provided by the conferees. The 1970 Reorganization Act attempted to tighten restrictions on conferees by forbidding them to introduce any language on a topic that neither chamber sent to conference or to modify any topic beyond the scope of the different House and Senate versions.

Frequently the ironing out of difficulties takes days or even weeks. Conferences on involved appropriations bills sometimes are particularly drawn out.

As a conference proceeds, conferees reconcile differences between the versions, but generally they grant concessions only insofar as they remain sure that the chamber they represent will accept the compromises. Occasionally, uncertainty over how either house will react, or the positive refusal of a chamber to back down on a disputed amendment, results in an impasse, and the bills die in conference even though each was approved by its sponsoring chamber.

Conferees sometimes go back to their respective chambers for further instructions, when they report certain portions in disagreement. Then the chamber concerned can either "recede and concur" in the amendment of the other house or "insist on its amendment."

When the conferees have reached agreement, they prepare a conference report embodying their recommendations (compromises). The report, in document form, must be submitted to each house.

The conference report must be approved by each house. Consequently, approval of the report is approval of the compromise bill. In the order of voting on conference reports, the chamber which asked for a conference yields to the other chamber the opportunity to vote first.

Final Steps. After a bill has been passed by both the House and Senate in identical form, all of the original papers are sent to the enrolling clerk of the chamber in which the bill originated. He then prepares an enrolled bill, which is printed on parchment paper. When this bill has been certified as correct by the secretary of the Senate or the clerk of the House, depending on which chamber originated the bill, it is signed first (no matter whether it originated in the Senate or House) by the Speaker of the House and then by the president of the Senate. It is next sent to the White House to await action.

If the president approves the bill, he signs it, dates it and usually writes the word "approved" on the document. If he does not sign it within 10 days (Sundays excepted) and Congress is in session, the bill becomes law without his signature.

However, should Congress adjourn before the 10 days expire, and the president has failed to sign the measure, it does not become law. This procedure is called the pocket veto.

A president vetoes a bill by refusing to sign it and, before the 10-day period expires, returning it to Congress with a message stating his reasons. The message is sent to the chamber that originated the bill. If no action is taken on the message, the bill dies. Congress, however, can attempt to override the president's veto and enact the bill, "the objections of the president to the contrary notwithstanding." Overriding a veto requires a two-thirds vote of those present, who must number a quorum and vote by roll call.

Debate can precede this vote, with motions permitted to lay the message on the table, postpone action on it or refer it to committee. If the president's veto is overridden by a two-thirds vote in both houses, the bill becomes law. Otherwise it is dead.

When bills are passed finally and signed, or passed over a veto, they are given law numbers in numerical order as they become law. There are two series of numbers, one for public and one for private laws, starting at the number "1" for each two-year term of Congress. They are then identified by law number and by Congress — for example, Private Law 21, 97th Congress; Public Law 250, 97th Congress (or PL 97-250).

Glossary of Congressional Terms

Act—The term for legislation once it has passed both houses of Congress and has been signed by the president or passed over his veto, thus becoming law. *(See also Pocket Veto.)* Also used in parliamentary terminology for a bill that has been passed by one house and engrossed. *(See Engrossed Bill.)*

Adjournment Sine Die—Adjournment without definitely fixing a day for reconvening; literally "adjournment without a day." Usually used to connote the final adjournment of a session of Congress. A session can continue until noon, Jan. 3, of the following year, when, under the 20th Amendment to the Constitution, it automatically terminates. Both houses must agree to a concurrent resolution for either house to adjourn for more than three days.

Adjournment to a Day Certain—Adjournment under a motion or resolution that fixes the next time of meeting. Under the Constitution, neither house can adjourn for more than three days without the concurrence of the other. A session of Congress is not ended by adjournment to a day certain.

Amendment—A proposal of a member of Congress to alter the language, provisions or stipulations in a bill or in another amendment. An amendment usually is printed, debated and voted upon in the same manner as a bill.

Amendment in the Nature of a Substitute—Usually an amendment that seeks to replace the entire text of a bill. Passage of this type of amendment strikes out everything after the enacting clause and inserts a new version of the bill. An amendment in the nature of a substitute also can refer to an amendment that replaces a large portion of the text of a bill.

Appeal—A member's challenge of a ruling or decision made by the presiding officer of the chamber. In the Senate, the senator appeals to members of the chamber to override the decision. If carried by a majority vote, the appeal nullifies the chair's ruling. In the House, the decision of the Speaker traditionally has been final; seldom are there appeals to the members to reverse the Speaker's stand. To appeal a ruling is considered an attack on the Speaker.

Appropriations Bill—A bill that gives legal authority to spend or obligate money from the Treasury. The Constitution disallows money to be drawn from the Treasury "but in Consequence of Appropriations made by Law."

By congressional custom, an appropriations bill originates in the House, and it is not supposed to be considered by the full House or Senate until a related measure authorizing the funding is enacted. An appropriations bill grants the actual money approved by authorization bills, but not necessarily the full amount permissible under the authorization. The 1985 Gramm-Rudman-Hollings law stipulated that the House is to pass by June 30 the last regular appropriations bill for the fiscal year starting the following Oct. 1. (There is no such deadline for the Senate.) However, for decades appropriations often have not been final until well after the fiscal year begins, requiring a succession of stopgap bills to continue the government's functions. In addition, much federal spending — about half of all budget authority, notably that for Social Security and interest on the federal debt — does not require annual appropriations; those programs exist under permanent appropriations. *(See also Authorization, Budget Process, Backdoor Spending Authority, Entitlement Program.)*

In addition to general appropriations bills, there are two specialized types. *(See Continuing Resolution, Supplemental Appropriations Bill.)*

Authorization—Basic, substantive legislation that establishes or continues the legal operation of a federal program or agency, either indefinitely or for a specific period of time, or which sanctions a particular type of obligation or expenditure. An authorization normally is a prerequisite for an appropriation or other kind of budget authority.

Under the rules of both houses, the appropriation for a program or agency may not be considered until its authorization has been considered. An authorization also may limit the amount of budget authority to be provided or may authorize the appropriation of "such sums as may be necessary." *(See also Backdoor Spending Authority.)*

Backdoor Spending Authority—Budget authority provided in legislation outside the normal appropriations process. The most common forms of backdoor spending are borrowing authority, contract authority, entitlements and loan guarantees that commit the government to payments of principal and interest on loans — such as Guaranteed Student Loans — made by banks or other private lenders. Loan guarantees only result in actual outlays when there is a default by the borrower.

In some cases, such as interest on the public debt, a permanent appropriation is provided that becomes available without further action by Congress.

Bills—Most legislative proposals before Congress are in the form of bills and are designated by HR in the House of Representatives or S in the Senate, according to the house in which they originate, and by a number assigned in the order in which they are introduced during the two-year period of a congressional term. "Public bills" deal with general questions and become public laws if approved by Congress and signed by the president. "Private bills" deal with individual matters such as claims against the government, immigration and naturalization cases or land titles, and become private laws if approved and signed. *(See also Concurrent Resolution, Joint Resolution, Resolution.)*

Bills Introduced—In both the House and Senate, any number of members may join in introducing a single bill or resolution. The first member listed is the sponsor of the bill, and all subsequent members listed are the bill's cosponsors.

Many bills are committee bills and are introduced under the name of the chairman of the committee or subcommittee. All appropriations bills fall into this category. A committee frequently holds hearings on a number of related bills and may agree to one of them or to an entirely new bill. *(See also Report, Clean Bill, By Request.)*

Bills Referred—When introduced, a bill is referred to the committee or committees that have jurisdiction over the subject with which the bill is concerned. Under the standing rules of the House and Senate, bills are referred by the Speaker in the House and by the presiding officer in the Senate. In practice, the House and Senate parliamentarians act for these officials and refer the vast majority of bills.

Borrowing Authority—Statutory authority that permits a federal agency to incur obligations and make payments for specified purposes with borrowed money.

Budget—The document sent to Congress by the president early each year estimating government revenue and expenditures for the ensuing fiscal year.

Budget Act—The common name for the Congressional Budget and Impoundment Control Act of 1974, which established the current budget process and created the Congressional Budget Office. The act also put limits on presidential authority to spend appropriated money. *(See Impoundments, Budget Process.)*

Budget Authority—Authority to enter into obligations that will result in immediate or future outlays involving federal funds. The basic forms of budget authority are appropriations, contract authority and borrowing authority. Budget authority may be classified by (1) the period of availability (one-year, multiple-year or without a time limitation), (2) the timing of congressional action (current or permanent) or (3) the manner of determining the amount available (definite or indefinite).

Budget Process—Congress in 1990 made far-reaching changes in its 1974 budget process law, called the Congressional Budget and Impoundment Control Act. The law continues to provide for congressional approval of budget resolutions and reconciliation bills, two mechanisms created by the 1974 law. *(See Budget Resolution, Reconciliation.)* The 1990 changes discarded provisions of 1985 and 1987 amendments to the Act that automatically cut federal spending in certain areas when pre-determined targets

were exceeded. Those amendments, collectively known as Gramm-Rudman-Hollings for their congressional sponsors, were intended to balance the federal budget by fiscal year 1991. Soaring deficits made the goal unachievable, threatening federal programs with almost random and massive cuts.

Congress stepped back from that brink and provided, instead, for spending caps in three categories: defense, domestic, and international for 1991-93; for the following two years the 1990 changes set overall discretionary spending caps. Each cap will increase automatically with inflation plus — for domestic spending only — an extra $20 billion. Moreover, spending that exceeds the cap due to factors beyond the control of Congress, such as a recession, will not trigger automatic cuts. Entitlement spending, such as for Medicare, was put on a "pay as you go" basis, requiring any expansion be paid for by a corresponding entitlement cut or revenue increase. Also, any tax cut must be paid for by a compensating tax increase or entitlement cut. But if all these provisions failed, automatic spending cuts could still occur. *(See Sequestration.)*

Budget Resolution—A concurrent resolution passed by both houses of Congress, but not requiring the president's signature, establishing the congressional budget plan. The resolution sets forth various budget totals and functional allocations. Its deadline is April 15 but if missed the Budget committees must report spending limits for the Appropriations committees based on discretionary spending in the president's budget.

By Request—A phrase used when a senator or representative introduces a bill at the request of an executive agency or private organization but does not necessarily endorse the legislation.

Calendar—An agenda or list of business awaiting possible action by each chamber. The House uses five legislative calendars. *(See Corrections, Discharge, House, Private, and Union Calendar.)*

In the Senate, all legislative matters reported from committee go on one calendar. They are listed there in the order in which committees report them or the Senate places them on the calendar, but they may be called up out of order by the majority leader, either by obtaining unanimous consent of the Senate or by a motion to call up a bill. The Senate also uses one non-legislative calendar; this is used for treaties and nominations. *(See Executive Calendar.)*

Calendar Wednesday—In the House, committees, on Wednesdays, may be called in the order in which they appear in Rule X of the House, for the purpose of bringing up any of their bills from either the House or the Union Calendar, except bills that are privileged. General debate is limited to two hours. Bills called up from the Union Calendar are considered in Committee of the Whole. Calendar Wednesday is not observed during the last two weeks of a session and may be dispensed with at other times by a two-thirds vote. This procedure is rarely used and routinely is dispensed with by unanimous consent.

Call of the Calendar—Senate bills that are not brought up for debate by a motion, unanimous consent or a unanimous consent agreement are brought before the Senate for action when the calendar listing them is "called." Bills must be called in the order listed. Measures considered by this method usually are non-controversial, and debate on the bill and any proposed amendments is limited to a total of five minutes for each senator.

Chamber—The meeting place for the membership of either the House or the Senate; also the membership of the House or Senate meeting as such.

Clean Bill—Frequently after a committee has finished a major revision of a bill, one of the committee members, usually the chairman, will assemble the changes and what is left of the original bill into a new measure and introduce it as a "clean bill." The revised measure, which is given a new number, then is referred back to the committee, which reports it to the floor for consideration. This often is a timesaver, as committee-recommended changes in a clean bill do not have to be considered and voted on by the chamber. Reporting a clean bill also protects committee amendments that could be subject to points of order concerning germaneness.

Clerk of the House—Chief administrative officer of the House of Representatives, with duties corresponding to those of the secretary of the Senate. *(See also Secretary of the Senate.)*

Cloture—The process by which a filibuster can be ended in the Senate other than by unanimous consent. A motion for cloture can apply to any measure before the Senate, including a proposal to change the chamber's rules. A cloture motion requires the signatures of 16 senators to be introduced. To end a filibuster, the cloture motion must obtain the votes of three-fifths of the entire Senate membership (60 if there are no vacancies), except when the filibuster is against a proposal to amend the standing rules of the Senate and a two-thirds vote of senators present and voting is required. The cloture request is put to a roll-call vote one hour after the Senate meets on the second day following introduction of the motion. If approved, cloture limits each senator to one hour of debate. The bill or amendment in question comes to a final vote after 30 hours of consideration (including debate time and the time it takes to conduct roll calls, quorum calls and other procedural motions). *(See Filibuster.)*

Committee—A division of the House or Senate that prepares legislation for action by the parent chamber or makes investigations as directed by the parent chamber. There are several types of committees. *(See Standing and Select or Special Committees.)* Most standing committees are divided into subcommittees, which study legislation, hold hearings and report bills, with or without amendments, to the full committee. Only the full committee can report legislation for action by the House or Senate.

Committee of the Whole—The working title of what is formally "The Committee of the Whole House [of Representatives] on the State of the Union." The membership is comprised of all House members sitting as a committee. Any 100 members who are present on the floor of the chamber to consider legislation comprise a quorum of the committee. Any legislation taken up by the Committee of the Whole, however, must first have passed through the regular legislative or Appropriations committee and have been placed on the calendar.

Technically, the Committee of the Whole considers only bills directly or indirectly appropriating money, authorizing appropriations or involving taxes or charges on the public. Because the Committee of the Whole need number only 100 representatives, a quorum is more readily attained, and legislative business is expedited. Before 1971, members' positions were not individually recorded on votes taken in Committee of the Whole. *(See Teller Vote.)*

When the full House resolves itself into the Committee of the Whole, it supplants the Speaker with a "chairman." A measure is debated and amendments may be proposed, with votes on amendments as needed. *(See Five-Minute Rule.)* The committee, however, cannot pass a bill. When the committee completes its work on the measure, it dissolves itself by "rising." The Speaker returns, and the chairman of the Committee of the Whole reports to the House that the committee's work has been completed. At this time members may demand a roll-call vote on any amendment adopted in the Committee of the Whole. The final vote is on passage of the legislation.

Committee Veto—A requirement added to a few statutes directing that certain policy directives by an executive department or agency be reviewed by certain congressional committees before they are implemented. Under common practice, the government department or agency and the committees involved are expected to reach a consensus before the directives are carried out. *(See also Legislative Veto.)*

Concurrent Resolution—A concurrent resolution, designated H Con Res or S Con Res, must be adopted by both houses, but it is not sent to the president for approval and therefore does not have the force of law. A concurrent resolution, for example, is used to fix the time for adjournment of a Congress. It also is used as the vehicle for expressing the sense of Congress on various foreign policy and domestic issues, and it serves as the vehicle for coordinated decisions on the federal budget under the 1974 Congressional Budget and Impoundment Control Act. *(See also Bills, Joint Resolution, Resolution.)*

Conference—A meeting between the representatives of the House and the Senate to reconcile differences between the two houses on provisions of a bill passed by both chambers. Members of the conference committee are appointed by the Speaker and the presiding officer of the Senate and are called "managers" for their respective chambers. A majority of the managers for each house must reach agreement on the provisions of the bill (often a compromise between the versions of the two chambers) before it can be considered by either chamber in the form of a "conference report." When the conference report goes to the floor, it cannot be amended, and, if it is not approved by both chambers, the bill may go back to conference under certain situations, or a new conference must be convened. Many rules and informal practices govern the conduct of conference committees.

Bills that are passed by both houses with only minor differences need not be sent to conference. Either chamber may "concur" in the other's amendments, completing action on the legislation. Sometimes leaders of the committees of jurisdiction work out an informal compromise instead of having a formal conference. *(See Custody of the Papers.)*

Confirmations—*(See Nominations.)*

Congressional Record—The daily, printed account of proceedings in both the House and Senate chambers, showing substantially verbatim debate, statements and a record of floor action. Highlights of legislative and committee action are embodied in a Daily Digest section of the *Record*, and members are entitled to have their extraneous remarks printed in an appendix known as "Extension of Remarks." Members may edit and revise remarks made on the floor during debate, and quotations from debate reported by the press are not always found in the Record.

The *Congressional Record* provides a way to distinguish remarks spoken on the floor of the House and Senate from undelivered speeches. In the Senate, all speeches, articles and other matter that members insert in the *Record* without actually reading them on the floor are set off by large black dots, or bullets. However, a loophole allows a member to avoid the bulleting if he delivers any portion of the speech in person. In the House, undelivered speeches and other material are printed in a distinctive typeface.*(See also Journal)*

Congressional Terms of Office—Normally begin on Jan. 3 of the year following a general election and are two years for representatives and six years for senators. Representatives elected in special elections are sworn in for the remainder of a term. A person may be appointed to fill a Senate vacancy and serves until a successor is elected; the successor serves until the end of the term applying to the vacant seat.

Continuing Resolution—A joint resolution, cleared by Congress and signed by the president (when the new fiscal year is about to begin or has begun), to provide new budget authority for federal agencies and programs to continue in operation until the regular appropriations acts are enacted. *(See Appropriations Bill.)*

The continuing resolution usually specifies a maximum rate at which an agency may incur obligations, based on the rate of the prior year, the president's budget request or an appropriations bill passed by either or both houses of Congress but not yet enacted. In recent years, most regular appropriations bills have not cleared and a full-year continuing resolution has taken their place. For fiscal 1987 and 1988, Congress intentionally rolled all 13 regular appropriations bills into one continuing resolution.

Continuing resolutions also are called "CRs" or continuing appropriations.

Contract Authority—Budget authority contained in an authorization bill that permits the federal government to enter into contracts or other obligations for future payments from funds not yet appropriated by Congress. The assumption is that funds will be available for payment in a subsequent appropriation act.

Controllable Budget Items—In federal budgeting this refers to programs for which the budget authority or outlays during a fiscal year can be controlled without changing existing, substantive law. The concept "relatively uncontrollable under current law" includes outlays for open-ended programs and fixed costs such as interest on the public debt, Social Security benefits, veterans' benefits and outlays to liquidate prior-year obligations. More and more spending for federal programs has become uncontrollable or relatively uncontrollable.

Correcting Recorded Votes—Rules prohibit members from changing their votes after the result has been announced. But, occasionally hours, days or months after a vote has been taken, a member may announce that he was "incorrectly recorded." In the Senate, a request to change one's vote almost always receives unanimous consent. In the House, members are prohibited from changing their votes if tallied by the electronic voting system. If the vote was taken by roll call, a change is permissible if consent is granted.

Corrections Calendar—Members of the House may place on this calendar bills reported favorably from committee that repeal rules and regulations considered excessive or unnecessary. Bills on the Corrections Calendar normally are called on the second and fourth Tuesday of each month at the discretion of the House Speaker in consultation with the minority leader. A bill must be on the calendar for at least three legislative days before it can be brought up for floor consideration. Once on the floor, a bill is subject to one hour of debate equally divided between the chairman and ranking member of the committee of jurisdiction. A vote may be called on whether to recommit the bill to committee with or without instructions. To pass, a three-fifths majority, or 261 votes if all House members vote, is required.

Cosponsor—*(See Bills Introduced.)*

Current Services Estimates—Estimated budget authority and outlays for federal programs and operations for the forthcoming fiscal year based on continuation of existing levels of service without policy changes. These estimates of budget authority and outlays, accompanied by the underlying economic and policy assumptions upon which they are based, are transmitted by the president to Congress when the budget is submitted.

Custody of the Papers—To reconcile differences between the House and Senate versions of a bill, a conference may be arranged. The chamber with "custody of the papers" — the engrossed bill, engrossed amendments, messages of transmittal — is the only body empowered to request the conference. By custom, the chamber that asks for a conference is the last to act on the conference report once agreement has been reached on the bill by the conferees.

Custody of the papers sometimes is manipulated to ensure that a particular chamber acts either first or last on the conference report.

Deferral—Executive branch action to defer, or delay, the spending of appropriated money. The 1974 Congressional Budget and Impoundment Control Act requires a special message from the president to Congress reporting a proposed deferral of spending. Deferrals may not extend beyond the end of the fiscal year in which the message is transmitted. A federal district court in 1986 struck down the president's authority to defer spending for policy reasons; the ruling was upheld by a federal appeals court in 1987. Congress can and has prohibited proposed deferrals by enacting a law doing so; most often cancellations of proposed deferrals are included in appropriations bills. *(See also Rescission.)*

Dilatory Motion—A motion made for the purpose of

killing time and preventing action on a bill or amendment. House rules outlaw dilatory motions, but enforcement is largely within the discretion of the Speaker or chairman of the Committee of the Whole. The Senate does not have a rule banning dilatory motions, except under cloture.

Discharge a Committee—Occasionally, attempts are made to relieve a committee from jurisdiction over a measure before it. This is attempted more often in the House than in the Senate, and the procedure rarely is successful.

In the House, if a committee does not report a bill within 30 days after the measure is referred to it, any member may file a discharge motion. Once offered, the motion is treated as a petition needing the signatures of 218 members (a majority of the House). After the required signatures have been obtained, there is a delay of seven days. Thereafter, on the second and fourth Mondays of each month, except during the last six days of a session, any member who has signed the petition must be recognized, if he so desires, to move that the committee be discharged. Debate on the motion to discharge is limited to 20 minutes, and, if the motion is carried, consideration of the bill becomes a matter of high privilege.

If a resolution to consider a bill is held up in the Rules Committee for more than seven legislative days, any member may enter a motion to discharge the committee. The motion is handled like any other discharge petition in the House.

Occasionally, to expedite non-controversial legislative business, a committee is discharged by unanimous consent of the House, and a petition is not required. *(Senate procedure, see Discharge Resolution.)*

Discharge Calendar—The House calendar to which motions to discharge committees are referred when they have the required number of signatures (218) and are awaiting floor action.

Discharge Petition—*(See Discharge a Committee.)*

Discharge Resolution—In the Senate, a special motion that any senator may introduce to relieve a committee from consideration of a bill before it. The resolution can be called up for Senate approval or disapproval in the same manner as any other Senate business. *(House procedure, see Discharge a Committee.)*

Division of a Question for Voting—A practice that is more common in the Senate but also used in the House, a member may demand a division of an amendment or a motion for purposes of voting. Where an amendment or motion can be divided, the individual parts are voted on separately when a member demands a division. This procedure occurs most often during the consideration of conference reports.

Division Vote—*(See Standing Vote.)*

Enacting Clause—Key phrase in bills beginning, "Be it enacted by the Senate and House of Representatives . . ." A successful motion to strike it from legislation kills the measure.

Engrossed Bill—The final copy of a bill as passed by one chamber, with the text as amended by floor action and certified by the clerk of the House or the secretary of the Senate.

Enrolled Bill—The final copy of a bill that has been passed in identical form by both chambers. It is certified by an officer of the house of origin (clerk of the House or secretary of the Senate) and then sent on for the signatures of the House Speaker, the Senate president pro tempore and the president of the United States. An enrolled bill is printed on parchment.

Entitlement Program—A federal program that guarantees a certain level of benefits to persons or other entities who meet requirements set by law, such as Social Security, farm price supports or unemployment benefits. It thus leaves no discretion with Congress on how much money to appropriate, and some entitlements carry permanent appropriations.

Executive Calendar—This is a non-legislative calendar in the Senate on which presidential documents such as treaties and nominations are listed.

Executive Document—A document, usually a treaty, sent to the Senate by the president for consideration or approval. Executive documents are identified for each session of Congress according to the following pattern: Executive A, 97th Congress, 1st Session; Executive B, and so on. They are referred to committee in the same manner as other measures. Unlike legislative documents, however, treaties do not die at the end of a Congress but remain "live" proposals until acted on by the Senate or withdrawn by the president.

Executive Session—A meeting of a Senate or House committee (or occasionally of either chamber) that only its members may attend. Witnesses regularly appear at committee meetings in executive session — for example, Defense Department officials during presentations of classified defense information. Other members of Congress may be invited, but the public and press are not to attend.

Expenditures—The actual spending of money as distinguished from the appropriation of funds. Expenditures are made by the disbursing officers of the administration; appropriations are made only by Congress. The two are rarely identical in any fiscal year. In addition to some current budget authority, expenditures may represent budget authority made available one, two or more years earlier.

Federal Debt—The federal debt consists of public debt, which occurs when the Treasury or the Federal Financing Bank (FFB) borrows money directly from the public or another fund or account, and agency debt, which is incurred when a federal agency other than Treasury or the FFB is authorized by law to borrow money from the public or another fund or account. The public debt comprises about 99 percent of the gross federal debt.

Filibuster—A time-delaying tactic associated with the Senate and used by a minority in an effort to prevent a vote on a bill or amendment that probably would pass if voted upon directly. The most common method is to take advantage of the Senate's rules permitting unlimited debate, but other forms of parliamentary maneuvering may be used. The stricter rules of the House make filibusters more difficult, but delaying tactics are employed occasionally through various procedural devices allowed by House rules. *(Senate filibusters, see Cloture.)*

Fiscal Year—Financial operations of the government are carried out in a 12-month fiscal year, beginning on Oct. 1 and ending on Sept. 30. The fiscal year carries the date of the calendar year in which it ends. (From fiscal year 1844 to fiscal year 1976, the fiscal year began July 1 and ended the following June 30.)

Five-Minute Rule—A debate-limiting rule of the House that is invoked when the House sits as the Committee of the Whole. Under the rule, a member offering an amendment is allowed to speak five minutes in its favor, and an opponent of the amendment is allowed to speak five minutes in opposition. Debate is then closed. In practice, amendments regularly are debated more than 10 minutes, with members gaining the floor by offering pro forma amendments or obtaining unanimous consent to speak longer than five minutes. *(See Strike Out the Last Word.)*

Floor Manager—A member who has the task of steering legislation through floor debate and the amendment process to a final vote in the House or the Senate. Floor managers usually are chairmen or ranking members of the committee that reported the bill. Managers are responsible for apportioning the debate time granted supporters of the bill. The ranking minority member of the committee normally apportions time for the minority party's participation in the debate.

Frank—A member's facsimile signature, which is used on envelopes in lieu of stamps, for the member's official outgoing mail. The "franking privilege" is the right to send mail postage-free.

Functions (Functional Classifications)—Categories of spending established for accounting purposes to keep track of specific expenditures. Each account is placed in the single function (such as national defense, agriculture, health, etc.) that best represents its major purpose, regardless of the agency administering the program. The functions do not correspond directly with appropriations or with the budgets of individual agencies. *(See also Budget Resolution.)*

Germane—Pertaining to the subject matter of the measure at hand. All House amendments must be germane to the bill being considered. The Senate requires that amendments be germane when they are proposed to general appropriation bills, bills being considered once cloture has been adopted or, frequently, when proceeding under a unanimous consent agreement placing a time limit on consideration of a bill. The 1974 budget act also requires that amendments to concurrent budget resolutions be germane. In the House, floor debate must be germane, and the first three hours of debate each day in the Senate must be germane to the pending business.

Gramm-Rudman-Hollings Deficit Reduction Act—*(See Budget Process, Sequestration.)*

Grandfather Clause—A provision exempting persons or other entities already engaged in an activity from rules or legislation affecting that activity. Grandfather clauses sometimes are added to legislation in order to avoid antagonizing groups with established interests in the activities affected.

Grants-in-Aid—Payments by the federal government to states, local governments or individuals in support of specified programs, services or activities.

Hearings—Committee sessions for taking testimony from witnesses. At hearings on legislation, witnesses usually include specialists, government officials and spokespersons for individuals or entities affected by the bill or bills under study. Hearings related to special investigations bring forth a variety of witnesses. Committees sometimes use their subpoena power to summon reluctant witnesses. The public and press may attend open hearings but are barred from closed, or "executive," hearings. The vast majority of hearings are open to the public. *(See Executive Session.)*

Hold-Harmless Clause—A provision added to legislation to ensure that recipients of federal funds do not receive less in a future year than they did in the current year if a new formula for allocating funds authorized in the legislation would result in a reduction to the recipients. This clause has been used most frequently to soften the impact of sudden reductions in federal grants.

Hopper—Box on House clerk's desk where members deposit bills and resolutions to introduce them. *(See also Bills Introduced.)*

Hour Rule—A provision in the rules of the House that permits one hour of debate time for each member on amendments debated in the House of Representatives sitting as the House. Therefore, the House normally amends bills while sitting as the Committee of the Whole, where the five-minute rule on amendments operates. *(See Committee of the Whole, Five-Minute Rule.)*

House—The House of Representatives, as distinct from the Senate, although each body is a "house" of Congress.

House as in Committee of the Whole—A procedure that can be used to expedite consideration of certain measures such as continuing resolutions and, when there is debate, private bills. The procedure only can be invoked with the unanimous consent of the House or a rule from the Rules Committee and has procedural elements of both the House sitting as the House of Representatives, such as the Speaker presiding and the previous question motion being in order, and the House sitting as the Committee of the Whole, such as the five-minute rule pertaining.

House Calendar—A listing for action by the House of public bills that do not directly or indirectly appropriate money or raise revenue.

Immunity—The constitutional privilege of members of Congress to make verbal statements on the floor and in committee for which they cannot be sued or arrested for slander or libel. Also, freedom from arrest while traveling to or from sessions of Congress or on official business. Members in this status may be arrested only for treason, felonies or a breach of the peace, as defined by congressional manuals.

Impoundments—Any action taken by the executive branch that delays or precludes the obligation or expenditure of budget authority previously approved by Congress. The Congressional Budget and Impoundment Control Act of 1974 was enacted after frequent use of impoundments by President Richard Nixon. In addition to creating the budget process currently used, the 1974 law established procedures for congressional approval or disapproval of temporary or permanent impoundments, which are called deferrals and rescissions.

Joint Committee—A committee composed of a specified number of members of both the House and Senate. A joint committee may be investigative or research-oriented, an example of the latter being the Joint Economic Committee. Others have housekeeping duties such as the joint committees on Printing and on the Library of Congress.

Joint Resolution—A joint resolution, designated H J Res or S J Res, requires the approval of both houses and the signature of the president, just as a bill does, and has the force of law if approved. There is no practical difference between a bill and a joint resolution. A joint resolution generally is used to deal with a limited matter such as a single appropriation.

Joint resolutions also are used to propose amendments to the Constitution. They do not require a presidential signature but become a part of the Constitution when three-fourths of the states have ratified them.

Journal—The official record of the proceedings of the House and Senate. The *Journal* records the actions taken in each chamber, but, unlike the *Congressional Record*, it does not include the substantially verbatim report of speeches, debates, statements and the like.

Law—An act of Congress that has been signed by the president or passed over his veto by Congress. Public bills, when signed, become public laws, and are cited by the letters PL and a hyphenated number. The two digits before the hyphen correspond to the Congress, and the one or more digits after the hyphen refer to the numerical sequence in which the bills were signed by the president during that Congress. Private bills, when signed, become private laws. *(See also Pocket Veto, Slip Laws, Statutes at Large, U.S. Code.)*

Legislative Day—The "day" extending from the time either house meets after an adjournment until the time it next adjourns. Because the House normally adjourns from day to day, legislative days and calendar days usually coincide. But in the Senate, a legislative day may, and frequently does, extend over several calendar days. *(See Recess.)*

Legislative Veto—A procedure, no longer allowed, permitting either the House or Senate, or both chambers, to review proposed executive branch regulations or actions and to block or modify those with which they disagreed.

The specifics of the procedure varied, but Congress generally provided for a legislative veto by including in a bill a provision that administrative rules or action taken to implement the law were to go into effect at the end of a designated period of time unless blocked by either or both houses of Congress. Another version of the veto provided for congressional reconsideration and rejection of regulations already in effect.

The Supreme Court June 23, 1983, struck down the legislative veto as an unconstitutional violation of the law-making procedure provided in the Constitution.

Loan Guarantees—Loans to third parties for which the federal government in the event of default guarantees, in whole or in part, the repayment of principal or interest to a lender or holder of a security.

Lobby—A group seeking to influence the passage or defeat of legislation. Originally the term referred to persons frequenting the lobbies or corridors of legislative chambers in order to speak to lawmakers.

The definition of a lobby and the activity of lobbying is a matter of differing interpretation. By some definitions, lobbying is limited to direct attempts to influence lawmakers through personal interviews and persuasion. Under other definitions, lobbying includes attempts at indirect, or "grass-roots," influence, such as persuading members of a group to write or visit their district's representative and state's senators or attempting to create a climate of opinion favorable to a desired legislative goal.

The right to attempt to influence legislation is based on the First Amendment to the Constitution, which says Congress shall make no law abridging the right of the people "to petition the government for a redress of grievances."

Majority Leader—The majority leader is elected by his party colleagues. In the Senate, in consultation with the minority leader and his colleagues, the majority leader directs the legislative schedule for the chamber. He also is his party's spokesperson and chief strategist. In the House, the majority leader is second to the Speaker in the majority party's leadership and serves as his party's legislative strategist.

Majority Whip—In effect, the assistant majority leader, in either the House or Senate. His job is to help marshal majority forces in support of party strategy and legislation.

Manual—The official handbook in each house prescribing in detail its organization, procedures and operations.

Marking Up a Bill—Going through the contents of a piece of legislation in committee or subcommittee to, for example, consider its provisions in large and small portions, act on amendments to provisions and proposed revisions to the language, and insert new sections and phraseology. If the bill is extensively amended, the committee's version may be introduced as a separate bill, with a new number, before being considered by the full House or Senate. *(See Clean Bill.)*

Minority Leader—Floor leader for the minority party in each chamber. *(See also Majority Leader.)*

Minority Whip—Performs duties of whip for the minority party. *(See also Majority Whip.)*

Morning Hour—The time set aside at the beginning of each legislative day for the consideration of regular, routine business. The "hour" is of indefinite duration in the House, where it is rarely used.

In the Senate it is the first two hours of a session following an adjournment, as distinguished from a recess. The morning hour can be terminated earlier if the morning business has been completed. Business includes such matters as messages from the president, communications from the heads of departments, messages from the House, the presentation of petitions, reports of standing and select committees and the introduction of bills and resolutions. During the first hour of the morning hour in the Senate, no motion to proceed to the consideration of any bill on the calendar is in order except by unanimous consent. During the second hour, motions can be made but must be decided without debate. Senate committees may meet while the Senate conducts morning hour.

Motion—In the House or Senate chamber, a request by a member to institute any one of a wide array of parliamentary actions. He "moves" for a certain procedure, such as the consideration of a measure. The precedence of motions, and whether they are debatable, is set forth in the House and Senate manuals.

Nominations—Presidential appointments to office subject to Senate confirmation. Although most nominations win quick Senate approval, some are controversial and become the topic of hearings and debate. Sometimes senators object to appointees for patronage reasons — for example, when a nomination to a local federal job is made without consulting the senators of the state concerned. In some situations a senator may object that the nominee is "personally obnoxious" to him. Usually other senators join in blocking such appointments out of courtesy to their colleagues. (See Senatorial Courtesy.)

Obligations—Orders placed, contracts awarded, services received and similar transactions during a given period that will require payments during the same or future period. Such amounts include outlays for which obligations had not been previously recorded and reflect adjustments for differences between obligations previously recorded and actual outlays to liquidate those obligations.

One-Minute Speeches—Addresses by House members at the beginning of a legislative day. The speeches may cover any subject but are limited to one minute's duration.

Outlays—Payments made (generally through the issuance of checks or disbursement of cash) to liquidate obligations. Outlays during a fiscal year may be for the payment of obligations incurred in prior years or in the same year.

Override a Veto—If the president disapproves a bill and sends it back to Congress with his objections, Congress may try to override his veto and enact the bill into law. Neither house is required to attempt to override a veto. The override of a veto requires a recorded vote with a two-thirds majority in each chamber. The question put to each house is: "Shall the bill pass, the objections of the president to the contrary notwithstanding?" (See also Pocket Veto, Veto.)

Oversight Committee—A congressional committee, or designated subcommittee of a committee, that is charged with general oversight of one or more federal agencies' programs and activities. Usually, the oversight panel for a particular agency also is the authorizing committee for that agency's programs and operations.

Pair—A voluntary, informal arrangement that two lawmakers, usually on opposite sides of an issue, make on recorded votes. In many cases the result is to subtract a vote from each side, with no effect on the outcome. Pairs are not authorized in the rules of either house, are not counted in tabulating the final result and have no official standing. However, members pairing are identified in the Congressional Record, along with their positions on such votes, if known. A member who expects to be absent for a vote can pair with a member who plans to vote, with the latter agreeing to withhold his vote.

There are three types of pairs: 1) A live pair involves a member who is present for a vote and another who is absent. The member in attendance votes and then withdraws the vote, announcing that he has a live pair with colleague "X" and stating how the two members would have voted, one in favor, the other opposed. A live pair may affect the outcome of a closely contested vote, since it subtracts one "yea" or one "nay" from the final tally. A live pair may cover one or several specific issues. 2) A general pair, widely used in the House, does not entail any arrangement between two members and does not affect the vote. Members who expect to be absent notify the clerk that they wish to make a general pair. Each member then is paired with another desiring a pair, and their names are listed in the Congressional Record. The member may or may not be paired with another taking the opposite position, and no indication of how the members would have voted is given. 3) A specific pair is similar to a general pair, except that the opposing stands of the two members are identified and printed in the Record.

Petition—A request or plea sent to one or both chambers from an organization or private citizens' group asking support of particular legislation or favorable consideration of a matter not yet receiving congressional attention. Petitions are referred to appropriate committees.

Pocket Veto—The act of the president in withholding his approval of a bill after Congress has adjourned. When Congress is in session, a bill becomes law without the president's signature if he does not act upon it within 10 days, excluding Sundays, from the time he gets it. But if Congress adjourns sine die within that 10-day period, the bill will die even if the president does not formally veto it.

The Supreme Court in 1986 agreed to decide whether the president can pocket veto a bill during recesses and between sessions of the same Congress or only between Congresses. The justices in 1987 declared the case moot, however, because the bill in question was invalid once the case reached the Court. (See also Veto.)

Point of Order—An objection raised by a member that the chamber is departing from rules governing its conduct of business. The objector cites the rule violated, the chair sustaining his objection if correctly made. Order is restored by the chair's suspending proceedings of the chamber until it conforms to the prescribed "order of business."

President of the Senate—Under the Constitution, the vice president of the United States presides over the Senate. In his absence, the president pro tempore, or a senator designated by the president pro tempore, presides over the chamber.

President Pro Tempore—The chief officer of the

Senate in the absence of the vice president; literally, but loosely, the president for a time. The president pro tempore is elected by his fellow senators, and the recent practice has been to elect the senator of the majority party with the longest period of continuous service.

Previous Question—A motion for the previous question, when carried, has the effect of cutting off all debate, preventing the offering of further amendmentsand forcing a vote on the pending matter. In the House, the previous question is not permitted in the Committee of the Whole. The motion for the previous question is a debate-limiting device and is not in order in the Senate.

Printed Amendment—A House rule guarantees five minutes of floor debate in support and five minutes in opposition, and no other debate time, on amendments printed in the *Congressional Record* at least one day prior to the amendment's consideration in the Committee of the Whole. In the Senate, while amendments may be submitted for printing, they have no parliamentary standing or status. An amendment submitted for printing in the Senate, however, may be called up by any senator.

Private Calendar—In the House, private bills dealing with individual matters such as claims against the government, immigration or land titles are put on this calendar. The private calendar must be called on the first Tuesday of each month, and the Speaker may call it on the third Tuesday of each month as well.

When a private bill is before the chamber, two members may block its consideration, which recommits the bill to committee. Backers of a recommitted private bill have recourse. The measure can be put into an "omnibus claims bill" — several private bills rolled into one. As with any bill, no part of an omnibus claims bill may be deleted without a vote. When the private bill goes back to the House floor in this form, it can be deleted from the omnibus bill only by majority vote.

Privilege—Relates to the rights of members of Congress and to the relative priority of the motions and actions they may make in their respective chambers. The two are distinct. "Privileged questions" deal with legislative business. "Questions of privilege" concern legislators themselves.

Privileged Questions—The order in which bills, motions and other legislative measures are considered by Congress is governed by strict priorities. A motion to table, for instance, is more privileged than a motion to recommit. Thus, a motion to recommit can be superseded by a motion to table, and a vote would be forced on the latter motion only. A motion to adjourn, however, takes precedence over a tabling motion and thus is considered of the "highest privilege." *(See also Questions of Privilege.)*

Pro Forma Amendment—*(See Strike Out the Last Word.)*

Public Laws—*(See Law.)*

Questions of Privilege—These are matters affecting members of Congress individually or collectively. Matters affecting the rights, safety, dignity and integrity of proceedings of the House or Senate as a whole are questions of privilege in both chambers.

Questions involving individual members are called questions of "personal privilege." A member rising to ask a question of personal privilege is given precedence over almost all other proceedings. An annotation in the House rules points out that the privilege rests primarily on the Constitution, which gives him a conditional immunity from arrest and an unconditional freedom to speak in the House. *(See also Privileged Questions.)*

Quorum—The number of members whose presence is necessary for the transaction of business. In the Senate and House, it is a majority of the membership. A quorum is 100 in the Committee of the Whole House. If a point of order is made that a quorum is not present, the only business that is in order is either a motion to adjourn or a motion to direct the sergeant-at-arms to request the attendance of absentees.

Readings of Bills—Traditional parliamentary procedure required bills to be read three times before they were passed. This custom is of little modern significance. Normally a bill is considered to have its first reading when it is introduced and printed, by title, in the *Congressional Record*. In the House, its second reading comes when floor consideration begins. (This is the most likely point at which there is an actual reading of the bill, if there is any.) The second reading in the Senate is supposed to occur on the legislative day after the measure is introduced, but before it is referred to committee. The third reading (again, usually by title) takes place when floor action has been completed on amendments.

Recess—Distinguished from adjournment in that a recess does not end a legislative day and therefore does not interrupt unfinished business. The rules in each house set forth certain matters to be taken up and disposed of at the beginning of each legislative day. The House usually adjourns from day to day. The Senate often recesses, thus meeting on the same legislative day for several calendar days or even weeks at a time.

Recognition—The power of recognition of a member is lodged in the Speaker of the House and the presiding officer of the Senate. The presiding officer names the member who will speak first when two or more members simultaneously request recognition.

Recommit to Committee—A motion, made on the floor after a bill has been debated, to return it to the committee that reported it. If approved, recommittal usually is considered a death blow to the bill. In the House, a motion to recommit can be made only by a member opposed to the bill, and, in recognizing a member to make the motion, the Speaker gives preference to members of the minority party over majority party members.

A motion to recommit may include instructions to the committee to report the bill again with specific amendments or by a certain date. Or, the instructions may direct that a particular study be made, with no definite deadline for further action. If the recommittal motion includes instructions to "report the bill back forthwith" and the motion is adopted, floor action on the bill continues; the committee does not actually reconsider the legislation.

Reconciliation—The 1974 budget act provides for a

"reconciliation" procedure for bringing existing tax and spending laws into conformity with ceilings enacted in the congressional budget resolution. Under the procedure, Congress instructs designated legislative committees to approve measures adjusting revenues and expenditures by a certain amount. The committees have a deadline by which they must report the legislation, but they have the discretion of deciding what changes are to be made. The recommendations of the various committees are consolidated without change by the Budget committees into an omnibus reconciliation bill, which then must be considered and approved by both houses of Congress. The orders to congressional committees to report recommendations for reconciliation bills are called reconciliation instructions, and they are contained in the budget resolution. Reconciliation instructions are not binding, but Congress must meet annual Gramm-Rudman deficit targets to avoid the automatic spending cuts of sequestration, which means it must also meet the goal of reconciliation. *(See also Budget Resolution, Sequestration.)*

Reconsider a Vote—A motion to reconsider the vote by which an action was taken has, until it is disposed of, the effect of putting the action in abeyance. In the Senate, the motion can be made only by a member who voted on the prevailing side of the original question or by a member who did not vote at all. In the House, it can be made only by a member on the prevailing side.

A common practice in the Senate after close votes on an issue is a motion to reconsider, followed by a motion to table the motion to reconsider. On this motion to table, senators vote as they voted on the original question, which allows the motion to table to prevail, assuming there are no switches. The matter then is finally closed and further motions to reconsider are not entertained. In the House, as a routine precaution, a motion to reconsider usually is made every time a measure is passed. Such a motion almost always is tabled immediately, thus shutting off the possibility of future reconsideration, except by unanimous consent.

Motions to reconsider must be entered in the Senate within the next two days of actual session after the original vote has been taken. In the House they must be entered either on the same day or on the next succeeding day the House is in session.

Recorded Vote—A vote upon which each member's stand is individually made known. In the Senate, this is accomplished through a roll call of the entire membership, to which each senator on the floor must answer "yea," "nay" or, if he does not wish to vote, "present." Since January 1973, the House has used an electronic voting system for recorded votes, including yea-and-nay votes formerly taken by roll calls.

When not required by the Constitution, a recorded vote can be obtained on questions in the House on the demand of one-fifth (44 members) of a quorum or one-fourth (25) of a quorum in the Committee of the Whole. *(See Yeas and Nays.)*

Report—Both a verb and a noun as a congressional term. A committee that has been examining a bill referred to it by the parent chamber "reports" its findings and recommendations to the chamber when it completes consideration and returns the measure. The process is called "reporting" a bill.

A "report" is the document setting forth the committee's explanation of its action. Senate and House reports are numbered separately and are designated S Rept or H Rept. When a committee report is not unanimous, the dissenting committee members may file a statement of their views, called minority or dissenting views and referred to as a minority report. Members in disagreement with some provisions of a bill may file additional or supplementary views. Sometimes a bill is reported without a committee recommendation.

Adverse reports occasionally are submitted by legislative committees. However, when a committee is opposed to a bill, it usually fails to report the bill at all. Some laws require that committee reports — favorable or adverse — be made.

Rescission—An item in an appropriations bill rescinding or canceling budget authority previously appropriated but not spent. Also, the repeal of a previous appropriation by Congress at the request of the president to cut spending or because the budget authority no longer is needed. Under the 1974 budget act, however, unless Congress approves a rescission within 45 days of continuous session after receipt of the proposal, the funds must be made available for obligation. *(See also Deferral.)*

Resolution—A "simple" resolution, designated H Res or S Res, deals with matters entirely within the prerogatives of one house or the other. It requires neither passage by the other chamber nor approval by the president, and it does not have the force of law. Most resolutions deal with the rules or procedures of one house. They also are used to express the sentiments of a single house such as condolences to the family of a deceased member or to comment on foreign policy or executive business. A simple resolution is the vehicle for a "rule" from the House Rules Committee. *(See also Concurrent and Joint Resolutions, Rules.)*

Rider—An amendment, usually not germane, that its sponsor hopes to get through more easily by including it in other legislation. Riders become law if the bills embodying them are enacted. Amendments providing legislative directives in appropriations bills are outstanding examples of riders, though technically legislation is banned from appropriations bills. The House, unlike the Senate, has a strict germaneness rule; thus, riders usually are Senate devices to get legislation enacted quickly or to bypass lengthy House consideration and, possibly, opposition.

Rules—The term has two specific congressional meanings. A rule may be a standing order governing the conduct of House or Senate business and listed among the permanent rules of either chamber. The rules deal with issues such as duties of officers, the order of business, admission to the floor, parliamentary procedures on handling amendments and voting and jurisdictions of committees.

In the House, a rule also may be a resolution reported by its Rules Committee to govern the handling of a particular bill on the floor. The committee may report a "rule," also called a "special order," in the form of a simple resolution. If the resolution is adopted by the House, the temporary rule becomes as valid as any standing rule and lapses only after action has been completed on the measure to which it pertains. A rule sets the time limit on general debate. It also may waive points of order against provisions of the bill in question such as non-germane language or against certain amendments intended to be proposed to the bill from the floor. It may even forbid all amendments or all amendments except those proposed by the legislative committee that handled the bill. In this instance, it is known as a "closed" or "gag" rule as opposed to an "open" rule, which puts no limitation on floor amendments, thus leaving the bill completely open to alteration by the adoption of germane amendments.

Secretary of the Senate—Chief administrative officer of the Senate, responsible for overseeing the duties of Senate employees, educating Senate pages, administering oaths, handling the registration of lobbyists and handling other tasks necessary for the continuing operation of the Senate. *(See also Clerk of the House.)*

Select or Special Committee—A committee set up for a special purpose and, usually, for a limited time by resolution of either the House or Senate. Most special committees are investigative and lack legislative authority — legislation is not referred to them and they cannot report bills to their parent chamber. *(See also Standing Committees.)*

Senatorial Courtesy—Sometimes referred to as "the courtesy of the Senate," it is a general practice — with no written rule — applied to consideration of executive nominations. Generally, it means that nominations from a state are not to be confirmed unless they have been approved by the senators of the president's party of that state, with other senators following their colleagues' lead in the attitude they take toward consideration of such nominations. *(See Nominations.)*

Sequestration—A procedure to cancel (or withhold) budgetary resources. Originally approved under the 1985 Gramm-Rudman-Hollings deficit reduction law, as amended in 1987, it threatened massive across-the-board cuts in federal programs in 1990 and later. Congress in late 1990 changed the law to provide a set of three sequesters, each of which kicks in 15 days after Congress adjourns. One offsets discretionary appropriations for the coming year that exceed statutory limitations and only affects discretionary spending. The second is triggered if Congress enacts entitlement spending increases or revenue decreases during the year and affects "non-exempt" entitlements. The third offsets an increase in the deficit above the limit set in law if the first two sequestions have not eliminated the excess deficit; it will cover all non-exempt spending. *(See Budget Process.)*

Sine Die—*(See Adjournment Sine Die.)*

Slip Laws—The first official publication of a bill that has been enacted and signed into law. Each is published separately in unbound single-sheet or pamphlet form. *(See also Law, Statutes at Large, U.S. Code.)*

Speaker—The presiding officer of the House of Representatives, selected by the caucus of the party to which he belongs and formally elected by the whole House.

Special Session—A session of Congress after it has adjourned sine die, completing its regular session. Special sessions are convened by the president.

Spending Authority—The 1974 budget act defines spending authority as borrowing authority, contract authority and entitlement authority for which budget authority is not provided in advance by appropriation acts.

Sponsor—*(See Bills Introduced.)*

Standing Committees—Committees permanently established by House and Senate rules. The standing committees of the House were extensively reorganized in 1995 by the 104th Congress. The last major realignment of Senate committees was in the committee system reorganization of 1977. The standing committees are legislative committees — legislation may be referred to them and they may report bills and resolutions to their parent chambers. *(See also Select or Special Committees.)*

Standing Vote—A non-recorded vote used in both the House and Senate. (A standing vote also is called a division vote.) Members in favor of a proposal stand and are counted by the presiding officer. Then members opposed stand and are counted. There is no record of how individual members voted.

Statutes at Large—A chronological arrangement of the laws enacted in each session of Congress. Though indexed, the laws are not arranged by subject matter, and there is not an indication of how they changed previously enacted laws. *(See also Law, Slip Laws, U.S. Code.)*

Strike From the Record—Remarks made on the House floor may offend some member, who moves that the offending words be "taken down" for the Speaker's cognizance, and then expunged from the debate as published in the *Congressional Record.*

Strike Out the Last Word—A motion whereby a House member is entitled to speak for five minutes on an amendment then being debated by the chamber. A member gains recognition from the chair by moving to "strike out the last word" of the amendment or section of the bill under consideration. The motion is pro forma, requires no vote and does not change the amendment being debated.

Substitute—A motion, amendment or entire bill introduced in place of the pending legislative business. Passage of a substitute measure kills the original measure by supplanting it. The substitute also may be amended. *(See also Amendment in the Nature of a Substitute.)*

Supplemental Appropriations Bill—Legislation appropriating funds after the regular annual appropriations bill for a federal department or agency has been enacted. A supplemental appropriation provides additional budget authority beyond original estimates for programs or activities, including new programs authorized after the enactment of the regular appropriation act, for which the need for funds is too urgent to be postponed until enactment of the next year's regular appropriation bill.

Suspend the Rules—Often a time-saving procedure for passing bills in the House. The wording of the motion, which may be made by any member recognized by the Speaker, is: "I move to suspend the rules and pass the bill . . ." A favorable vote by two-thirds of those present is required for passage. Debate is limited to 40 minutes and no amendments from the floor are permitted. If a two-thirds favorable vote is not attained, the bill may be considered later under regular procedures. The suspension procedure is in order every Monday and Tuesday and is intended to be reserved for non-controversial bills.

Table a Bill—Motions to table, or to "lay on the table," are used to block or kill amendments or other parliamentary questions. When approved, a tabling motion is considered the final disposition of that issue. One of the most widely used parliamentary procedures, the motion to table is not debatable, and adoption requires a simple majority vote.

In the Senate, however, different language sometimes is used. The motion may be worded to let a bill "lie on the table," perhaps for subsequent "picking up." This motion is more flexible, keeping the bill pending for later action, if desired. Tabling motions on amendments are effective debate-ending devices in the Senate.

Teller Vote—This is a largely moribund House procedure in the Committee of the Whole. Members file past tellers and are counted as for or against a measure, but they are not recorded individually. In the House, tellers are ordered upon demand of one-fifth of a quorum. This is 44 in the House, 20 in the Committee of the Whole.

The House also has a recorded teller vote, now largely supplanted by the electronic voting procedure, under which the votes of each member are made public just as they would be on a recorded vote.

Treaties—Executive proposals — in the form of resolutions of ratification — which must be submitted to the Senate for approval by two-thirds of the senators present. Treaties are normally sent to the Foreign Relations Committee for scrutiny before the Senate takes action. Foreign Relations has jurisdiction over all treaties, regardless of the subject matter. Treaties are read three times and debated on the floor in much the same manner as legislative proposals. After approval by the Senate, treaties are formally ratified by the president.

Trust Funds—Funds collected and used by the federal government for carrying out specific purposes and programs according to terms of a trust agreement or statute such as the Social Security and unemployment compensation trust funds. Such funds are administered by the government in a fiduciary capacity and are not available for the general purposes of the government.

Unanimous Consent—Proceedings of the House or Senate and action on legislation often take place upon the unanimous consent of the chamber, whether or not a rule of the chamber is being violated. Unanimous consent is used to expedite floor action and frequently is used in a routine fashion such as by a senator requesting the unanimous consent of the Senate to have specified members of his staff present on the floor during debate on a specific amendment.

Unanimous Consent Agreement—A device used in the Senate to expedite legislation. Much of the Senate's legislative business, dealing with both minor and controversial issues, is conducted through unanimous consent or unanimous consent agreements. On major legislation, such

agreements usually are printed and transmitted to all senators in advance of floor debate. Once agreed to, they are binding on all members unless the Senate, by unanimous consent, agrees to modify them. An agreement may list the order in which various bills are to be considered, specify the length of time bills and contested amendments are to be debated and when they are to be voted upon and, frequently, require that all amendments introduced be germane to the bill under consideration. In this regard, unanimous consent agreements are similar to the "rules" issued by the House Rules Committee for bills pending in the House.

Union Calendar—Bills that directly or indirectly appropriate money or raise revenue are placed on this House calendar according to the date they are reported from committee.

U.S. Code—A consolidation and codification of the general and permanent laws of the United States arranged by subject under 50 titles, the first six dealing with general or political subjects, and the other 44 alphabetically arranged from agriculture to war. The *U.S. Code* is updated annually, and a new set of bound volumes is published every six years. *(See also Law, Slip Laws, Statutes at Large.)*

Veto—Disapproval by the president of a bill or joint resolution (other than one proposing an amendment to the Constitution). When Congress is in session, the president must veto a bill within 10 days, excluding Sundays, after he has received it; otherwise, it becomes law without his signature. When the president vetoes a bill, he returns it to the house of origin along with a message stating his objections. *(See also Pocket Veto, Override a Veto.)*

Voice Vote—In either the House or Senate, members answer "aye" or "no" in chorus, and the presiding officer decides the result. The term also is used loosely to indicate action by unanimous consent or without objection.

Whip—*(See Majority and Minority Whip.)*

Without Objection—Used in lieu of a vote on non-controversial motions, amendments or bills that may be passed in either the House or Senate if no member voices an objection.

Yeas and Nays—The Constitution requires that yea-and-nay votes be taken and recorded when requested by one-fifth of the members present. In the House, the Speaker determines whether one-fifth of the members present requested a vote. In the Senate, practice requires only 11 members. The Constitution requires the yeas and nays on a veto override attempt. *(See Recorded Vote.)*

Yielding—When a member has been recognized to speak, no other member may speak unless he obtains permission from the member recognized. This permission is called yielding and usually is requested in the form, "Will the gentleman yield to me?" While this activity occasionally is seen in the Senate, the Senate has no rule or practice to parcel out time.

Constitution of the United States

We the People of the United States, in Order to form a more perfect Union, establish Justice, insure domestic Tranquility, provide for the common defence, promote the general Welfare, and secure the Blessings of Liberty to ourselves and our Posterity, do ordain and establish this Constitution for the United States of America.

ARTICLE I

Section 1. All legislative Powers herein granted shall be vested in a Congress of the United States, which shall consist of a Senate and House of Representatives.

Section 2. The House of Representatives shall be composed of Members chosen every second Year by the People of the several States, and the Electors in each State shall have the Qualifications requisite for Electors of the most numerous Branch of the State Legislature.

No Person shall be a Representative who shall not have attained to the age of twenty five Years, and been seven Years a Citizen of the United States, and who shall not, when elected, be an Inhabitant of that State in which he shall be chosen.

[Representatives and direct Taxes shall be apportioned among the several States which may be included within this Union, according to their respective Numbers, which shall be determined by adding to the whole Number of free Persons, including those bound to Service for a Term of Years, and excluding Indians not taxed, three fifths of all other Persons.]¹ The actual Enumeration shall be made within three Years after the first Meeting of the Congress of the United States, and within every subsequent Term of ten Years, in such Manner as they shall by Law direct. The Number of Representatives shall not exceed one for every thirty Thousand, but each State shall have at Least one Representative; and until such enumeration shall be made, the State of New Hampshire shall be entitled to chuse three, Massachusetts eight, Rhode-Island and Providence Plantations one, Connecticut five, New-York six, New Jersey four, Pennsylvania eight, Delaware one, Maryland six, Virginia ten, North Carolina five, South Carolina five, and Georgia three.

When vacancies happen in the Representation from any State, the Executive Authority thereof shall issue Writs of Election to fill such Vacancies.

The House of Representatives shall chuse their Speaker and other Officers; and shall have the sole Power of Impeachment.

Section 3. The Senate of the United States shall be composed of two Senators from each State, [chosen by the Legislature thereof,]² for six Years; and each Senator shall have one Vote.

Immediately after they shall be assembled in Consequence of the first Election, they shall be divided as equally as may be into three Classes. The Seats of the Senators of the first Class shall be vacated at the Expiration of the second Year, of the second Class at the Expiration of the fourth Year, and of the third Class at the Expiration of the sixth Year, so that one third may be chosen every second Year; [and if Vacancies happen by Resignation, or otherwise, during the Recess of the Legislature of any State, the Executive thereof may make temporary Appointments until the next Meeting of the Legislature, which shall then fill such Vacancies.]³

No Person shall be a Senator who shall not have attained to the Age of thirty Years, and been nine Years a Citizen of the United States, and who shall not, when elected, be an Inhabitant of that State for which he shall be chosen.

The Vice President of the United States shall be President of the Senate, but shall have no Vote, unless they be equally divided.

The Senate shall chuse their other Officers, and also a President pro tempore, in the Absence of the Vice President, or when he shall exercise the Office of President of the United States.

The Senate shall have the sole Power to try all Impeachments. When sitting for that Purpose, they shall be on Oath or Affirmation. When the President of the United States is tried, the Chief Justice shall preside: And no Person shall be convicted without the Concurrence of two thirds of the Members present.

Judgment in Cases of Impeachment shall not extend further than to removal from Office, and disqualification to hold and enjoy any Office of honor, Trust or Profit under the United States: but the Party convicted shall nevertheless be liable and subject to Indictment, Trial, Judgment and Punishment, according to Law.

Section 4. The Times, Places and Manner of holding Elections for Senators and Representatives, shall be prescribed in each State by the Legislature thereof; but the Congress may at any time by Law make or alter such Regulations, except as to the Places of chusing Senators.

The Congress shall assemble at least once in every Year, and such Meeting shall [be on the first Monday in December],[4] unless they shall by Law appoint a different Day.

Section 5. Each House shall be the Judge of the Elections, Returns and Qualifications of its own Members, and a Majority of each shall constitute a Quorum to do Business; but a smaller Number may adjourn from day to day, and may be authorized to compel the Attendance of absent Members, in such Manner, and under such Penalties as each House may provide.

Each House may determine the Rules of its Proceedings, punish its Members for disorderly Behaviour, and, with the Concurrence of two thirds, expel a Member.

Each House shall keep a Journal of its Proceedings, and from time to time publish the same, excepting such Parts as may in their Judgment require Secrecy; and the Yeas and Nays of the Members of either House on any question shall, at the Desire of one fifth of those Present, be entered on the Journal.

Neither House, during the Session of Congress, shall, without the Consent of the other, adjourn for more than three days, nor to any other Place than that in which the two Houses shall be sitting.

Section 6. The Senators and Representatives shall receive a Compensation for their Services, to be ascertained by Law, and paid out of the Treasury of the United States. They shall in all Cases, except Treason, Felony and Breach of the Peace, be privileged from Arrest during their Attendance at the Session of their respective Houses, and in going to and returning from the same; and for any Speech or Debate in either House, they shall not be questioned in any other Place.

No Senator or Representative shall, during the Time for which he was elected, be appointed to any civil Office under the Authority of the United States, which shall have been created, or the Emoluments whereof shall have been encreased during such time; and no Person holding any Office under the United States, shall be a Member of either House during his Continuance in Office.

Section 7. All Bills for raising Revenue shall originate in the House of Representatives; but the Senate may propose or concur with Amendments as on other Bills.

Every Bill which shall have passed the House of Representatives and the Senate, shall, before it become a Law, be presented to the President of the United States; If he approve he shall sign it, but if not he shall return it, with his Objections to that House in which it shall have originated, who shall enter the Objections at large on their Journal, and proceed to reconsider it. If after such Reconsideration two thirds of that House shall agree to pass the Bill, it shall be sent, together with the Objections, to the other House, by which it shall likewise be reconsidered, and if approved by two thirds of that House, it shall become a Law. But in all such Cases the Votes of both Houses shall be determined by yeas and Nays, and the Names of the Persons voting for and against the Bill shall be entered on the Journal of each House respectively. If any Bill shall not be returned by the President within ten Days (Sundays excepted) after it shall have been presented to him, the Same shall be a Law, in like Manner as if he had signed it, unless the Congress by their Adjournment prevent its Return, in which Case it shall not be a Law.

Every Order, Resolution, or Vote to which the Concurrence of the Senate and House of Representatives may be necessary (except on a question of Adjournment) shall be presented to the President of the United States; and before the Same shall take Effect, shall be approved by him, or being disapproved by him, shall be repassed by two thirds of the Senate and House of Representatives, according to the Rules and Limitations prescribed in the Case of a Bill.

Section 8. The Congress shall have Power To lay and collect Taxes, Duties, Imposts and Excises, to pay the Debts and provide for the common Defence and general Welfare of the United States; but all Duties, Imposts and Excises shall be uniform throughout the United States;

To borrow Money on the credit of the United States;

To regulate Commerce with foreign Nations, and among the several States, and with the Indian Tribes;

To establish an uniform Rule of Naturalization, and uniform Laws on the subject of Bankruptcies throughout the United States;

To coin Money, regulate the Value thereof, and of foreign Coin, and fix the Standard of Weights and Measures;

To provide for the Punishment of counterfeiting the Securities and current Coin of the United States;

To establish Post Offices and post Roads;

To promote the Progress of Science and useful Arts, by securing for limited Times to Authors and Inventors the exclusive Right to their respective Writings and Discoveries;

To constitute Tribunals inferior to the supreme Court;

To define and punish Piracies and Felonies committed on the high Seas, and Offences against the Law of Nations;

To declare War, grant Letters of Marque and Reprisal, and make Rules concerning Captures on Land and Water;

To raise and support Armies, but no Appropriation of Money to that Use shall be for a longer Term than two Years;

To provide and maintain a Navy;

To make Rules for the Government and Regulation of the land and naval Forces;

To provide for calling forth the Militia to execute the Laws of the Union, suppress Insurrections and repel Invasions;

To provide for organizing, arming, and disciplining, the Militia, and for governing such Part of them as may be employed in the Service of the United States, reserving to the States respectively, the Appointment of the Officers, and the Authority of training the Militia according to the discipline prescribed by Congress;

To exercise exclusive Legislation in all Cases whatsoever, over such District (not exceeding ten Miles square) as may, by Cession of particular States, and the Acceptance of Congress, become the Seat of the Government of the United States, and to exercise like Authority over all Places purchased by the Consent of the Legislature of the State in which the Same shall be, for the Erection of Forts, Magazines, Arsenals, dock-Yards, and other needful Buildings; —And

To make all Laws which shall be necessary and proper for carrying into Execution the foregoing Powers, and all other Powers vested by this Constitution in the Government of the United States, or in any Department or Officer thereof.

Section 9. The Migration or Importation of such Persons as any of the States now existing shall think proper to admit, shall not be prohibited by the Congress prior to the Year one thousand eight hundred and eight, but a Tax or duty may be imposed on such Importation, not exceeding ten dollars for each Person.

The Privilege of the Writ of Habeas Corpus shall not be suspended, unless when in Cases of Rebellion or Invasion the public Safety may require it.

No Bill of Attainder or ex post facto Law shall be passed.

No Capitation, or other direct, Tax shall be laid, unless in Proportion to the Census or Enumeration herein before directed to be taken.[5]

No Tax or Duty shall be laid on Articles exported from any State.

No Preference shall be given by any Regulation of Commerce or Revenue to the Ports of one State over those of another; nor shall Vessels bound to, or from, one State, be obliged to enter, clear, or pay Duties in another.

No Money shall be drawn from the Treasury, but in Consequence of Appropriations made by Law; and a regular Statement and Account of the Receipts and Expenditures of all public Money shall be published from time to time.

No Title of Nobility shall be granted by the United States: And no Person holding any Office of Profit or Trust under them, shall, without the Consent of the Congress, accept of any present, Emolument, Office, or Title, of any kind whatever, from any King, Prince, or foreign State.

Section 10. No State shall enter into any Treaty, Alliance, or Confederation; grant Letters of Marque and Reprisal; coin Money; emit Bills of Credit; make any Thing but gold and silver Coin a Tender in Payment of Debts; pass any Bill of Attainder, ex post facto Law, or Law impairing the Obligation of Contracts, or grant any Title of Nobility.

No State shall, without the Consent of the Congress, lay any Imposts or Duties on Imports or Exports, except what may be absolutely necessary for executing it's inspection Laws: and the net Produce of all Duties and Imposts, laid by any State on Imports or Exports, shall be for the Use of the Treasury of the United States; and all such Laws shall be subject to the Revision and Controul of the Congress.

No State shall, without the Consent of Congress, lay any Duty of Tonnage, keep Troops, or Ships of War in time of Peace, enter into any Agreement or Compact with another State, or with a foreign Power, or engage in War, unless actually invaded, or in such imminent Danger as will not admit of delay.

ARTICLE II

Section 1. The executive Power shall be vested in a President of the United States of America. He shall hold his Office during the Term of four Years, and, together with the Vice President, chosen for the same Term, be elected, as follows

Each State shall appoint, in such Manner as the Legislature thereof may direct, a Number of Electors, equal to the whole Number of Senators and Representatives to which the State may be entitled in the Congress: but no Senator or Representative, or Person holding an Office of Trust or Profit under the United States, shall be appointed an Elector.

[The Electors shall meet in their respective States, and vote by Ballot for two Persons, of whom one at least shall not be an Inhabitant of the same State with themselves. And they shall make a List of all the Persons voted for, and of the Number of Votes for each; which List they shall sign and certify, and transmit sealed to the Seat of the Government of the United States, directed to the President of the Senate. The President of the Senate shall, in the Presence of the Senate and House of Representatives, open all the Certificates, and the Votes shall then be counted. The Person having the greatest Number of Votes shall be the President, if such Number be a Majority of the whole Number of Electors appointed; and if there be more than

one who have such Majority, and have an equal Number of Votes, then the House of Representatives shall immediately chuse by Ballot one of them for President; and if no Person have a Majority, then from the five highest on the list the said House shall in like Manner chuse the President. But in chusing the President, the Votes shall be taken by States, the Representation from each State having one Vote; A quorum for this Purpose shall consist of a Member or Members from two thirds of the States, and a Majority of all the States shall be necessary to a Choice. In every Case, after the Choice of the President, the Person having the greatest Number of Votes of the Electors shall be the Vice President. But if there should remain two or more who have equal Votes, the Senate shall chuse from them by Ballot the Vice President.][6]

The Congress may determine the Time of chusing the Electors, and the Day on which they shall give their Votes; which Day shall be the same throughout the United States.

No Person except a natural born Citizen, or a Citizen of the United States, at the time of the Adoption of this Constitution, shall be eligible to the Office of President; neither shall any Person be eligible to that Office who shall not have attained to the Age of thirty five Years, and been fourteen Years a Resident within the United States.

In Case of the Removal of the President from Office, or of his Death, Resignation, or Inability to discharge the Powers and Duties of the said Office,[7] the Same shall devolve on the Vice President, and the Congress may by Law provide for the Case of Removal, Death, Resignation or Inability, both of the President and Vice President, declaring what Officer shall then act as President, and such Officer shall act accordingly, until the Disability be removed, or a President shall be elected.

The President shall, at stated Times, receive for his Services, a Compensation, which shall neither be encreased nor diminished during the Period for which he shall have been elected, and he shall not receive within that Period any other Emolument from the United States, or any of them.

Before he enter on the Execution of his Office, he shall take the following Oath or Affirmation:—"I do solemnly swear (or affirm) that I will faithfully execute the Office of President of the United States, and will to the best of my Ability, preserve, protect and defend the Constitution of the United States."

Section 2. The President shall be Commander in Chief of the Army and Navy of the United States, and of the Militia of the several States, when called into the actual Service of the United States; he may require the Opinion, in writing, of the principal Officer in each of the executive Departments, upon any Subject relating to the Duties of their respective Offices, and he shall have Power to grant Reprieves and Pardons for Offences against the United States, except in Cases of Impeachment.

He shall have Power, by and with the Advice and Consent of the Senate, to make Treaties, provided two thirds of the Senators present concur; and he shall nominate, and by and with the Advice and Consent of the Senate, shall appoint Ambassadors, other public Ministers and Consuls, Judges of the supreme Court, and all other Officers of the United States, whose Appointments are not herein otherwise provided for, and which shall be established by Law: but the Congress may by Law vest the Appointment of such inferior Officers, as they think proper, in the President alone, in the Courts of Law, or in the Heads of Departments.

The President shall have Power to fill up all Vacancies that may happen during the Recess of the Senate, by granting Commissions which shall expire at the End of their next Session.

Section 3. He shall from time to time give to the Congress Information of the State of the Union, and recommend to their Consideration such Measures as he shall judge necessary and expedient; he may, on extraordinary Occasions, convene both Houses, or either of them, and in Case of Disagreement between them, with Respect to the Time of Adjournment, he may adjourn them to such Time as he shall think proper; he shall receive Ambassadors and other public Ministers; he shall take Care that the Laws be faithfully executed, and shall Commission all the Officers of the United States.

Section 4. The President, Vice President and all civil Officers of the United States, shall be removed from Office on Impeachment for, and Conviction of, Treason, Bribery, or other high Crimes and Misdemeanors.

ARTICLE III

Section 1. The judicial Power of the United States, shall be vested in one supreme Court, and in such inferior Courts as the Congress may from time to time ordain and establish. The Judges, both of the supreme and inferior Courts, shall hold their Offices during good Behaviour, and shall, at stated Times, receive for their Services, a Compensation, which shall not be diminished during their Continuance in Office.

Section 2. The judicial Power shall extend to all Cases, in Law and Equity, arising under this Constitution, the Laws of the United States, and Treaties made, or which shall be made, under their Authority; — to all Cases affecting Ambassadors, other public Ministers and Consuls; — to all Cases of admiralty and maritime Jurisdiction; — to Controversies to which the United States shall be a Party; — to Controversies between two or more States; — between a State and Citizens of another State;[8] — between Citizens of different States; — between Citizens of the same State claiming Lands under Grants of different States, and between a State, or the Citizens thereof, and foreign States, Citizens or Subjects.[8]

In all Cases affecting Ambassadors, other public Ministers and Consuls, and those in which a State shall be Party, the supreme Court shall have original Jurisdiction. In all the other Cases before mentioned, the supreme Court shall have appellate Jurisdiction, both as to Law and Fact, with such Exceptions, and under such Regulations as the Congress shall make.

The Trial of all Crimes, except in Cases of Impeachment, shall be by Jury; and such Trial shall be held in the State where the said Crimes shall have been committed; but when not committed within any State, the Trial shall be at such Place or Places as the Congress may by Law have directed.

Section 3. Treason against the United States, shall consist only in levying War against them, or in adhering to their Enemies, giving them Aid and Comfort. No Person shall be convicted of Treason unless on the Testimony of two Witnesses to the same overt Act, or on Confession in open Court.

The Congress shall have Power to declare the Punishment of Treason, but no Attainder of Treason shall work Corruption of Blood, or Forfeiture except during the Life of the Person attainted.

ARTICLE IV

Section 1. Full Faith and Credit shall be given in each State to the public Acts, Records, and judicial Proceedings of every other State. And the Congress may by general Laws prescribe the Manner in which such Acts, Records and Proceedings shall be proved, and the Effect thereof.

Section 2. The Citizens of each State shall be entitled to all Privileges and Immunities of Citizens in the several States.

A Person charged in any State with Treason, Felony, or other Crime, who shall flee from Justice, and be found in another State, shall on Demand of the executive Authority of the State from which he fled, be delivered up, to be removed to the State having Jurisdiction of the Crime.

[No Person held to Service or Labour in one State, under the Laws thereof, escaping into another, shall, in Consequence of any Law or Regulation therein, be discharged from such Service or Labour, but shall be delivered up on Claim of the Party to whom such Service or Labour may be due.][9]

Section 3. New States may be admitted by the Congress into this Union; but no new State shall be formed or erected within the Jurisdiction of any other State; nor any State be formed by the Junction of two or more States, or Parts of States, without the Consent of the Legislatures of the States concerned as well as of the Congress.

The Congress shall have Power to dispose of and make all needful Rules and Regulations respecting the Territory or other Property belonging to the United States; and nothing in this Constitution shall be so construed as to Prejudice any Claims of the United States, or of any particular State.

Section 4. The United States shall guarantee to every State in this Union a Republican Form of Government, and shall protect each of them against Invasion; and on Application of the Legislature, or of the Executive (when the Legislature cannot be convened) against domestic Violence.

ARTICLE V

The Congress, whenever two thirds of both Houses shall deem it necessary, shall propose Amendments to this Constitution, or, on the Application of the Legislatures of two thirds of the several States, shall call a Convention for proposing Amendments, which, in either Case, shall be valid to all Intents and Purposes, as Part of this Constitution, when ratified by the Legislatures of three fourths of the several States, or by Conventions in three fourths thereof, as the one or the other Mode of Ratification may be proposed by the Congress; Provided [that no Amendment which may be made prior to the Year One thousand eight hundred and eight shall in any Manner affect the first and fourth Clauses in the Ninth Section of the first Article; and][10] that no State, without its Consent, shall be deprived of its equal Suffrage in the Senate.

ARTICLE VI

All Debts contracted and Engagements entered into, before the Adoption of this Constitution, shall be as valid against the United States under this Constitution, as under the Confederation.

This Constitution, and the Laws of the United States which shall be made in Pursuance thereof; and all Treaties made, or which shall be made, under the Authority of the United States, shall be the supreme Law of the Land; and the Judges in every State shall be bound thereby, any Thing in the Constitution or Laws of any State to the Contrary notwithstanding.

The Senators and Representatives before mentioned, and the Members of the several State Legislatures, and all executive and judicial Officers, both of the United States and of the several States, shall be bound by Oath or Affirmation, to support this Constitution; but no religious Test shall ever be required as a Qualification to any Office or public Trust under the United States.

ARTICLE VII

The Ratification of the Conventions of nine States, shall be sufficient for the Establishment of this Constitution between the States so ratifying the Same.

Done in Convention by the Unanimous Consent of the States present the Seventeenth Day of September in the Year of our Lord one thousand seven hundred and Eighty seven and of the Independence of the United States of America the Twelfth. IN WITNESS whereof We have hereunto subscribed our Names,

George Washington,
President and
deputy from Virginia.

New Hampshire: John Langdon,
Nicholas Gilman.

Massachusetts: Nathaniel Gorham,
Rufus King.

Connecticut: William Samuel Johnson,
Roger Sherman.

New York: Alexander Hamilton.

New Jersey: William Livingston,
David Brearley,
William Paterson,
Jonathan Dayton.

Pennsylvania: Benjamin Franklin,
Thomas Mifflin,
Robert Morris,
George Clymer,
Thomas FitzSimons,
Jared Ingersoll,
James Wilson,
Gouverneur Morris.

Delaware: George Read,
Gunning Bedford Jr.,
John Dickinson,
Richard Bassett,
Jacob Broom.

Maryland: James McHenry,
Daniel of St. Thomas Jenifer,
Daniel Carroll.

Virginia: John Blair,
James Madison Jr.

North Carolina: William Blount,
Richard Dobbs Spaight,
Hugh Williamson.

South Carolina: John Rutledge,
Charles Cotesworth Pinckney,
Charles Pinckney,
Pierce Butler.

Georgia: William Few,
Abraham Baldwin.

[The language of the original Constitution, not including the Amendments, was adopted by a convention of the states on September 17, 1787, and was subsequently ratified by the states on the following dates: Delaware, December 7, 1787; Pennsylvania, December 12, 1787; New Jersey, December 18, 1787; Georgia, January 2, 1788; Connecticut, January 9, 1788; Massachusetts, February 6, 1788; Maryland, April 28, 1788; South Carolina, May 23, 1788; New Hampshire, June 21, 1788.

Ratification was completed on June 21, 1788.

The Constitution subsequently was ratified by Virginia, June 25, 1788; New York, July 26, 1788; North Carolina, November 21, 1789; Rhode Island, May 29, 1790; and Vermont, January 10, 1791.]

Amendments

Amendment I

(First ten amendments ratified December 15, 1791.)

Congress shall make no law respecting an establishment of religion, or prohibiting the free exercise thereof; or abridging the freedom of speech, or of the press; or the right of the people peaceably to assemble, and to petition the Government for a redress of grievances.

Amendment II

A well regulated Militia, being necessary to the security of a free State, the right of the people to keep and bear Arms, shall not be infringed.

Amendment III

No Soldier shall, in time of peace be quartered in any house, without the consent of the Owner, nor in time of war, but in a manner to be prescribed by law.

Amendment IV

The right of the people to be secure in their persons, houses, papers, and effects, against unreasonable searches and seizures, shall not be violated, and no Warrants shall issue, but upon probable cause, supported by Oath or affirmation, and particularly describing the place to be searched, and the persons or things to be seized.

Amendment V

No person shall be held to answer for a capital, or otherwise infamous crime, unless on a presentment or indictment of a Grand Jury, except in cases arising in the land or naval forces, or in the Militia, when in actual service in time of War or public danger; nor shall any person be subject for the same offence to be twice put in jeopardy of life or limb; nor shall be compelled in any criminal case to be a witness against himself, nor be deprived of life, liberty, or property, without due process of law; nor shall private property be taken for public use, without just compensation.

Amendment VI

In all criminal prosecutions, the accused shall enjoy the right to a speedy and public trial, by an impartial jury of the State and district wherein the crime shall have been committed, which district shall have been previously ascertained by law, and to be informed of the nature and cause of the accusation; to be confronted with the witnesses against him; to have compulsory process for obtaining witnesses in his favor, and to have the Assistance of Counsel for his defence.

Amendment VII

In Suits at common law, where the value in controversy shall exceed twenty dollars, the right of trial by jury shall be preserved, and no fact tried by a jury, shall be otherwise re-examined in any Court of the United States, than according to the rules of the common law.

Amendment VIII

Excessive bail shall not be required, nor excessive fines imposed, nor cruel and unusual punishments inflicted.

Amendment IX

The enumeration in the Constitution, of certain rights, shall not be construed to deny or disparage others retained by the people.

Amendment X

The powers not delegated to the United States by the Constitution, nor prohibited by it to the States, are reserved to the States respectively, or to the people.

Amendment XI *(Ratified February 7, 1795)*

The Judicial power of the United States shall not be construed to extend to any suit in law or equity, commenced or prosecuted against one of the United States by Citizens of another State, or by Citizens or Subjects of any Foreign State.

Amendment XII *(Ratified June 15, 1804)*

The Electors shall meet in their respective states and vote by ballot for President and Vice-President, one of whom, at least, shall not be an inhabitant of the same state with themselves; they shall name in their ballots the person voted for as President, and in distinct ballots the person voted for as Vice-President, and they shall make distinct lists of all persons voted for as President, and of all persons voted for as Vice-President, and of the number of votes for each, which lists they shall sign and certify, and transmit sealed to the seat of the government of the United States, directed to the President of the Senate; — The President of the Senate shall, in the presence of the Senate and House of Representatives, open all the certificates and the votes shall then be counted; — The person having the greatest number of votes for President, shall be the President, if such number be a majority of the whole number of Electors appointed; and if no person have such majority, then from the persons having the highest numbers not exceeding three on the list of those voted for as President, the House of Representatives shall choose immediately, by ballot, the President. But in choosing the President, the votes shall be taken by states, the representation from each state having one vote; a quorum for this purpose shall consist of a member or members from two-thirds of the states, and a majority of all the states shall be necessary to a choice. [And if the House of Representatives shall not choose a President whenever the right of choice shall devolve upon them, before the fourth day of March next following, then the Vice-President shall act as President, as

in the case of the death or other constitutional disability of the President. —][11] The person having the greatest number of votes as Vice-President, shall be the Vice-President, if such number be a majority of the whole number of Electors appointed, and if no person have a majority, then from the two highest numbers on the list, the Senate shall choose the Vice-President; a quorum for the purpose shall consist of two-thirds of the whole number of Senators, and a majority of the whole number shall be necessary to a choice. But no person constitutionally ineligible to the office of President shall be eligible to that of Vice-President of the United States.

Amendment XIII *(Ratified December 6, 1865)*

Section 1. Neither slavery nor involuntary servitude, except as a punishment for crime whereof the party shall have been duly convicted, shall exist within the United States, or any place subject to their jurisdiction.

Section 2. Congress shall have power to enforce this article by appropriate legislation.

Amendment XIV *(Ratified July 9, 1868)*

Section 1. All persons born or naturalized in the United States, and subject to the jurisdiction thereof, are citizens of the United States and of the State wherein they reside. No State shall make or enforce any law which shall abridge the privileges or immunities of citizens of the United States; nor shall any State deprive any person of life, liberty, or property, without due process of law; nor deny to any person within its jurisdiction the equal protection of the laws.

Section 2. Representatives shall be apportioned among the several States according to their respective numbers, counting the whole number of persons in each State, excluding Indians not taxed. But when the right to vote at any election for the choice of electors for President and Vice President of the United States, Representatives in Congress, the Executive and Judicial officers of a State, or the members of the Legislature thereof, is denied to any of the male inhabitants of such State, being twenty-one years of age,[12] and citizens of the United States, or in any way abridged, except for participation in rebellion, or other crime, the basis of representation therein shall be reduced in the proportion which the number of such male citizens shall bear to the whole number of male citizens twenty-one years of age in such State.

Section 3. No person shall be a Senator or Representative in Congress, or elector of President and Vice President, or hold any office, civil or military, under the United States, or under any State, who, having previously taken an oath, as a member of Congress, or as an officer of the United States, or as a member of any State legislature, or as an executive or judicial officer of any State, to support the Constitution of the United States, shall have engaged in insurrection or rebellion against the same, or given aid or comfort to the enemies thereof. But Congress may by a vote of two-thirds of each House, remove such disability.

Section 4. The validity of the public debt of the United States, authorized by law, including debts incurred for payment of pensions and bounties for services in suppressing insurrection or rebellion, shall not be questioned. But neither the United States nor any State shall assume or pay any debt or obligation incurred in aid of insurrection or rebellion against the United States, or any claim for the loss or emancipation of any slave; but all such debts, obligations and claims shall be held illegal and void.

Section 5. The Congress shall have power to enforce, by appropriate legislation, the provisions of this article.

Amendment XV *(Ratified February 3, 1870)*

Section 1. The right of citizens of the United States to vote shall not be denied or abridged by the United States or by any State on account of race, color, or previous condition of servitude.

Section 2. The Congress shall have power to enforce this article by appropriate legislation.

Amendment XVI *(Ratified February 3, 1913)*

The Congress shall have power to lay and collect taxes on incomes, from whatever source derived, without apportionment among the several States, and without regard to any census or enumeration.

Amendment XVII *(Ratified April 8, 1913)*

The Senate of the United States shall be composed of two Senators from each State, elected by the people thereof, for six years; and each Senator shall have one vote. The electors in each State shall have the qualifications requisite for electors of the most numerous branch of the State legislatures.

When vacancies happen in the representation of any State in the Senate, the executive authority of such State shall issue writs of election to fill such vacancies: *Provided,* That the legislature of any State may empower the executive thereof to make temporary appointments until the people fill the vacancies by election as the legislature may direct.

This amendment shall not be so construed as to affect the election or term of any Senator chosen before it becomes valid as part of the Constitution.

Amendment XVIII *(Ratified January 16, 1919)*

Section 1. After one year from the ratification of this article the manufacture, sale, or transportation of intoxicating liquors within, the importation thereof into, or the exportation thereof from the United States and all territory subject to the jurisdiction thereof for beverage purposes is hereby prohibited.

Section 2. The Congress and the several States shall have concurrent power to enforce this article by appropriate legislation.

Section 3. This article shall be inoperative unless it shall have been ratified as an amendment to the Constitution by the legislatures of the several States, as provided in the Constitution, within seven years from the date of the submission hereof to the States by the Congress.][13]

Amendment XIX *(Ratified August 18, 1920)*

The right of citizens of the United States to vote shall not be denied or abridged by the United States or by any State on account of sex.

Congress shall have power to enforce this article by appropriate legislation.

Amendment XX *(Ratified January 23, 1933)*

Section 1. The terms of the President and Vice President shall end at noon on the 20th day of January, and the terms of Senators and Representatives at noon on the 3d day of January, of the years in which such terms would have ended if this article had not been ratified; and the terms of their successors shall then begin.

Section 2. The Congress shall assemble at least once in every year, and such meeting shall begin at noon on the 3d day of January, unless they shall by law appoint a different day.

Section 3.[14] If, at the time fixed for the beginning of the term of the President, the President elect shall have died, the Vice President elect shall become President. If a President shall not have been chosen before the time fixed for the beginning of his term, or if the President elect shall have failed to qualify, then the Vice President elect shall act as President until a President shall have qualified; and the Congress may by law provide for the case wherein neither a President elect nor a Vice President elect shall have qualified, declaring who shall then act as President, or the manner in which one who is to act shall be selected, and such person shall act accordingly until a President or Vice President shall have qualified.

Section 4. The Congress may by law provide for the case of the death of any of the persons from whom the House of Representatives may choose a President whenever the right of choice shall have devolved upon them, and for the case of the death of any of the persons from whom the Senate may choose a Vice President whenever the right of choice shall have devolved upon them.

Section 5. Sections 1 and 2 shall take effect on the 15th day of October following the ratification of this article.

Section 6. This article shall be inoperative unless it shall have been ratified as an amendment to the Constitution by the legislatures of three-fourths of the several States within seven years from the date of its submission.

Amendment XXI *(Ratified December 5, 1933)*

Section 1. The eighteenth article of amendment to the Constitution of the United States is hereby repealed.

Section 2. The transportation or importation into any State, Territory, or possession of the United States for delivery or use therein of intoxicating liquors, in violation of the laws thereof, is hereby prohibited.

Section 3. This article shall be inoperative unless it shall have been ratified as an amendment to the Constitution by conventions in the several States, as provided in the Constitution, within seven years from the date of the submission hereof to the States by the Congress.

Amendment XXII *(Ratified February 27, 1951)*

Section 1. No person shall be elected to the office of the President more than twice, and no person who has held the office of President, or acted as President, for more than two years of a term to which some other person was elected President shall be elected to the office of the President more than once. But this Article shall not apply to any person holding the office of President when this Article was proposed by the Congress, and shall not prevent any person who may be holding the office of President, or acting as President, during the term within which this Article become operative from holding the office of President or acting as President during the remainder of such term.

Section 2. This article shall be inoperative unless it shall have been ratified as an amendment to the Constitution by the legislatures of three-fourths of the several States within seven years from the date of its submission to the States by the Congress.

Amendment XXIII *(Ratified March 29, 1961)*

Section 1. The District constituting the seat of Government of the United States shall appoint in such manner as the Congress may direct:

A number of electors of President and Vice President equal to the whole number of Senators and Representatives in Congress to which the District would be entitled if it were a State, but in no event more than the least populous State; they shall be in addition to those appointed by the States, but they shall be considered, for the purposes of the election of President and Vice President, to be electors appointed by a State; and they shall meet in the District and perform such duties as provided by the twelfth article of amendment.

Section 2. The Congress shall have power to enforce this article by appropriate legislation.

Amendment XXIV *(Ratified January 23, 1964)*

Section 1. The right of citizens of the United States to vote in any primary or other election for President or Vice President, for electors for President or Vice President, or for Senator or Representative in Congress, shall not be denied or abridged by the United States or any State by reason of failure to pay any poll tax or other tax.

Section 2. The Congress shall have power to enforce this article by appropriate legislation.

Amendment XXV *(Ratified February 10, 1967)*

Section 1. In case of the removal of the President from office or of his death or resignation, the Vice President shall become President.

Section 2. Whenever there is a vacancy in the office of the Vice President, the President shall nominate a Vice President who shall take office upon confirmation by a majority vote of both Houses of Congress.

Section 3. Whenever the President transmits to the President pro tempore of the Senate and the Speaker of the House of Representatives his written declaration that he is unable to discharge the powers and duties of his office, and until he transmits to them a written declaration to the contrary, such powers and duties shall be discharged by the Vice President as Acting President.

Section 4. Whenever the Vice President and a majority of either the principal officers of the executive departments or of such other body as Congress may by law provide, transmit to the President pro tempore of the Senate and the Speaker of the House of Representatives their written declaration that the President is unable to discharge the powers and duties of his office, the Vice President shall immediately assume the powers and duties of the office as Acting President.

Thereafter, when the President transmits to the President pro tempore of the Senate and the Speaker of the House of Representatives his written declaration that no inability exists, he shall resume the powers and duties of his office unless the Vice President and a majority of either the principal officers of the executive department or of such other body as Congress may by law provide, transmit within four days to the President pro tempore of the Senate and the Speaker of the House of Representatives their written declaration that the President is unable to discharge the powers and duties of his office. Thereupon Congress shall decide the issue, assembling within forty-eight hours for that purpose if not in session. If the Congress, within twenty-one days after receipt of the latter written declaration, or, if Congress is not in session, within twenty-one days after Congress is required to assemble, determines by two-thirds vote of both Houses that the President is unable to discharge the powers and duties of his office, the Vice President shall continue to discharge the same as Acting President; otherwise, the President shall resume the powers and duties of his office.

Amendment XXVI *(Ratified July 1, 1971)*

Section 1. The right of citizens of the United States, who are eighteen years of age or older, to vote shall not be denied or abridged by the United States or by any State on account of age.

Section 2. The Congress shall have power to enforce this article by appropriate legislation.

Amendment XXVII *(Ratified May 7, 1992)*

No law varying the compensation for the services of the Senators and Representatives shall take effect, until an election of Representatives shall have intervened.

Notes

1. The part in brackets was changed by section 2 of the Fourteenth Amendment.
2. The part in brackets was changed by the first paragraph of the Seventeenth Amendment.
3. The part in brackets was changed by the second paragraph of the Seventeenth Amendment.
4. The part in brackets was changed by section 2 of the Twentieth Amendment.
5. The Sixteenth Amendment gave Congress the power to tax incomes.
6. The material in brackets has been superseded by the Twelfth Amendment.
7. This provision has been affected by the Twenty-fifth Amendment.
8. These clauses were affected by the Eleventh Amendment.
9. This paragraph has been superseded by the Thirteenth Amendment.
10. Obsolete.
11. The part in brackets has been superseded by section 3 of the Twentieth Amendment.
12. See the Nineteenth and Twenty-sixth Amendments.
13. This Amendment was repealed by section 1 of the Twenty-first Amendment.
14. See the Twenty-fifth Amendment.

Source: U.S. Congress, House, Committee on the Judiciary, *The Constitution of the United States of America, as Amended,* 100th Cong., 1st sess., 1987, H Doc 100-94.

INDEX